Anāhitā

Anāhitā

A History and Reception of the Iranian Water Goddess

Manya Saadi-nejad

I.B. TAURIS

LONDON • NEW YORK • OXFORD • NEW DELHI • SYDNEY

I.B. TAURIS
Bloomsbury Publishing Plc
50 Bedford Square, London, WC1B 3DP, UK
1385 Broadway, New York, NY 10018, USA

BLOOMSBURY, I.B. TAURIS and the I.B. Tauris logo
are trademarks of Bloomsbury Publishing Plc

First published in Great Britain 2021

Cover design: Adriana Brioso
Cover image © World History Archive / Alamy Stock Photo

A catalogue record for this book is available from the British Library.

A catalog record for this book is available from the Library of Congress.

ISBN:	HB:	978-1-8386-0159-1
	PB:	978-1-8386-0111-9
	ePDF:	978-1-8386-0157-7
	eBook:	978-1-8386-0156-0

Typeset by Integra Software Services Pvt. Ltd.

To find out more about our authors and books visit www.bloomsbury.com
and sign up for our newsletters.

Contents

List of Illustrations

Acknowledgments

First and foremost, I would like to extend my warmest, heartfelt thanks to Professor Maria Macuch and Professor Almut Hintze, who were my supervisors during my Ph.D. at Freie Universität, Berlin, for their support and helpful comments. I am grateful to Professors Mark Hale, Jean Kellens, and James R. Russell for discussions that were as helpful as they were encouraging. I am eternally grateful to my parents Dr. Reza Saadi nejad and Azam Sadati, for their unconditional love and support. I would like to thank my son, Persia Shahdi, for his patience and support throughout the years I spent in writing this book.

And Finally, I would like to take this opportunity to thank Dr. Richard Foltz for his help and support, encouragement, and our valued conversation during many years.

A Note on Transcriptions

The transcription of Avestan is based on the system of Karl Hoffman (Hoffmann 1975). For Pahlavi I have used the system of D. N. Mackenzie (Mackenzie 1986). I have based my transcriptions from New Persian on those of the *Encyclopædia Iranica* (Yarshater 1982–).

Abbreviations

AM	*Andarz ī Ādurbād ī Mahraspandān*
AS	*Abdīh ud Sahīgīh ī Sagistān*
Av	Avestan
AW	*Ayādgār ī Wuzurgmihr*
AWN	*Ardā Wīrāz-Nāmag*
Bd	*Bundahišn*
ČAP	*Čīdag Andarz ī Pōryōtkēšān*
Dk	*Dēnkard*
GBd	*Greater Bundahišn*
HN	*Hāδōxt Nask*
HR	*Husraw ī Kawādān ud Rēdag-ē*
KAP	*Kārnāmag ī Ardaxšīr ī Pāpagān*
MP	*Middle Persian*
MX	*Mēnōg ī xrad*
N	*Nērangestān*
NM	*Nāmagīhā ī Manuščihr*
NP	New Persian
Phl	Pahlavi
PIE	Proto-Indo-European
RV	*Ṛg Veda*
ŠĒ	*Šahrestānīhā ī Ērānšahr*
Skt	Sanskrit

ŠN   *Šāh-nāmeh*

Vd   *Vīdēvdād*

WZ   *Wizīdagīhā ī Zādsprām*

Y   *Yasna*

Yt   *Yašt*

ZWY   *Zand ī Wahman Yašt*

Introduction

This is a study of how the most important goddess of pre-Islamic Iran, Anāhitā, was transformed over time. Possibly having roots in the prehistoric river goddess(es) of the ancient proto-Indo-European peoples of the fifth millennium BCE or earlier, she emerges by the late Achaemenid period as one of the three principal deities of the Iranian pantheon, alongside Ahura Mazdā and Miθra. An important Avestan hymn, the *Ābān Yašt,* is composed in the honor of Anāhitā, establishing her role within the Zoroastrian religion. During the course of this process, she acquires additional functions, presumably from preexisting goddesses in the regions where Iranians came to live. Variations on the Iranian Anāhitā are found in the religious cultures of neighboring lands, such as Armenia, Bactria, and Sogdiana. With the coming of Islam, her cult disappeared, yet numerous aspects of it survived in female figures from Persian literature and through folk tales and rituals, usually Islamicized, which are often connected with water. This study aims to schematize these variations over time and space, in order to trace Anāhitā's development as a major figure in Iranian religion and the constantly evolving mix of her roles and attributes within culturally diverse communities throughout Greater Iran.

According to both the Avesta and the royal inscriptions of three successive Iranian empires, Anāhitā (along with Miθra) was the most powerful deity created by the supreme being, Ahura Mazdā.[1] Being originally a water-river goddess, Anāhitā likely incorporated aspects of preexisting water deities in the areas where her cult flourished. She was specifically goddess of the rivers and the lakes. Temples devoted to her have been identified at Sardis, Babylon, Damascus, Persepolis, Bīšāpūr, and Hamadan, as well as in Afghanistan and Armenia, usually alongside rivers.[2] More such sites are being identified all the time, and numerous place names throughout Iran (Pol-e doxtar, Qale-ye doxtar, etc.) may reflect her memory. Many holy sites across the Middle East are thought to have been originally temples devoted to Anāhitā.[3] The Čâr Stên temple on a hillside near Duhok in Iraqi Kurdistan, excavated only as recently as 2006, is a particularly illustrative example: a square chamber containing the main firepit is circumscribed by a knee-high water channel, fed by run-off, carved into the rock walls and running from there into an open-air sacrificial area, which Kurdish archaeologists have attributed to Anāhitā.[4]

In the context of ancient Iranian religion, Anāhitā is noteworthy in a number of respects. First, she is the most prominent female deity among the Iranian goddesses, "being worthy of worship,"[5] within a largely male pantheon of Iranian deities. Second, her visual aspect is more fully developed than of any other Iranian deity: she is a shape-shifter, alternately a goddess and a river, and has been described fully in both forms. Physical descriptions of her in the Avesta are very extensive and detailed. Some of the other deities mentioned in the Yašts do occasionally take on various shapes (animals and human beings). However, since in the Iranian belief system deities are not usually perceived in human forms, they are not generally anthropomorphized to the extent one sees in Greek and Mesopotamian mythology.

In her original form as a water goddess, Anāhitā is more involved in fertility, support, and healing. Over time, however, and perhaps partly through influence from non-Indo-European goddesses, she acquired additional functions and characteristics which tied her to the warrior and priestly functions as well. In contrast to the norm according to which a deity was connected to a particular social group, Anāhitā came to be associated with all of the three major social categories of ancient Iranian society: priests/rulers, warriors, and "producers."[6] By the historical period—specifically her appearance in the Avestan hymn devoted to her, the *Ābān Yašt*—Anāhitā as the female *yazata* of the waters[7] comes to possess three very different aspects: she is simultaneously (1) a spiritual ruler, (2) a mighty deity who supports warriors, and (3) a fertility goddess.[8] Thus, through the acquisition of new characteristics, which were likely taken over from preexisting local, non-Iranian goddesses, Anāhitā assumed functions associated with the full range of her devotees' needs and concerns at all social levels, giving her a uniquely important role in the emerging Iranian society.

There is much evidence of Anāhitā's popularity in ancient times, when she was an object of devotion among the Iranian peoples, but the details of this are less clear than one might wish. Specifically, Anāhitā's features, functions, and place in the pantheon varied considerably from one historical period to the next, and also among the various regions of Iranian cultural influence—in Asia Minor including Armenia, Anatolia, and possibly even Arabia[9]—where her cult was active. This study aims to schematize these variations over time and space, in order to trace Anāhitā's development as a major figure in Iranian religion and the constantly evolving mix of her roles and attributes within culturally diverse communities throughout Greater Iran.

We may never know the exact details concerning Anāhitā's historical transformation and development. Nor can we assess with any certainty the extent to which her importance was due to her taking over the position of a preexisting local goddess or goddesses—although her original identity as a river goddess did not disappear—when the Iranians moved into southwestern Asia.

A comparative study of the mythologies of the various Indo-European peoples suggests that in the common period (*c.* 5000 years BP) there existed a river goddess who was the object of religious devotion. (It is not possible given our data to reconstruct with certainty what her name may have been, although at least one of her epithets appears to be very ancient as will be shown in Chapter Four.) As the Iranian version of this hypothetical deity, Anāhitā had one important mythological and ritual role among many. Through a series of historical encounters with devotees of different (i.e., non-Iranian) cultural backgrounds, Anāhitā's client base of devotees was dramatically expanded—her expanding transfunctionality giving her the potential to encompass all levels of society.[10] As a result, her status was unrivalled by any other Iranian goddess throughout the course of three successive Iranian empires over a period of a thousand years.

As the most important Iranian goddess, Anāhitā, or *Arəduuī Sūrā Anāhitā*, as she is referred to in the Avesta, has been the focus of numerous scholarly studies both in Iran and in the West, mostly in the form of brief articles focusing on specific issues regarding her identity and functions in terms of their various possible influences. To date, however, no study has sought to treat questions regarding her origins or her transformation and development over time in a unified way that attempts to construct a full picture of the goddess throughout her evolving contexts over time. Such, therefore, is the aim of the present study.

In charting out Anāhitā's historical transformations, a number of questions emerge. What exactly does Anāhitā represent, in religio-mythological terms, at the various stages of her transformation? Can her original identity as an Indo-European water goddess be convincingly established? And if so, what, if anything, do Anāhitā and these goddesses have in common, and to what extent? How and when were these similarities transmitted? And how is her essential nature as a water goddess connected to her assimilation of other functions over time?

Other questions arise when looking at the evolving roles and representations of Anāhitā during her periods of greatest popularity under the (late?) Achaemenids. What can we conclude from her presence in the Iranian pantheon? A similar question arises when looking at the role of Anāhitā, especially during the Parthian and Sasanian periods. Did she remain important during the last two Iranian monarchies? What was her role in the Avesta and in the Middle Persian texts? What differences exist between the two in terms of how they portray her? Are any sociopolitical forces behind this transformation?

More broadly, what can we conclude by the prominence of female deities in the Iranian pantheon? Can this be taken as a reflection of gender relations in ancient Iranian societies, or is the presence of goddesses merely a projection of male ideas about femininity? Should Anāhitā's importance in the religious life of Iranians be seen as reflecting an improved position of women in Iranian society, or does her apparent demotion in the priestly Pahlavi texts actually reflect the opposite? Finally, with the Islamization of the Iranian peoples, what aspects of Anāhitā's legacy survive, whether in literature, or in popular religious rituals and legends, and how can they be detected?

The similarities (and differences) between different goddesses that we will discuss in this study demand that one identify certain shared themes and characteristics between them through the use of comparative mythology. This involves exploring the relationship between the goddesses' various myths (from diverse cultural contexts) in order to identify any underlying similarities and trace their possible common origins. This is necessary to provide a starting point for the evolution and transformation of the goddess known as "Anāhitā."

The importance of fertility—that of both the tribe members and their domesticated animals—was paramount among all of the ancient peoples and reflected in their religious traditions (although importance of the goddesses does not necessarily mean women had social power). Accordingly, the female life-giving principle was central to their ritual life. The best-known visual representations of fertility and women from the ancient period are nude figurines, generically referred to as "Venuses," featuring prominent breasts, large buttocks, and thick thighs, probably symbolizing fertility. Modern feminist scholarship has often sought to reconstruct a "matriarchal," goddess-centered world prior to the fourth millennium BCE, which is said to have been superseded by patriarchy.[11] Our aim is to consider the data available for analyzing and assessing the feminine elements in the religious life of ancient societies without relying on such preconceptions.

Clearer evidence of goddess worship can be found in the oldest mythological texts, such as those pertaining to the Sumerian goddess Inanna, but the written versions of these materials do not go back to any presumed "matriarchal" period, and they likely bear editorial transformations reflecting the perspectives of their male writers at a time when patriarchy had already become firmly established.[12] At best, one can attempt to "read between the lines" of these texts in an attempt to discern possible, older oral versions and the values they may have promoted.

In our case, vital importance of water in all forms (river, lake, stream, etc.) for human survival was also involved. As we will see, fertility and healing were common functions of water goddesses, and many rituals and offering were connected to them. In fact, much of this evidence would indicate that water was a central focus in the rituals of many cultures descended from the proto-Indo-European people. Ritual ceremonies and sacrifices were offered on the banks of the rivers and lakes, cast into the water (which was usually associated with female deities) as gifts honoring the supernatural powers of water and its associated deity.

To understand the importance of these religious symbols and rituals, we may consider the role of these rituals in the ancient societies. They reflected the deepest needs, concerns, and thus, values of a society. Is there any common "plot structure" between the various mythological stories and tales of water goddesses? In our case, the theology of Zoroastrianism (like other religions), its symbols, and worldview were created primarily from a male elite monopoly of discourse and functioned to legitimize them. Therefore, in an attempt to represent diverse perspectives, this study seeks to discover the role of the goddesses—more precisely the water goddess, and in this case Anāhitā—asking whether Anāhitā's gender is an important analytic category for this study.

This study is thus consciously and necessarily selective: it does not attempt a comprehensive discussion of the philological issues of the Avestan and Pahlavi texts—which will be analyzed only in terms of what they can offer to our topic. Rather, we have sought to understand Anāhitā's transformations over time. Our research focuses in the first instance on the evidence for the worship of female deities, particularly Indo-European water goddesses. We compare these goddesses and their rituals with Anāhitā, incorporating methods borrowed from gender studies, in an effort to uncover any possible common origins and/or any absorption of characteristics and functions. Second, we attempt to understand the goddess according to how she is described in her most important texts: the *Ābān Yašt*, the Middle Persian texts, as well as other sources, with regard to her phenomenology in Mazdaean religion and to understand her transformation and its circumstances from a water goddess with (possibly) limited functions to her multifunctional features. In connection with this, we also compare her with the most important female deities in the Avesta. Finally, we analyze her transformations over time and place and trace her possible survivals, which can be detected in the literature and folk rituals of Islamic Iran.

Goddesses in the Ancient World

The worship of goddesses was central to the religious practice of the various early societies that predated the migration of the Iranians into central and southwest Asia during the second half of the second millennium BCE, when Iranian speakers began moving into these regions.[1] These pre-Iranian societies included those of the Bactriana-Margiana Archaeological Complex (BMAC) in Central Asia (*c.* 2300 and 1700 BCE), the Elamites in Southwestern Asia, the various peoples of Mesopotamia, and numerous pastoral-nomadic groups of the Zagros Mountains and the plateau further east.

Goddesses and their functions and rituals in any tradition transform themselves over time, and always represent a composite drawn from a range of sources. Thus, Anāhitā, as a composite goddess (as will be discussed in Chapter Five), shows many different characteristics, which may have been absorbed from goddesses who existed before her arrival on the Iranian plateau. The existence of these goddesses from prehistoric time will be discussed shortly, with the aim of better understanding Anāhitā's functions, features, and rituals, which may represent a combination of Iranian and non-Iranian origin and the goal of contextualizing her within the larger framework of goddesses.

"Venus" Figurines

The best-known visual representations of women from the ancient period are figurines, generically referred to as "Venuses," which have been found over a wide territory across western Eurasia and cover a vast historical time span, from the Upper Paleolithic Age (*c.* 25000 BCE) to the Bronze Age (*c.* 2000 BCE).[2] Venus figurines are usually nude, having different shapes but usually featuring prominent breasts (or sometimes the opposite), large buttocks, and thick thighs.

Some appear to be pregnant. These features have led many archaeologists to assume that they might represent mother goddesses and are connected to fertility rites.[3] A number of other explanations are possible, however.[4]

Although there exists some measure of agreement among scholars regarding the rather broad scope of what these figurines may represent and the possible functions of them—which include ancestor worship, successful agriculture, sex objects or guides to the underworld for the dead, substitutes for human sacrifice, and teaching social codes to children or simply as toys for them[5]—these functions most likely differed from one spatio-temporal context to another.

Venus Figurines in Iran

As the Indo-European-speaking peoples began to migrate outward from their presumed home on the southern Russian steppes beginning some 5,000 to 6,000 years ago,[6] their dispersal among a wide range of other cultures led to transformation, adaptation, and assimilation with the beliefs and practices of the latter. At the same time, all of the peoples descended from the proto-Indo-Europeans retained aspects of their ancestors' language and culture, allowing us to speak of a common Indo-European heritage.

The presence of Venus figurines throughout the territory of the Iranian plateau, including Tappeh Sarāb, east of Kermanshah in north-west Iran, Giyān Tappeh, near Nahāvand in the west, Tappeh Alī-kosh, near Dēzfūl in Khuzestan to the southwest, Tappeh Sīalk, near Kāshān in central Iran, Kalūraz, near Tappeh Jalāliyeh in Gilan in north,[7] and Turang Tappeh, near Gorgan in the northeast,[8] may attest to the existence of a goddess worship across the region prior to the arrival of the Indo-European-speaking Iranians by the end of the second millennium BCE.

Contemporary studies of Iranian history have combined archeology, linguistics, and textual approaches in an attempt to fill out the historical narrative for Western Asia. Referring to the history of this region "Iranian," however, tends to obscure the fact that there were already people living in the area before the Iranians arrived, in some cases, with long-established civilizations of their own. Cultural exchanges between their culture(s) and that of the newcomers (Indo-Iranians, with their own goddesses) can be assumed and, in many cases, demonstrated.

As Iranians migrated southward and then westward onto the Iranian plateau during the second millennium BCE,[9] one may assume some level of mutual influence between the new arrivals and the preexisting local peoples of the region. Nasab and Kazzazi have detected distinct changes in style and body proportions between figurines over both time—from the Paleolithic to the Neolithic periods—and space, that is, between those from Central Europe and those found in Iran. These changes likely reflect an ongoing process of cultural encounter and mutual influence among different ancient peoples.[10]

Pre-Iranian Goddess Worship in the Iranian Lands

Much of the material culture from the historical Iranian heartlands identified with goddess worship dates to the period prior to the arrival of Iranian speakers in the region. Moreover, the fact that we do not know for sure how any given artifact should be interpreted means we can only guess at the extent to which female figurines might have been connected to any kind of goddess worship.

In some cases, textual materials can be connected with physical evidence such as objects or rock reliefs. Perhaps the most promising connection between written and material sources for ancient goddess worship can be found in western Anatolia, where female figures from Çatal Hüyük—a site occupied from around 6250 to 5400 BCE—appear compatible with a prominent goddess-centered fertility cult, which persisted in the region well into historical times.[11] As Ehrenberg notes, "the worship of a fertility goddess is attested in historical records in Anatolia, some several thousand years after the Neolithic figurines were produced in the area, and this strengthens the possibility that the earlier Anatolian figurines are representations of the same goddess, particularly when their form and context are examined."[12]

Elam

Of the various pre-Iranian inhabitants of Western Asia, the Elamites are among the most significant. The "Persian" society that developed during the Achaemenid period (550–330 BCE) was in essence a hybrid between the native Elamites and intrusive Iranians associated with the Parsa tribe.[13] The Elamite presence covered a wide area, from their homeland in the southern Zagros Mountains and Khuzestan at the southeastern edge of the Mesopotamian plain to the east, as far as Kerman on the southeastern part of the Iranian plateau. Their culture was heavily influenced by those of Mesopotamia—the Sumerian, Babylonian, and Assyrian civilizations—and at the beginning appears to have been goddess-centered,[14] suggesting the possibility that ancient Elamite society was initially goddess-centered.[15]

The Elamites were a major political force in the region for more than 2,000 years, from around 2600 to 640 BCE. Their home territory is named as "Elam" (the "high land," referring to its position within the southern part of the Zagros Mountain range) in the Hebrew Bible (from the Sumerian transcription *elam(a)*, Akkadian *elamtu*, Elamite *haltamti*). In their own cuneiform texts, the Elamites referred to their country as "*Ha(l)-tamti*"; this may have been pronounced something like "Haltamti," meaning "gracious lord-land" or just "high land."[16] It has been suggested that since *Hal* means "land," and *tamti* means "god," it would seem that they called their place "God's Country."[17]

Two specific features of Elamite belief are the ritual importance of women and the holiness of the snake, both possibly vestiges of an earlier goddess-centered period. Representations of the snake are found in inscriptions, seals, and various objects such as water containers. Snakes were seen as offering protection from evil powers. They were symbols of fertility and wealth. In Iranian folkloric tales even today, snakes have two-sided features: beneath their generally frightening appearance, snakes can also be symbols of treasure and wisdom.

The prevalence of Elamite figurines of the so-called "naked goddesses"[18] indicates that goddesses were important in this area. This hypothesis is supported by written sources, such as a contract from 2280 BCE on which the list of Elamite deities begins with the goddess Pinikir.[19] She was the great mother-goddess of Elam, and the Babylonians identified her with their own goddess Ištar.[20] Pinikir's importance appears to have decreased somewhat over the subsequent millennium, perhaps reflecting changing gender relations within Elamite society. At some point, she was displaced as the head of the Elamite pantheon by a male deity, Humban, yet she remained an important object of devotion, as is shown in later Elamite texts.[21] Hinz argues that "the fact that precedence was given to a goddess, who stood above and apart from the other Elamite gods, indicates a matriarchal approach in the devotees of the religion."[22]

The existence of a large number of female figurines dating from around 2000 BCE suggests that Pinikir was still very important at that time. She gradually came to be worshipped mostly in the south of Elam, where she was conflated with an existing local goddess, Kiririša, "the Great Goddess," who was Humban's wife. Kiririša was also known as the local goddess of a place near Bushehr on the northern side of the Persian Gulf. Shrines were dedicated to her at Susa, Čoga Zanbīl, and Tappeh Liyān, all three of which came to be part of Persian territory.

She often was referred as Kiririša-of-Liyān. Some evidence exists regarding ceremonies connected to water and flowing streams in Elamite religion, particularly the rock relief at Dā o Do<u>k</u>tar in western Fars province which Potts associates with Kiririša.[23]

Over time Susa became more and more important as a center for Elamite culture, and Susa's patron deity, In-Šušin-ak, rose in importance as well. Humban, as the great creator god, Kiririša, the goddess, and In-Šušin-ak thus came to constitute the supreme triad within the Elamite pantheon.[24] It would seem that this relationship was later transposed onto the Persian pantheon and influenced the triad Ahura Mazdā–Anāhitā–Miθra, as will be discussed in Chapter Seven. Hinz states that In-Šušin-ak "occasionally replace Kiririša in second place after Humban,"[25] but neither he nor Miθra ever gained complete supremacy.

Sumer and Mesopotamia

The Sumerians, like the Elamites, a non-Semitic people of Western Asia, who called themselves *ùĝ saĝ gíg-ga*, literally meaning "the black-headed people,"[26] are credited with establishing one of the earliest urban civilizations by around 5000 BCE. Like their neighbors, the Elamites, their racial and linguistic affiliations remain open to debate, and their geographic origins are rather unclear.

Establishing themselves between the Tigris and Euphrates rivers, in modern Iraq, to the Persian Gulf in Iran[27] and Syria, the Sumerians built a large number of cities, each of which had its own local gods and goddesses. They built their temples, called "ziggurats," to resemble mountains rising up above the flat Mesopotamian plain, and imagined their gods on top. This practice suggests that they may originally have come from a mountainous area.[28] The Sumerian worldview, enshrined in their myths which were written down as the earliest cuneiform texts, formed the basis of later Mesopotamian civilization.

The Sumerian creation myth centers on a primordial couple, a god and a goddess who produced the younger generation of gods.[29] This myth first appears in cuneiform clay tablets dated to the end of fourth millennium BCE, found in a temple dedicated to the goddess Inanna (*nin-an-ak*, "Lady of Heaven"), in the city of Uruk. Scholars have pondered the location of the mythical city of Dilmun mentioned in the Sumerian creation myth. Some have associated it with excavations of ruins on the island of Bahrain[30] in the Persian Gulf. Since the Elamit goddess Kiririša was the goddess of the southern coastal region by the Persian Gulf,[31] can this be taken as a possible cultural exchange between these goddesses?

Mesopotamian civilization affected the development of Iranian culture both indirectly through the Elamite population, which the Persian polity ultimately absorbed, and directly through ongoing encounters between Iranians and Mesopotamians. The economic and political dimensions of their relationship contained some religious rituals and ideological influences that shaped their cultural exchanges. This may be understood via the methodological framework related to the field of religious studies: "religions are embedded in culture and that 'culture' is inclusive of political and economic influences."[32]

The Achaemenid kings wrote their inscriptions in Elamite, Babylonian, and Old Persian; this fact demonstrates the enduring cosmopolitanism of the Persian Empire. It is, therefore, not surprising that Iranians might have absorbed some religio-cultural influences from these other civilizations, including the role of goddesses.

Mesopotamian Goddesses

The ancient Mesopotamian peoples had a number of important goddesses, whose roles and functions were slowly taken over by male deities. Yet the importance of these goddesses survived for many centuries and influenced the Elamite people and later the Iranians.[33] The Sumerian goddess Inanna and the Babylonian Ištar, with many similarities in their functions and associated rituals, are two examples of goddesses who held central importance in their respective societies. Their functions and popularity show some similarities to those of Anāhitā, and raise some questions about their possible connection.

As Iranian tribes began to come into contact with the peoples of Mesopotamia, beginning in the late second millennium BCE, the process of cultural interaction and religious syncretism continued to affect their understanding of their deities, including Anāhitā. From this new encounter, Anāhitā began to assume the form by which she is best known through descriptions from the Achaemenid period onward. It is quite natural that with the arrival of Iranian speakers in Mesopotamia the identity of the primary goddess of the region would come to be conflated to some extent with that of an existing Iranian goddess, Anāhitā. From one region to another, the specific visible identity of the goddess, as well as her particular blend of functions, might differ. Chaumont is among those who have suggested that at an early stage of the Iranian-Mesopotamian encounter (*c.* 1000 BCE or later) the Iranian river goddess Anāhitā acquired some of attributes of the Mesopotamian Ištar/(I)nana, in particular, her warlike character.[34] The fact that the sanctuary in Rabātak in Afghanistan was dedicated to Nana, as was the Sasanian sanctuary in Ēstaxr to Anāhitā, can be considered as additional evidence of the possible connection between the two goddesses as will be discussed below.[35]

Inanna/Ištar and Nanai/Nana/Nanā

Nana and Inanna were long assumed by scholars to be one goddess, with Nana being a later incarnation of Inanna.[36] However, recent research has cast doubt on such claims. It is not clear whether these names were originally different— their resemblance being due to cultural exchanges—or whether they were counterparts of one ancient goddess. Potts (along with some other contemporary scholars) argues that Inanna/Ištar must be strictly distinguished from Nana, and that she (Nana) was not identical to Inanna.[37] He also notes that Nana "is frequently identified with the Iranian divinity Anāhitā and/or the Greek goddess Artemis."[38]

Inanna/Ištar

Inanna was a Sumerian goddess who was worshipped from ancient times. The Babylonians knew her as the counterpart of Ištar. It seems that she was associated with war, nature (water), and sex (but not marriage), possibly involving sacred prostitution at her temples and perhaps even the sacrifice of the male partner.[39] She was identified as the anthropomorphic projection of the planet Venus. The terms "Inanna-HUD" and "Inanna-SIG" have been translated as "Inanna of the Morning" and "Inanna of the Evening," representing the two appearances of the planet Venus as the morning and the evening star.[40] This leads us to one example of cultural exchange between Anāhitā and Inanna, or more precisely what Anāhitā absorbed from Inanna. Anāhitā, who is presented as Ardwī-sūr-Anāhīd in the Pahlavi texts, was identified with the planet Venus (in a precisely astronomical position -GBd.VA.8). This clearly shows her syncretization with the goddess Inanna, which is important for our argument since Anāhitā's transformation cannot accurately be understood without grasping and analyzing these mythological comparisons (as will be discussed further in Chapter Nine).

The influences of Mesopotamian culture and rituals on the Indo-European Iranian-speaking tribes happened gradually. Perhaps the strongest example of this influence can be seen in the annual mourning ritual associated with the sacrificial "death" of the vegetation god, Dumuzi, in connection to the goddess

Inanna; this symbolized the annual regeneration of nature and was thus centrally important to the Mesopotamian civilization which depended heavily on agriculture. One of the main components of the annual religious cycle connected with this myth was ritual mourning over the death of this divine lover, who was considered to have died a martyr. Variations on this myth and its attendant rituals can be detected throughout subsequent Iranian history, from the *Šāhnāmeh* to Shi'ism and will be discussed in Chapter Ten.

A more perplexing question concerns the alleged emergence of henotheism, among the Iranians as well among the peoples of Mesopotamia. The rise of the god Marduk to his supreme position within the pantheon of the Babylonians, like that of Yahweh in the Israelite context, is best explained, where a particular deity is championed as the patron of a specific group at the expense of its (and their) rivals. Cyrus II's attempt to associate himself with Marduk upon conquering Babylon in 539 BCE is the clearest example of how Iranian migrants deliberately appropriated Mesopotamian religion for their own purposes, but this is surely only the tip of the iceberg. From the elite classes down to the level of the general population, Iranians must have taken what they needed from Mesopotamian culture and adapted it into forms familiar to themselves.

The divine couple of Marduk and the goddess Ištar show some interesting similarities with the Iranian pairing of Miθra and Anāhitā. In fact, Miθra and Anāhitā are the only deities who have been documented along with Ahura Mazdā in the inscriptions of the Persian kings (e.g., those of Artaxerxes II, r. 404–358 BCE). The transformations undergone by Anāhitā during the Achaemenid period, during which she first comes into historical prominence, can be explained according to this model, as will be discussed in Chapter Eight.

Nana/Nanai/Nanā

As an originally Mesopotamian goddess and probably having undergone a degree of conflation with some other female deity, Nana eventually became popular in the South, especially at Uruk, Susa, and Kušān,[41] as well as to the East within the pantheon of Bactria.[42] Associated with war, fertility, wisdom, and water, the goddess Nana was worshiped at Dura-Europos as "Artemis Nanaia," reflecting the mixed Hellenistic-Semitic-Iranian culture there. In 2004 BCE, a coalition of Elamites and "Su-people" from Shimaski (possibly the BMAC region in Central Asia) captured Ur and took a statue of Nanna back to Anshan "as a captive." She was returned to Ur after 1984 BCE.[43]

She appears as Nanai on Kušan coins (first to fourth centuries CE), indicating that her cult had spread as far eastward as the territories of the Indus valley and beyond. The Bactrian Rabātak inscription of Kušan king Kaniška I (first half of the first century CE) calls Nanai *amsa Nana*; in Kušan coins, she is *Nanašan* ("royal Nana")—"she is the goddess who rules and thus ordains kingship."[44] Nana was the principal deity in Kaniška pantheon and the leader of the gods in the Rabatak inscription, and the Rabatak sanctuary was dedicated to her.[45] The idea that Nana was the principal deity in Kaniška's pantheon was challenged by Gnoli,[46] who argued that she, like Anāhitā, was indeed the deity to whom the sanctuary was dedicated but that neither she nor Anāhitā ever were the heads of the pantheon. Michael Shenkar, however, disagrees with Gnoli's opinion, arguing that: "Contrary to Gnoli, there are no sufficient grounds to doubt that Nana was the most important deity worshiped by Kaniška and the head of the royal dynastic pantheon of his time. This is confirmed by her place in Rabatac inscription, the popularity of her image on coins and in personal names, and the fact that Nana was almost the most important goddess in neighboring Soghdiana and Chorasmia."[47]

Grenet notes that Nana(ia) appears on the selection of five gods represented on Kaniška's gold coins, where they receive Iranian names: *Nana* or *Nanašao*, *Miiro* (Mithra), *Mao* (Māh), *Athšo* (Ādur), and *Oado* (Wād).[48] These selected deities are all connected to natural elements, directly or indirectly: to the Sun, Moon, fire, and wind. So where is the deity of water? Water figures not only in Herodotus's list of the Persians' prayers, but also in Y 1.16 and the *Niyāyišn*'s daily prayers to the Sun, Moon, fire, and water. It seems that for the Kušans Nana has replaced the concept of the water deity (Anāhitā). Grenet states that she was the patron and protector of royalty, another similarity to Anāhitā. In the Sogdian pantheon, meanwhile, Anāhitā appears separately from Nana "on a few occasions."[49]

The prevalence of Sogdian coins bearing Nana's name suggests that she was the major deity of Sogdiana in pre-Islamic times.[50] Despite her Mesopotamian origin, she was the deity most frequently represented in Sogdiana during the seventh and eighth centuries.[51] Since many of the ancient peoples living across this wide expanse of territory practiced agriculture, deities and rituals related to fertility are widely attested among them. The Indo-European Iranian-speaking tribes were relative latecomers to this region, and it is inevitable that their culture would have been shaped and influenced by those of the peoples already living there.

The spread of Nana's cult over such vast distances vividly illustrates the cultural connections (presumably stemming mostly from trade) that existed from prehistoric times, linking the Mediterranean world to that of Central Asia and beyond, with the Iranian plateau at its center. She was worshiped in Susa from the third millennium BCE, and her cult continued during the Seleucid and Parthian period as the principal deity of the city, known as Artemis-Nanaia cult.[52]

Azarpay notes:

> The symbols and attributes of the early medival [sic] Soghdian and Khwarezmian images of Nanā, though influenced by Indian formal models, indicate that the goddess preserved both her early Mesopotamian affiliation with the sun and the moon, and her identity as a love and war deity.[53]

The cult of Nana may have already existed in Central Asia prior to the arrival of the Indo-Iranians in the region, since she appears on a BMAC seal dating to the early second millennium BCE.[54] Similarly, her cult in Bactria may predate her appearance in the Kušan pantheon by over two millennia.[55]

The cults of Nana and Anāhitā were also present in Armenia. Nana was worshipped as Nane in a temple at the small town of Thil. She was believed to be the daughter of Aramazd (the Avestan Ahura Mazdā). Her cult was closely tied to that of Anahit (the counterpart of Avestan Anāhitā), and was the iconographic prototype for several goddesses on the Indo-Iranian pantheon.[56] Rosenfield notes, "As the feminine personifications of abundance among the Kušāns, Nana-Anāhitā had much in common with Ardoxšo, but the cult of Ardoxšo seems to have been centered upon dynastic and political abundance, whereas that of Nana emphasized natural phenomena."[57] In Bactria, the goddess Ardoxšo (Avestan Aši vaŋʰhī) was worshipped by Kušāns, appearing on their coins (as will be discussed in Chapter Six). Azarpay states that Nana was also equated with the Iranian goddess Ārmaiti, and that the cult of Nana-Ārmaiti was widely spread throughout eastern Iran.[58]

It seems that all of these goddesses had some functions in common, most likely through cultural borrowing. Since these borrowings were often only partial, they should be analyzed with caution when attempting to document Anāhitā's transformations.

The Steppes

The culture of the steppe-dwelling proto-Indo-Europeans (around fifth millennium BCE) from whom the Iranians descended focused primarily on male gods, particularly those connected with war, rule, and related activities.

The goddesses of the proto-Indo-Europeans were mostly associated with natural phenomena, such as the dawn, rivers, and the decomposition of bodies, as well as fertility, healing, childbirth, love, and sex.[59] Over time the proto-Indo-European deities, gods and goddesses alike, acquired new functions and shifting status depending on the different locations to which the various proto-Indo-European tribes migrated and the other cultures with which they interacted.

For example, the indigenous peoples who lived around Caspian and Azov Seas in prehistoric times worshipped goddesses.[60] By the late second millennium BCE, they developed a close relationship with the nomadic Iranian Sakas, influencing them through their lifestyle and their rituals. This may help account for the fact that among the Sakas women had important roles, including governance and going to war, to a greater extent than among other Indo-Iranian groups.

On the list of Saka deities provided by Herodotus, the most important is the goddess of the hearth-fire, whom he refers to as "Hestia/Tabiti": "The gods whom they propitiate by worship are … Hestia most of all."[61] While the position of "Hestia" among the Sakas does not necessarily reflect gender roles in their society, it does raise the question of why the supreme deity of this warrior people would be a goddess, given that this is not the norm among the descendants of the proto-Indo-Europeans. The most plausible explanation is that the Sakas' special reverence for a female deity possibly was adopted from some of the non-Indo-European peoples they encountered on the steppes.

Other goddesses from Herodotus's list are Api-Gē, the earth-goddess (who generally reminds one of the Zoroastrian Spəṇtā Ārmaiti), who figures third in importance, and "Urania" ("heavenly") Aphrodite Argimpasa, the goddess of fertility and love, who comes fifth. In comparison to the pantheons of other Iranian groups, it is remarkable that of the five most important Saka deities mentioned by Herodotus, three are goddesses.

These three goddesses, moreover, seem to be related to each other. Hestia-Tabiti and Api-Gē are less anthropomorphized than Argimpasa-Aphrodite Urania, however. Of the three, Argimpasa seems most similar to Anāhitā, with her tripartite characteristics as a multifunctional goddess with fertility, military, and sacerdotal aspects.[62] Furthermore, Argimpasa-Aphrodite *Urania* and Anāhitā were both worshipped as the divine patronesses of the kings, bestowing royal power.[63] Ultimately, all three major Saka goddesses seem to be connected in varying degrees to Anāhitā.[64]

Indo-European Water Goddesses

A central aim of this study is to untangle and clarify Anāhitā's roots. In her original form as a water goddess, she appears to share a number of similar functions with other Indo-European water goddesses, including Arnemetia, Nemetona, Sirona, Brigantia, and others. Can these similarities be shown to be fundamental and thematic? How can they be explained? Can Anāhitā's original identity as an Indo-European water goddess be established in a convincing way?

Celtic Goddesses

There exists a range of evidence from across Indo-European societies that a goddess related to and personified as water in the form of rivers, lakes, and streams was present since ancient times. Indeed, much of this evidence would indicate that water was a central focus in the rituals of many cultures throughout Europe by around 1300 BC at the latest, and probably well before that. As a religious symbol, water was used as a healing, purifying, and sanctifying element in rituals.[1] The Celts, in particular, built sanctuaries at the sources of rivers and lakes, as did the Aryans in Iran. Sacrifices were offered on the banks of the rivers and cast into the water as gifts, honoring its supernatural powers, which was mostly associated with female deities. Items offered included such things as swords, and often the severed heads of vanquished enemies, which were believed to hold special powers.

Many Celtic sites throughout Europe are considered to have been religious in nature; La Tène on the edge of Lake Neuchâtel in Switzerland is a particularly rich example.[2] Investigations at La Tène uncovered thousands of weapons, tools, jewelry, and coins at the bottom of the lake, suggesting that the lake was used for sacrificial offering.[3] A large quantity of objects—mostly weapons—thrown into the water as offerings have been found in European rivers,[4] which demonstrates that these rivers were considered as an abode of sacredness. The fact that these offerings were mostly connected with war suggests that the warriors of the time, according to their belief system, were seeking the support and protection of a water deity.

Indo-European cosmology posited a connection between water, earth, and sky, as reflected in their myths. Along with rivers and lakes, springs and wells were also considered sacred places and were associated with many functions, notably healing. Among the Germanic peoples including the Scandinavians, the shores of lakes and waterfalls as well as the banks of rivers were used as sacred locations for offerings, and they cast their sacrifices into the lakes.[5]

These sacred water sites were typically connected to female deities. Widespread evidence for water goddess cults during the early first millennium AD is based upon iconographical, epigraphic, and archaeological discoveries and records.[6] A large number of river/lake goddesses in ancient Europe gave their names to rivers or received the rivers' names. Many major European rivers had goddess-spirits; that of the Seine, for example, was called "Sequana."[7] The river Marne and the goddess Matrona, the river Saône and the goddess Souconna, the river Yonne and the goddess Icauni, the river Boyne and the goddess Bóinn, the river Shannon and the goddess Sionnan, the river Inny and the goddess Eithne, and the river (or Lough) Érne and the goddess Érne are further examples of such associations. Thus, water-river goddesses were widely distributed across Europe, from Ireland and England to France, Germany, and into Russia. These goddesses were usually associated with rivers, springs, and lakes, and possessed some similar functions and water-based rituals. Healing was one of these functions, and certain springs, which were considered to be sacred, were believed to have healing properties.

Since water was symbolic of health and healing, the goddesses who were related to water usually had a healing function as well. These goddesses were also sometimes represented with animals such as snakes or dogs. Snakes, due to the shedding of their skin, may have been a symbol of rebirth and thus fertility; alternatively, their winding nature may have suggested the meandering of a river. Dogs, for their part, were associated with self-healing.[8] There were sacred dogs in some healing sanctuaries,[9] which remind us of the fact that in Zoroastrianism dogs were seen as righteous, sacred animals and were used in some rituals; they possessed purifying features and could exorcise demons.[10]

In his account of the Gallic Wars, the Roman emperor Julius Caesar provides a list of Celtic deities which he identified with those of the Roman pantheon.[11] Among these he mentions Minerva, identified with various Celtic goddesses as a protector of rivers and springs.[12] As noted above, there is strong evidence for the association of flowing water with goddesses in the Celtic belief system.[13] Water goddesses were very popular among the Celts, whose migrations left traces all across Europe. These goddesses not only ensured fertility but also were able to cure the ill, a capacity embodied in the sacred power of water. The strength and vital necessity of rivers, springs, and lakes were seen as demonstrations of the supernatural powers of the goddesses who inhabited the waters. The belief in the sacredness of water (wells/springs/lakes/rivers) survived in Christian Europe through the association of water sites with female saints.[14]

Dānu

One of the main proto-Indo-European word for "river-water" and "water-basin" is the stem *dānu-*,[15] which also is connected to the concept of a water goddess. A widely recurring term connected with rivers in Indo-European, *dānu*, from *dehanu*, was apparently the name given to a proto-Indo-European river goddess since she also appears in the Vedas, as Dānu.[16] In Avestan, *dānu-* means "river, stream"; this sense survives in the modern Ossetic *don*.[17] The Irish Danu and the Welsh Dôn both come from the same linguistic root, which means "abundant, giving." The Indo-European *dā-* and its suffixed derivative *dānu-* means "river."[18] Reflexes of this term can be found in the myths of many of the Indo-European peoples, often in connection with a river goddess.

It is noteworthy for our discussion that the word *dānu-* (river-water), apart from providing theophoric names and categories, also embodies the very concept of water-river goddess. This shows that the words for "water" in proto-Indo-European languages could be connected with the deity associated with it. Hence, it is also possible to connect another proto-Indo-European word, *ap-* "current (of water)," with Anāhitā.

The term *dānu* survives most famously in the names of several European rivers, including the Danube, the Don (one in Russia and another in England), the Dnieper, the Dniester,[19] and others. Indo-European *deh2nu-* "river" is reconstructed from Sanskrit *dānu*, Irish *dānu*, Welsh *dôn*, and Ossetic *donbettys*. A shortened form of the name appears to have been *dā-*.[20]

A water goddess named Dānu is found in Germanic as well as Celtic mythology (cf. proto-Celtic *Danona*). She was thus very likely a proto-Indo-European water goddess. The wide range of attestations for this term may indicate that Dānu was originally a title rather than a particular goddess, and was bestowed on various rivers by various Indo-European peoples during the course of their migrations into and across Europe over time. The Greek goddess Demeter (*dā-*

mater, "river-mother") is likewise connected to water,[21] and the goddess Dānu in the Vedas would seem to be related as well.

In Irish tradition, Dānu was the goddess of the waters, as well as of the first Celtic tribes to settle in Ireland, the *Tuatha Dé Danann* (the "people of the Goddess Dānu/Danann").[22] Human beings (or, more specifically, the Indo-European peoples) are even considered as "The children of Dānu"; she, as the mother-water goddess, has given them life.[23] There exist many folk myths about "Dānu's people."[24] The Celtic scholar Peter Ellis notes that "The Dānube, first recorded as the Dānuvius, was named after the Celtic goddess Dānu, whose name means 'divine waters.'"[25] Classicist Arthur Bernard Cook affirms that "Dānuvius and its cognates must moreover be connected with the Avestan *dānu-*, 'river.'"[26]

The Celtic creation story mentions the "heavenly water" which floods downward.[27] Dānu is thus the divine water flowing down from heaven; the parallel with Anāhitā, who is described in exactly the same way, is too clear to be coincidental. Miriam Robbins Dexter has suggested that Dānu was originally a non-Indo-European river and earth goddess who was adopted at an early stage of proto-Indo-European religion.[28] In any case, at least some of the notions associated with this goddess must be very ancient. Dānu can also be connected to Brigit, the Celtic goddess of wisdom, war, healing, and fertility.[29]

The Goddesses

Some of the major Celtic water goddesses include: Arnemetia, who was a water and spring goddess; Nemetona, a goddess of springs; the spring-water goddess Sirona in Hochscheid in Germany; Sulis, a goddess of healing springs including those at Bath in England;[30] and Brigantia who was the goddess of war, healing, water, and also fertility and prosperity. All of these goddesses had a variety of functions, similar to Anāhitā's, among which fertility and healing were especially prominent. Some were popular over a wide area and possessed a range of characteristics and purposes, while the others were simply local goddesses. Very often a Celtic goddess is portrayed in company of a god of differing origin (e.g., Roman).[31] The pairing of a temple to Mithras with one to a water goddess also has widespread parallels in Iran.

Coventina/Conventina

An important Romano-Celtic water goddess was Coventina/Conventina, represented both as a single river goddess and as a triple nymph.[32] Originally a local Celtic water goddess, Coventina was associated with the functions of healing and childbirth, and possibly war as well. She became popular among Roman soldiers following the establishment of Roman power in Britain. At least ten inscriptions related to Coventina have been found at the Roman site of Carrawburgh, near Hadrian's wall in Northumberland.[33] These inscriptions were accompanied by a number of statues and coins. The goddess has sometimes been identified as Brigantia in another guise, or even Venus.[34] Based on the date of coinage bearing her image, it would appear that Coventina's cult flourished during the second and third centuries CE. Several stone altars have been found bearing dedications to her as well, where she was referred to as *Dea nympha Coventina*.[35] The remains of a Roman temple devoted to Mithras (a Mithræum) have also been found and excavated at Carrawburgh, near Hadrian's Wall in Northumberland, including three adjacent altars. This would seem to indicate a triad of deities, providing an interesting parallel with the Iranian grouping of Mazdā-Miθra-Anāhitā.

The association of Coventina with Mithras at Carrawburgh thus raises the following question: Why did these two deities, a water goddess who also is a healer with clear functional and cultic commonalities with Anāhitā (e.g., both goddesses received the severed heads as offering), and Mithras, a martial deity whose cult was centered on the tauroctony or bull sacrifice, have adjacent temples and inscriptions? Can there have been a relationship between them similar to what we see in the pairing of Anāhitā and Miθra in the Iranian context? Cumont states that the Roman soldiers who followed the cult of Miθra had borrowed him (via the frontier zone of eastern Anatolia/northern Mesopotamia) from the Iranian pantheon,[36] but this is still a matter of discussion among scholars, and as Richard Gordon notes, several scholars have argued that the Roman cult of Mithras has no substantial connection with Iran.[37] These questions merit a separate study, but for our purposes it may be noted that the possible connection between the Iranian and European cases in terms of the Miθra–water goddess pairing is striking, and may support Cumont's position.

Although Coventina was seen as a healing goddess, based on the springs dedicated to her for both male and female devotees, she was not simply a typical Celtic healer deity; she had many other functions as well, related to spirituality, war, and fertility, and even to the personal lives of her devotees.[38] Some of the Carrawburgh relics, such as the small bronze masks, the head on the spout of a pottery jug, the head of a male statue, and the heads on the front of one of the altars, may suggest the presence of the kind of human head cult discussed above.[39]

Brigantia/Bríg/Brigan

Among the ancient Celtic goddesses who often had similar functions, a few names occur in many different locations, an indication that these goddesses were honored by diverse groups of Celts. Brigantia, "the eponymous deity associated with principle tribe of north Britain," is one.[40] Variations of her name are found throughout Europe. An interesting connection to Anāhitā can be found in Brigantia's name itself, which is derived from the root **bhergh-* "high," which also occurs in **Brigentī*, **brigant-*, "high person/place," **bhr̥ĝh-n̥t-ī* "the eminent," proto-Celtic form **Brĭgantī* (from *brig-* high), as is the old Irish *Brigit*.[41] The term has Indo-Iranian reflexes, including the Sanskrit *br̥hatī* and the Avestan *bərəzaitī*, both of which are feminine adjectives meaning "high, lofty." *Bərəzaitī*, "the lofty one," is one of Anāhitā's most common adjectives, with which it would appear to be cognate; the name Brigantia comes from a root meaning "high," "the high one,"[42] or "mountainous, tall; the high, lofty one."[43] This provides an exact linguistic correspondence with Anāhitā's Irish counterpart, and is entirely fitting for a "celestial river,"[44] which is symbolized by the Milky Way.

A widely attested Celtic goddess connected to victory, water, wisdom, fire, war, healing, fertility (by protecting cattle),[45] and prosperity, Brigantia was specifically connected with sacred waters and wells, just like many other Celtic goddesses.[46] Jolliffe notes that Victory was a goddess worshipped by the Roman soldiers, and that equation of Brigantia with Victory might well have been made by them at the time.[47]

Brigantia was the daughter of Dagda, the protector god of the Celtic tribes.[48] She was worshipped in the Celtic regions of Ireland, Scotland, Wales, and Brittany, as well as other locations in Europe where Celts were present. The wide area of her popularity led to an expansion of her functions, transforming her into a more powerful multifunctional goddess, as was the case with Anāhitā in Iran.

Brigantia was also worshipped widely throughout the Roman Empire, according to a Roman version of her cult. Her martial functions would have been particularly appealing to Roman soldiers and may have led to her conflation with certain Roman martial deities.[49] Variants of her can be detected in Brigindo of Gaul, Brigantia of northern England, and Bríg of Ireland. Her various names and functions ultimately derive from a common ancestor Brigantii, who was connected to Lake Constance around the river Rhine in central Europe.[50]

The Gallic deity Bricta may also be related to her. The rivers Brent in England, Braint in Wales, and Brigid in Ireland are all linguistically connected to this goddess—and most likely religiously as well—through the root Brig/Brigant.[51]

This strongly suggests that Brigantia, like Anāhitā, originated as a water goddess who absorbed some additional functions over time.

Like Anāhitā, Brigantia was associated with the juxtaposition of fire and water. The water from many of her wells was believed to be effective against eye diseases, which points to another of her functions. She was also connected with wisdom, and it was said that (like the Norse god Odin) she lost her sight in order to gain wisdom and inner sight. Blinded, she restored her sight by washing her eyes in the sacred waters.[52]

The greatest number of sacred wells in Ireland are dedicated to Brigit, who became Christianized as the island's patron saint.[53] In Roman times she was identified with Minerva, the Latin goddess of war, wisdom, and crafts. She was also identified with victory, and described as "celestial," possibly under influence of *Dea Caelestis*,[54] a fertility goddess sometimes identified as Aphrodite Urania, and who was worshipped by Romans as the "heavenly goddess." This provides yet another similarity with Anāhitā, who carried the same epithet. She acquired a cosmic character since she was identified and Romanized as *Dea Caelestis Brigantia* (Goddess of the Heavens Brigantia).[55]

The second-century geographer Ptolemy mentions a tribe in Leinster, Ireland, calling itself the Brigantes, who gave their name to the river Brigid.[56] Taken together, these signs suggest that similar to Anāhitā, Brigantia/Brigid may at some point have united the three Indo-European social group functions within herself. We may, therefore, suppose her to have originated as a local water goddess, and absorbing additional functions over time, such as protection of the royalty and warriors during the war, and fertility functions such as healing. The Romans worshipped her primarily as a war goddess.[57] Apart from sharing many functions with Anāhitā, including water and wisdom, she was of particular importance for the imperial family (like Anāhitā), as Jolliffe suggests.[58]

An archaeological site at Luxeuil in France has produced the remains of an ancient Celtic temple associated with healing, combining hot springs and sanctuaries. Several deities are depicted in the iconography at this site, including Bricta and Sirona (a goddess of fertility and healing), who were both worshipped widely and were associated with rivers and healing springs. Since Bricta appears to have been a variant of Bríg, she was probably a goddess of healing, protection, and fertility with both water and perpetual fire associations (like Anāhitā). One may note that the combination of healing water and perpetual fire was very widespread in ancient Europe,[59] suggesting that this combination was characteristically connected to proto-Indo-European water goddesses whose descendants include Anāhitā.

Based on evidence given by Strabo,[60] the pairing of fire and water cults seems to have ancient precedents in Indo-Iranian religion, including temples devoted to Anāhitā (Anaïtis). We may recall that in Iran the so-called Adur Anahid fire temple in Eṣṭaxr, which was under the custodianship of the Sasanian royal family, can be seen as combining fire and water symbolism in the cult of Anāhitā.

It is worth noting that the goddess Brigantia is referred to in one of her inscriptions as "the goddess the Nymph Brigantia"[61] (recalling the goddess Coventina, who was mentioned as *Dea Nimfa Coventina* in a Carrawburgh inscription[62]), reminiscent of the possible connection between Anāhitā and the *pairika*s who also had "nymph" functions.

Brigantia appears in many inscriptions and reliefs, including the so-called Birrens relief (dated to 210 CE), where she appears as a winged goddess.[63] This is interesting because the goddesses Ostia-Minerva and Victory sometimes have wings in their sculptures, who, in turn, remind us of the Mesopotamian Innana/Ištar. These wings may have been an icon symbolizing of the power of flight through the heavens.

Imbolc, the festival dedicated to Brigantia which is held on February 1 in Ireland, was the principal pagan spring festival in pre-Christian times,[64] celebrating the "return of spring and of the reawakening of the fire that would purify the land for the new season."[65]

Other Celtic Goddesses

Sulis or Sul was a native Celtic deity who was equated with Roman goddess Minerva; her cult was popular over a wide area, and is attested for a period of nearly four centuries.[66] "Sulis" is philologically linked to the sun.[67] Her sacred spring in Bath with its hot mineral water, *Aquae Sulis*, which remains a popular tourist site to this day, appears to have served as the principal connection with the goddess, where her devotees requested her support. These requests sometimes included vengeance and curses, showing another possible function of the goddess.[68] In this respect, they are highly reminiscent of those made by villainous characters mentioned in the *Ābān Yašt*, who ask (in vain) for Anāhitā's support in pursuing their destructive activities. Moreover, in the *Aquae Sulis*, there was a perpetual fire,[69] which reminds one of Anāhitā's temples in the Iranian world.

Arnemetia was a Romano-Celtic water goddess associated with a spring in Buxton, England. Water from this spring was supposed to cure diseases and illnesses. Celtic mythology also includes a local river goddess named Verbeia. She was worshipped as a deification of the river Wharfe in England, as was the case with many other rivers in Europe associated with a female deity. The root of her name may represent a Celtic or British term (probably reflex of the proto-Indo-European root *wer-bhe-*) of "bend, turn," and so might have meant "(she who is) constantly bending and turning."[70] An image of a woman with an oversized head and two huge snakes in her hands may represent this goddess. Again, the presence of snakes may have to do with rebirth, symbolized by the snake's habit of sloughing off its skin, or the "serpentine" winding of rivers.[71] In Indo-European tradition, dragons/snakes are the symbol of drought and chaos, embodiments of the destructive potential of rivers. This symbol is also present in depictions of another Celtic spring goddess, Sirona (whose name possibly is philologically related to "star"[72]), who is represented with a snake wrapped around her right forearm.

A number of legends associate female spirits, sometimes negative ones, with England's river Wharfe. It was said that sometimes the goddess of the river appears as a white horse and claims a victim in her waters.[73] The concept of river goddesses having a negative form could be related to opposing aspects of the waters and their ambivalent role in the lives of humans. Rivers have two opposing aspects: they bring fertility and blessing to life, but in their dragon shape they can also cause destruction through flooding. As we will discuss later, it is noteworthy that two Vedic goddesses, Aditi and Dānu, also embody the opposing concepts of cosmic and non-cosmic waters.

Another Irish river goddess is Boann or Boand, goddess of the river Boyne in Ireland. In a poem from the early Irish onomastic literature, known as the *Dindshenchas*, she is equated with several well-known rivers including the Tigris and the Euphrates.[74] The fact that the *Dindshenchas* mentions such far-off rivers recalls a section of the *Bundahišn* (11.6), which provides a catalogue of the world's major rivers.

Other Celtic river goddesses include Shannon, memorialized in the name of Ireland's longest river, and Clota, which is associated with the river Clyde in Scotland. Yet another was Ancama, who is the subject of some inscriptions found in Germany. At Möhn, near Trier, a temple around a spring with sacred water was dedicated to her.[75] The goddess Damona was mostly worshipped in the French region of Burgundy; her main sanctuary, at Alesia, was a shrine connected to water. Her name means "divine/great cow"; she may thus have some connection to the Vedic goddess Aditi, whose symbol is a sacred cow. This concept, moreover, connects them both with fertility.

The Celtic goddess Epona, goddess of horses and fertility, whose name etymologically connects her with horses, may draw our interest here. She may be compared with the Avestan goddess Druuāspā, whose name also connects her to horses (Druuāspā = "wild solid horses"[76]). Epona was a very popular goddess whose cult was found in Gaul, Britain, Rhine and Danube limes, Macedonia, Italy, Spain, and Portugal.[77] She is depicted in several reliefs with horses surrounding her. Her iconography shows that horse symbols are central to her, since she invariably appears with them.

One of the best-known depictions of Epona has been found in a damaged small marble relief from Viminiacium dated to the second or third centuries CE.[78] Although the relief has suffered heavy damage, to Epona's right and left, one may still discern horses turning toward the goddess. There are two horses to her right and it seems the left side was the same, but due to damage, the figure of the second horse on the left side is missing. In another relief, from fourth-century CE Salonica, the goddess similarly appears between four horses, with two on either side. The iconography of a goddess with four horses provides a clear parallel with Anāhitā. Moreover, there is connection between Epona and water: she occurs at a number of spring sites in Gaul. In one relief, she appears as a water nymph with horse and water-lily leaf.[79] Epona had still other functions in common with Anāhitā: she was linked to the underworld and thus with regeneration and rebirth, and by extension with water and healing. Other motifs accompanying her are fruits, the dog, and the raven,[80] each connecting her to different functions.

All of these goddesses who are associated with water illustrate the fact that water's power and its connection with female deities are very old within the Celtic belief system, and their many similarities with Iranian and Indic examples suggest these associations may go back to proto-Indo-European times. Throughout much of Western Europe (especially in France), the major river names are all feminine.[81] Many of these water goddesses are recorded only in inscriptions, and are often paired with a male deity, offering a further parallel to the pairing of Arəduuī Sūrā Anāhitā with Miθra as represented and documented in Iranian inscriptions such as those of Artaxerxes II (r. 404–358 BCE).

The Cult of the Head

The shrine of Sequana, goddess of the river Seine in France, was located at the river's source in Burgundy, near Dijon.[82] The goddess was envisaged,[83] since she appears as large bronze figure of a goddess with a diadem standing in a boat. Several votive items were dedicated to the goddess, some of them showing her healing function.[84] Over one hundred carvings have been found in the marshes nearby, including a figure of Sequana herself as well as many others representing human heads. A considerable number of these, which appear to have been votive offerings in a religious or a ritual context, were found at the source of the Seine; carvings of human heads have been found there as well, possibly representing a method to honoring the goddess.[85] This leads us to another point about the warlike function of some Celtic goddesses, which is the Celtic "cult of the head" or "cult of the severed head" offering the head as sacrifice to their deities.[86] The Celts considered the head to be the source of body life (what we might call the "soul") and the power center for the humans.[87] The head was thus identified with the source and origin of all of the waters, river streams and lakes, and these headwater locations were usually considered as sacred. Human skulls have been discovered at a number of wells and springs, leading to speculation that there may have been a connection between the head cult and the sacred waters. Accordingly, the Celts' sacrifices and offerings to the water goddesses (e.g., the Irish goddess Brigit, Coventina, etc.) sometimes included real human heads.[88] The Iranians, as we shall see below, had the same practice.

Collecting the heads of slain enemies was believed to enable the warriors to absorb their powers. Heads severed in battle seem to have been dedicated to goddesses with warlike functions. Evidence of this kind of sacrificial ritual has been found from the Roquepertuse (Bouches-du-Rhône) and Entremont, near Aix-en-Provence, as well as in a large-scale excavation of the hill fort of Danebury in central Britain. Many complete human bodies have been found as well, along with both severed human heads and head-shaped carvings.[89] In the caves at Wookey Hole where the River Axe rises, fourteen skulls with no bodies have been found.[90] The human head also played a role in the cult of the Coventina, the river and water goddess described above, whose well is adjacent to a Mithraeum in Northumberland, England,[91] suggesting that the cult of the head was not without significance to worshippers of Coventina. Water also had connection to the Celtic "cult of head." Severed heads were among the many offerings left at the bottoms of lakes.[92]

A strikingly similar phenomenon is found in ancient Iran, where, for example, the Sāsānian king Ardešīr demonstrated his devotion to Anāhitā by sending the severed heads of defeated enemies to her temple at Eṣṭaxr.[93] Two centuries later, in 430 CE, the severed heads of Christian martyrs were exposed there, demonstrating the continuity of this tradition.[94] The Iranian form of the "head cult" clearly emphasizes Anāhitā's warrior aspect. (This will be discussed more fully in Chapter Five.) The close similarity between these rituals in Europe and Iran can hardly be accidental, and must point to a common origin.

Slavic

The word *bog*, meaning "god" in various Slavic languages, is a loan from the Iranian *baga-*, and this fact should remind us of the longstanding geographical and cultural proximity between Slavs and Iranians throughout history.

Mokosha (the patron of horses) was a pagan Slavic-Ukrainian goddess who was associated with water. Mokosha, however (who may have been originally a goddess of the Finno-Ugric tribes[95]), was first and foremost an earth goddess, called "Moist Mother Earth." Her name is derived from the Slavic root (*mokryi/*mok*) "moist" or "wet,"[96] which suggests her connection with water and moisture. She ruled over fertility and possessed all the aspects of a mother goddess.[97] She also was associated with childbirth, as well as with warriors; the horse was sacred to her. Although her cult was more prevalent in the north, she left her mark on all of the Russian-inhabited lands. Her multiple functions are common between most Indo-European mother goddesses, who were associated with water and fertility, women and childbirth, as well as warriors.

Mokosha's great feast was held in the beginning of autumn.[98] In Ukraine, in late August every year it was customary for locals to honor her by swimming in a river to cleanse themselves of evil; this practice continued after the introduction of Christianity. Her cult continued among Slavic women up to the nineteenth century.[99]

Non-Indo-European Neighbors of the Slavs

Some of the Finno-Ugric peoples, who are northern non-Indo-European neighbors to the Slavs, had a water goddess who shared some similarities with Indo-European river goddesses. For example, in Western Russia, the Mordvins worshipped Ved'ava, a "water mother" goddess who ruled the waters. Although Ved'ava was originally related to fertility, over time she came to be associated with drowning, and was envisioned as a mermaid; she was thus perceived as a sign of misfortune.[100]

As the Water Mother, Ved'ava provided life-giving moisture: she was the protector of love, marriage, and childbirth. Family, calendar, and especially wedding traditions refer to her.[101] A ritual considered integral to the marriage ceremony was to immerse the bride in water: the bride was taken to the river directly from the nuptial bed. The Mordvins believed that this ritual would assist in the delivery of children. We may recall, for example, that according to Zoroastrian belief three maids will swim in a lake containing Zaraθuštra's sperm, thereby becoming impregnated so as to give birth to three future saviors. Also, like Daēnā, Ved'ava could appear either as a young girl (naked or clothed) with long, loose hair, or as a dreadful woman with hanging breasts.[102]

Another striking parallel connecting Anāhitā with non-Indo-Europeans of the Ural region is found among certain Ugric peoples. As noted by Kuz'mina, they have a river goddess who, like Anāhitā, wears clothing made from beaver skins.[103] Since the proto-Indo-Iranians inhabited the southern Urals during the late third and early second millennia BCE, a connection between the water goddess in the two cultures seems likely.

Armenian

The Armenians, an Indo-European people who have long inhabited the southern Caucasus and western Anatolia, have undergone centuries if not millennia of influences from their Iranian neighbors. It appears that prior to their conversion to Christianity in the early fourth century, the religion of the Armenians was permeated with Zoroastrian features probably absorbed by them sometime during the Achaemenid period. Zoroastrian elements remain present in Armenian culture up to the present day.

Like the Iranians, the Armenians seemed to have referred to adherents of Zoroastrianism as "Mazdā-worshippers." Aramazd (a loan form from Parthian) was the principal deity of pre-Christian Armenia.[104] They also worshipped a goddess named Anahit (*bānūg*, "the Lady"), a fertility and healing goddess clearly derived from the Iranian Anāhitā. In addition, the Armenians worshipped familiar Iranian deities such as Mihr (Miθra), Spantaramet (Sepanta-armaiti), and Nanē (Nanai/Inanna). At the same time, the Armenian pantheon differed somewhat from that of the Iranians.

Anahit

Influenced by the other goddesses in the area, the Armenian Anahit was very important and popular, like her Iranian peer Anāhitā, with many temples dedicated to her. She was considered to be the daughter of Aramazd (the Armenian corruption of Ahura-Mazdā). Recalling many other Indo-European water goddesses who were associated with springs, on the slopes of Mt. Ararat there is a spring called *Anahtakan albiwr*, "spring of Anāhīd," an identification that remains up to the present day.[105] Thus, ancient Armenian religion preserved in their beliefs about Anahit what was likely a proto-Indo-European association between a water goddess and healing. Anahit is also associated with Armenian temples built high in the mountains.

According to Greek historians such as Strabo, there existed some ceremonies connected with Anahit that involved sacred prostitution.[106] Tiridates III, before his conversion to Christianity, prayed officially to the triad Aramazd–Anahit–Vahagn (Vərəθrayna). He specifically prayed to "the great lady Anahit ... the benefactress of the whole human race, mother of all knowledge, daughter of the great Aramazd."[107]

After Aramazd, Anahit was the most important deity of Armenia. As in western Iran, she seems to have held a special place in the hearts of the common people. She was referred to as "the Glory," "the Great Queen," or "the Lady." Unlike the Iranians, Armenians made statues of their deities, probably a sign of Hellenistic influence.[108] The symbol of ancient Armenian medicine was the head of the bronze-gilded statue of Anahit, currently in the British Museum.[109] She was also called the "one born of gold" or the "golden-mother," perhaps because her statues were made from solid gold in Erēz, which was the main center for her cult.[110] At other Armenian cult centers associated with the god Vahagn and the goddess Astlik, Anahit was worshiped in the guise of a golden idol apparently known as *oskemayr*, "the Golden Mother."[111]

Anahit was referred to as the "noble Lady and mother of all knowledge, daughter of the great and mighty Aramazd."[112] There are references to offerings at her altars, and in 36 BCE one of the Roman commander Mark Antony's soldiers carried off the famous gold statue of her from the temple at Erēz. The bronze head mentioned above, originally discovered at Satala, is similar to that of the Greek Aphrodite, recalling that according to Classical sources all statues in Armenia were made by Greek craftsmen.[113]

Although Armenian rituals connect Anahit with water, she does not appear to have been connected to support warriors unlike in Iran. This difference can be explained by the theory that Anāhitā's martial functions might have been a later Mesopotamian influence accruing to the Iranian goddess from Inanna/Ištar, and furthermore suggests that the Armenians had already adopted her prior to that time. The Armenians seem rather to have adopted the Mesopotamian martial goddess as a distinct figure in her own right.

Nanē and Astlik

It is noteworthy that whereas in western Iran Anāhitā seems to have become conflated with the Mesopotamian goddess Inanna/Ištar, in the Armenian pantheon, Anahit is distinct from Nanē, the Armenian version of the Sumerian Inanna. In contrast to the Iranian case, in Armenia the functions of the two goddesses were not conflated, and each had her separate role. At the same time, the Armenian Nanē absorbed some of the functions of another Iranian goddess, Aši. The relationship between Anahit and Nanē was mythologized by the Armenians as the two being "daughters" of Aramazd.[114]

In Hellenistic times the Armenians identified Nanē with Athena, perhaps indicating that she had come to be seen as austere and warlike. It is possible that the Armenians may have originally had a single goddess possessing a range of functions—love, fertility, beauty, motherhood, and war—which were later divided between different goddesses. Anahit acquired the functions of healing and motherhood, and Nanē those of war, while another goddess, Astghik or Astlik, who was identified with Aphrodite and Ištar, became the goddess of love and beauty.

Astlik means "little star" (*astl*, "star" + "ik," the diminutive suffix).[115] This goddess probably has ancient Indo-European roots. Vahagn, the Armenian version of the Iranian Vərəθrayna, was her lover. In addition to her astral nature, Astlik was also connected with water and springs, and some water rituals were related to her. During the nineteenth century, an Armenian priest recorded a legend according to which at the source of the Euphrates in the mountains there is a pool where Astlik bathes. Young men used to climb and light a fire in order to behold the beauty of the naked goddess, and this is why the waters send up a mist there to shield her from their prying eyes.[116] Although this story indicates Astlik's possible Mesopotamian roots, the presence of the Euphrates and a pool at its source also connects her to water and water rituals. A closely related myth exists today among the Iranian-speaking Zaza of Bingöl in eastern Turkey.[117]

Armenians today have preserved an ancient ritual called "Vardavar" in which people sprinkle water on each other, echoing similar *āb-pāšī* rituals that survive in contemporary Iran. In the past, this ritual was devoted either to Anahit or to Astlik. Russell reports that it was believed by the inhabitants of the region that on the morning of Vardavar Anahit bathed in a place where two rivers meet, and that a similar story exists about Astlik.[118] Until a century ago, during this festival the Armenians of Dersim, Turkey, slaughtered cattle bearing the brand of a star or half moon; it is thus possible that Anahit absorbed these cult symbols from the Mesopotamian goddess Ištar. Chaumont, on the other hand, considers that Astlik is the "local equivalent of Aphrodite,"[119] but the two assertions are not mutually exclusive.

If we accept that the sky light was considered as a personification of Astlik—and we should recall that Anāhitā is also a celestial river, the Milky Way, and was later identified with the planet Venus—and also accept Astlik's water-related features, then it is not difficult to find a connection between her and Anāhitā. Actually, it seems that the Armenian Anahit, especially in her function as a healer goddess, and Astlik both possessed some of Anāhitā's characteristics; in fact, each of the three major Armenian goddesses have some functions and rituals in common with her.

Sandaramet (Spandaramet) and Dainanazdayašniš

The Avestan female deities Spəṇta Ārmaiti and Daēnā both appear in Armenian forms during the pre-Christian period. The Aramaic Arebsun inscriptions from late Achaemenid Cappadocia refer to Dainanazdayašniš as the wife of the god Bel.[120] The fifth-century CE Armenian historian Yeghishe Vardapet refers to the Aməša Spəṇtas as "adjutant gods" (*hamharz astuatsk'*), which raises the question of whether in looking at Armenian goddesses and their functions we may, in fact, be dealing with a "complex" of goddesses, in which functions between them may appear to overlap simply because on some level they represent a divine unity.[121]

It is also possible to detect survivals of Anāhitā and other pre-Christian goddesses in later Armenian Christianity. For example, the tenth-century *Book of Lamentations* by St. Gregory of Narek refers to the Virgin Mary as *barjr*, "lofty," recalling Anāhitā's cognate epithet *bərəzaitī*.[122] Similarly, in the Armenian epic tradition, the Holy Virgin of Maruťa possesses a shrine both on top of a mountain *and* under water.[123] Valentina Calzolari has identified a strong substrate of Anāhitā's cult in that of the Armenian saint Thekla of Iconium, who was a close associate of St. Paul.[124]

Indo-Iranian

The grouping of Indo-European tribes collectively known as Indo-Iranian began moving southward from east of the Ural Mountains presumably from the end of the third millennium BCE onward. Some continued on to the Indian subcontinent, bringing with them the culture known from the Rig Vedā, while others pushed southwestward onto the Iranian plateau and eventually to the edges of the densely populated Mesopotamian plain.

According to the analysis of Georges Dumezil (which continues to be a matter of debate among scholars), the Indo-Iranian pantheon of deities and their relationships to humans reflect the tripartite class structure of Indo-European society—priests/rulers, warriors, and producers—with each class being associated with a particular group of deities.[125] The tripartite pantheon is predominantly male. Goddesses are most frequently associated with the third function, especially fertility, but some "synthesize" with other deities to cover all three functions. Thus, in Dumézil's view, goddesses typically have a "base" in the third function, but have "extensions" into the other two.[126]

Two groups of Indo-Iranian deities are common to the Indian (Vedic) and Iranian (Avestic) traditions; however, in each of the two, their status is inverted. One is the *devas* (Skt) or *daēuuas* (Av), who are viewed positively in the Vedas but considered as false deities/demons in the Avesta. The other is the *asuras* (Skt) or *ahuras* (Av), seen negatively in the Vedas but positively in the Avesta. Exactly how this inversion came about remains a matter of speculation and controversy among scholars. In the Iranian pantheon, the main deities, including Anāhitā, belong to the *ahuras* group. As Hintze points out, "in Old Persian inscriptions and the Gaϑas the cultic competitors of Ahura Mazdā are the *daēuuas* the Iranian equivalent of the Vedic 'gods' (*deva-*), rather than Angra Mainyu."[127] In Vedic mythology, the Sky and Earth have *devas* as their children.[128]

In the Vedas, there are two smaller groups of deities related to *asuras*, the Dānavas (the children of Dānu, of dragon-shaped appearance) and the Ādityas (the children of Aditi, whose appearance is like men). Both Dānu and Aditi are feminine, and considered as goddesses. (Recall that Aditi is the mother of the Ādityas, the latter term being derived from Aditi.) Their functions are quite different, however.

Conceived as demonic, the Dānavas bind the cosmic waters, and are connected to cold, darkness, and chaos. The demonic dragon, Vṛtra, belongs to the Dānavas. The Ādityas, on the other hand, possess the characteristics of liberation and unbinding, and are connected to light, cosmic water, and order (*ṛtá*).[129]

Vedic Deities

Aditi: The Goddess of Infinite Expanse

Following the linguistic discussion of the term *anāhitā* in the Introduction, it may be noted that an exact parallel exists in Vedic Sanskrit: *aditi*, who, moreover, is also a goddess and is related to the concept of the cosmic Waters. She is a universal abstract goddess who represents or is connected to the physical creation.[130] The Vedic term *diti* comes from the root √*dā*, meaning "to bind." *A-diti*, therefore, like *A-nāhitā* (but from a different verbal root), as an adjective means "unbounded" or "boundlessness" and is the expression of the visible Infinite and what is free from bonds.[131] *A-diti* and *A-nāhitā* both are described as "mighty," a linguistic parallel too striking to be merely coincidental.

As a goddess, Aditi seems to have many different aspects. As the mother goddess, she is mother of Varuna and Mitra (whose names are paired in many Vedic verses); she was originally distinct from the sky, and was mentioned as being "on the side" of heaven.[132] Aditi seems to be more than an individual goddess: she is a broadly multifunctional figure, and on an abstract level, she is equated with aspects of the cosmos. In the *Ṛg Veda*, she is said to be the "heavens," and interestingly (like Anāhitā but more abstractly), she is also the "mother," the "father," and indeed all the gods. She is what has been born and what will be born.[133] Thus, not only is the Vedic Aditi the original mother goddess, she is mother not just of all the gods, but of everything in creation. She embodied everything: the sky, the earth, the heaven, the waters, and all the other deities.

Aditi's symbol is a sacred cow, or *dhenu*, which offers "unlimited milk." This cow is related to the seven basic rivers of Vedic geography. The sacred cow is something in common between the Iranian and Vedic traditions. It is interesting to note that in the Avestan world, as represented in the Pahlavi sources—just as in the Zoroastrian Creation myth—there exists a sacred cow (the gāw ī ēk-dād), who is killed by Ahriman, but since Ohrmazd had first created the world in spirit form (*mēnog*), he had preserved Creation's prototypes (*ēwēnag*) in the Sun and the Moon, which enabled the "soul" of the cow to survive within the Moon as emphasized by Hintze.[134] The Pahlavi *Wizīdagīhā ī Zādspram* (The Selections of Zādspram) specifies the female gender of this cow:

(WZ 2. 8–9)
pas ō gāw mad ī ēk- dād.

...ud mādag spēd rošn būd čiyōn māh.
and he (Ahriman) came to the sole-created cow[135]...
And it was a female, white and bright like the moon.[136]

The female gender of the "sole-created" cow is similar to that of the goddess Aditi's symbol. The common connection between the cow in the Avestan and Vedic traditions, which points to a common origin, can be taken together with the linguistic parallel between the terms *anāhitā* and *aditi* to show that the very notion of a water goddess, along with its various ritual and mythological associations, was itself part of the common Indo-Iranian tradition.

A further point is, Aditi also represents "the wide horizon." She is the goddess of both the past and the future, of life events, the seven dimensions of the universe, and of consciousness. Some sources mention her as the consort of Brahma, though in later Hinduism she was downgraded in importance, taking on the role of guardian and guide.

Diti

In Vedic mythology, Diti is contrasted with Aditi, as a "being without any definite conception."[137] Originally, they may have represented a cosmic pair, with Aditi being the endless sky and Diti the earth. While Aditi is a positive figure, as are her children the Ādityas, Diti and her children are classified as *asuras*, or demons.

Taking into consideration the well-known process by which certain classes of Indo-Iranian deities were downgraded to demonic status, while others were elevated as beneficent beings, Diti's negative status may be a Vedic innovation; accordingly, her being identified as mother to the *asuras* would not have been a bad thing at an earlier time in Indo-Iranian history when those of deities were not seen as demonic. It might even be speculated that the name Aditi did not originally represent Diti's opposite, but came about through a renaming process so as to justify the maintaining of rituals devoted to a mother goddess now demoted to a demon.[138] At any rate, the "demonic" children of the *asuras* were broken into two family groups: the children of Dānu, who were called "Dānavas," and the children of Diti (Dānu's sister and sometimes identified with her), who were called "Daityas." These two groups do not demonstrate any notable differences.[139]

In several instances, Vṛtra (the personified "dragon" who guarded the waters) is called "Dānava," the son of the goddess Dānu who is connected to the sea (RV I.32.9; II.11.10; III.30.8; V.30.4; V.32). Vṛtra is referred both as *áhi-* (Av. *aži-*, "dragon") and *dāsá-* (Av. *dahāka-*). A passage in the *Ṛg Veda* (1.32.11) describes the "bound waters" as having Vṛtra-dragon as their husband-guardian; this reflects a widespread and presumably ancient Indo-European myth of a dragon preventing access to a water source.[140]

There may also be a connection between *vaŋʰhī dāitiiā*, "the (good) Dāityā," which is the name of a sacred river in the Avesta,[141] and the children of the Vedic Diti, a wife of Kaśyapa, who is sometimes equated with Dānu. Her children are called the "Daityas," which might be connected to the name of the river.

According to Gnoli, the name Dāityā is related to religious law. He states that the river has mythical characteristics, which can be explained within the framework of the notion of *Airiiana Vaēĵah*, the traditional concept of a world center with a world mountain, the peak of the Harā (according to the old Iranian cosmology).[142] It was also mythologically recognized as a heavenly river, though perhaps in reality it referred to the Oxus.

The Avestan term *vaŋhuiiā° dāitiiaiiā°* "of the good Dāiti" qualifies *airiiana-vaēĵah*; the entire phrase *airiianəm vaēĵō vaŋhuiiā° dāitiiaiiā°*, "the Aryan expanse of the good Dāiti," is the original name of the district *Airiiana Vaēĵah*.[143] In the *Bundahišn* the river is described as the "(spiritual) chief of the running waters" (*dāitī rōd tazāgān ābān rad*).[144] This river is also the location where Zaraθuštra is said to have sacrificed to Anāhitā.

Dānu

Dānu or **deh*ₐ*nu-*, the Indo-European river goddess, also appears in the Vedas as Dānu whose sons hold back the heavenly waters.[145] Somewhat ambiguously, Diti is either identified with Dānu or the two are described as sisters. Dānu, too (and contrary to the term *dānu-* in Indo-European myth), is considered to be a demonic goddess in the Vedic texts (as the mother of the dragon Vṛtra). From this Dānu there is the derivative Dānava, again meaning "demon." When and why the demons conquered by Indra came to be called Dānu is not clear,[146] and the meaning of the term Dānu is even less so. It has been suggested that it derives from a root meaning "to cut" or "to drip"; the second meaning could be more connected to the Indo-European *dānu-* and less to the Vedic goddess. However, Brown argues that from the root √*dha*, Dānu could mean "wise or powerful," "bondage," or "restraint,"[147] which fits precisely with Dānu's function.[148] It may be that there are two distinct meanings for the word: "good water," derived from **dānu-* (water or rain), and the second from **dânú-* (giving).[149]

Diti's children, the Daityas, and those of Dānu, the Dānavas, were the two races of demonic *asura*s; the Dānavas, however, are divided into good and bad. One of the Dānavas mentioned in the *Ŗg Veda* (I.32.9) is Vŗtra, the demonic serpent dragon, who is killed by the god Indra. One can see a connection here between Dānu, now a demon but originally a water goddess, and the proto-Indo-European myth of the hero who kills the serpent guarding the water source.[150] (The relevance to Anāhitā will be discussed in Chapter Seven.)

A number of other elements in the *Ŗg Veda* indicate that Dānu was not always a demonic figure, and that at least the term *dānū-* itself retained a positive meaning. Mitra-Varuna and the Aśvins are said to be *srprá-dānū* (RV VIII.25.5–6). The Asvins are called *dānūnaspati*, "lords of Dānuna" (RV VIII.8.16). The god Soma is also called *dānūda* and *dānūpinva*, "giving *dānū*" or "overflowing with *dānū*" (RV IX.97.23). A number of terms are derived from Dānu: "*dānukitra*," for example, applied to the dawn, "water of the clouds," which connects Dānu with water or with rivers. Soma, the deity and sacred beverage, is referred to as "*danuda*" and "*danupinva*," again connecting Danu to water/liquid (RV IX.97.23). There is thus hardly any doubt that from the beginning *dānu-* had some strong conceptual connection with water or liquid.[151] We may note that the word exists in the Avesta (as well as throughout Europe, as previously mentioned) as a river, suggesting that *dānu-*, like *asura-*, was originally a positive word among the Indo-Europeans.

The Sanskrit term *su-dānava-* has been translated as "good (or bounteous) water," and *su-dānu-* as "good river." Also the word *su- dānu-* is applied to various deities in the sense of "bounteous" or "wise."[152] The Vishvedevas—universal deities conceived negatively—are called *su-dānava*s (RV VIII.83.6, 8, 9), as are the Ādityas (RV VIII.67.16), Vishnu (RV VIII.24.12), and the Aśvins (RV I.117.10, 24). The term also occurs in a hymn to Sárasvatī (RV VII.96.4). In the *Ŗg Veda*, positive references to the *su-dānava*s are far more frequent than negative references to *danava* or *sadānuvās*.[153] The Sanskritic connection may survive on the Hindu island of Bali in Indonesia, where there is a temple in Pura Ulun Dānu in Bratan, which is dedicated to Dānu.

Sárasvatī

Many of the rivers in ancient India were considered sacred, and all of the holy rivers were worshiped in Vedic mythology. Being identified with Anāhitā on a number of grounds,[154] Sárasvatī is one of the most notable. Related to fertility, she is hailed both as a divinity and as the mythical river, which she personifies, exactly like Anāhitā. In the *Ṛg Veda*, her movement is described as that of a chariot; she is "the greatest of all the waters" (RV VIII, 95, 1–2) and "the mother of all rivers" (RV VIII, 36, 6).[155] Her name probably means "to flow; she who has flow" or "she who possesses waters."[156] Thus, she was presumably at first associated with flowing water; at some later time, she came also to be associated with knowledge and wisdom, and her water origin was forgotten.

As the goddess of wisdom Sárasvatī was a very powerful deity, a warrior, believed to protect and support her devotees by annihilating their enemies. She is represented as a beautiful young woman, with four arms, or occasionally with two arms, seated on a lotus which, significantly, is a water-based plant. She is usually depicted near a flowing river, further evidence of her origin as a river goddess. It is likely that Sárasvatī was originally the name of one of the branches of the river Sind (the sky/heaven river), now disappeared; it has also been suggested that she is to be identified with the Ganges, or perhaps a small but very holy river in Madhyadeśa.[157] Her Iranian equivalent is Harahvatī (Av. Haraxᵛaitī), which was applied to a region with various rivers.[158]

She later surpasses all other rivers, and like Anāhitā was said to flow from the mountains down to the sea. In other verses she is called to descend from the sky, again like Anāhitā.[159] Bahar states that Sárasvatī (like Anāhitā) may have some connection with Ištar, since apparently people performed sacrificial ceremonies around the river and prepared a holy fire to present to the deity Agni (fire).[160]

Conclusions

Almost all of the female deities discussed in this chapter are directly or indirectly associated with water. They thus held central and vital roles in their respective societies given the vital importance of water for human survival; even the earth (which was also most often associated with a female deity) could not be fertile without water. Water in all its forms (river, lake, streams, well, etc.) was considered as the source of the life, and the water deity followed the same concept. Fertility and healing were common functions of water goddesses; however, a vague link between these goddesses and death and the underworld sometimes existed as well. This could be connected to the uncontrolled and sometimes destructive power of water in its more violent forms, such as floods which cause destruction and drowning, or simply because water often disappears underground. In this way, water represented the threshold between life and death, suggesting that water goddesses, in contrast to other kinds of more specialized deities, were connected with the complete circle of life.

Many (or perhaps even all) of the rivers, lakes, and streams in ancient Europe, India, and Iran were considered sacred, and all of the sacred water and watery places were worshiped according to the mythologies preserved throughout these regions. Lakes, rivers, and springs were therefore chosen as the sites of important sanctuaries and rituals, which were most often identified with a female deity. River goddesses, who also were connected with fertility, were hailed both as divinities and as the mythical river(s) which they personified.

The Indo-European river goddess Dānu (*$Deh^a nu$-*), the Iranian river-lake deity Anāhitā, the Vedic Sárasvatī, the Celtic Sequana, Verbeia, and Shannon and the Irish Boann are merely some of the best-known examples of these water goddesses. The compatibility of their shared functions is easy to reconcile with the practices and worldview found in Iranian mythology, specifically with the goddess Anāhitā. All of these ancient goddesses (Anāhitā included) were associated with rivers, springs, and lakes, and were associated with similar functions and water-based rituals. These functions included fertility and healing, and streams, rivers, and lakes that were considered to be sacred were believed to ensure both.

The commonalities and similarities between these various water goddesses express themselves in a variety of ways. One is through the etymology of their names or epithets. As noted, the Indo-European *da-* ("to flow, flowing") and its suffixed derivative *$danu$-*, meaning "river," exists in Avestan as *dānu-* "river, stream." According to the Iranian cosmic framework, Anāhitā as a river is the ultimate source of all watercourses. She is originally a heavenly river symbolized by the Milky Way (as will be discussed in the following chapter), which flows down from a high mountain range. Similarly, Celtic mythology mentions the "heavenly water," which floods downward.[161] Dānu is one such watercourse flowing down from heaven; Anāhitā is described in exactly the same way.

Related to the flow of the river is the sense that the water is "unbound." The morphological component "*hi-*" in the name Anāhitā means "to bind." Thus, "*hita-*" is a verbal adjective meaning "bound." *Anāhitā*, therefore, means "unbound [to anything]."[162] One may compare this with Aditi in Vedic Sanskrit, where the term *diti* comes from the root √*dā*, meaning "to bind." Thus, while the two are derived from different verbal roots, their semantic meaning is the same: *Aditi*, like *Anāhitā*, means "the unbound."

As has been shown, these connections extend beyond proper names and include epithets as well. The example has been given of the Celtic goddess

Brigantia (*brigant*, "high person," *bhṛ̂gʰ -ṇt-ī*, "(the) eminent")[163] and the Avestan adjective *bərəzaitī-*, meaning "high, lofty," which is one of Anāhitā's most common epithets.

Connections among the water goddesses can also be discerned through the rituals associated with them. In most cases, sacrifices to them were offered on the banks of rivers, streams, or other watery places. Often, offerings were thrown directly into the water. In many cases, these offerings were items connected with war, suggesting that the warrior classes of these ancient societies relied on the support and protection of a water goddess. In support of this contention, warriors are frequently mentioned in inscriptions and hymns devoted to these water goddesses.

Yet, even more than war, these goddesses were associated with fertility and childbirth. The Iranian Anāhitā and the Celtic Coventina are good examples of this. It is surely not accidental that for each of these goddesses physical remains of temples exist today where one can identify a ritual pairing with the martial deity Mithra/Mithras.

Indeed, water goddesses represented so many different aspects of life that they commonly absorbed additional functions over time. In some cases, notably those of Brigantia and Anāhitā, these additional functions came eventually to overshadow and even obscure the goddess's original nature and function as a water deity.

This accumulation of functions could lead, as it did in the cases of both Brigantia and Anāhitā, to their coming to encompass all three of the major social castes—priests, warriors, and "producers"—among their devotees. In this way, goddesses such as Brigantia and Anāhitā developed in ways that gave them almost universal importance across ancient society, relied upon by the ruling class to maintain their rule, the warriors for victory in battle, and by "producers" for ensuring fertility and health.

Finally, parallels among goddesses including Brigantia, Sequana, and Anāhitā suggest the existence of a "cult of the head" with roots in the pagan age. As late as the historical period, Ardešīr demonstrated his devotion to Anāhitā by sending the severed heads of defeated enemies to her temple at Eṣṭaxr.[164] This recorded fact probably followed an earlier existing tradition and may have been one of the factors uniting the ancient water goddesses.

Arəduuī Sūrā Anāhita in the Avesta

The *Yašts* (a Middle Persian term derived from the Avestan verb *yaz-* "to worship ritually"/Av. *yazata-* "worthy of worship"), which preserve the Young Avestan oral tradition, are a collection of twenty-one devotional hymns to the various Iranian divinities (*yazata*s), dating back to approximately 1000 to 600 BCE.[1]

The most extensive appearance of *Arəduuī Sūrā Anāhitā* in the Zoroastrian texts is found in the fifth *Yašt*, the *Ābān Yašt*, which is an entire Avestan hymn devoted to her. The *Ābān Yašt* has 30 sections or *karde* and 133 stanzas, making it the third longest *Yašt* after the *Farwardīn Yašt* and the *Mihr Yašt*. The hymn (like much of the Avesta) is a dialogue between Ahura Mazdā and Zaraϑuštra; each section begins with the refrain "O Spitama Zaraϑuštra, may you sacrifice to her, *Arəduuī Sūrā Anāhitā*." The fifth *Yašt* is especially remarkable due to its richly descriptive verses of the Iranian goddess; it also includes some legendary epic material from ancient times. Although some of the material in the *Ābān Yašt* seems to be extremely archaic while parts might have been borrowed from other *Yašt*s,[2] yet the whole hymn displays a masterful harmony of content.

One of the important features of the *Ābān Yašt* is that it contains the names of legendary figures from Iranian myths, including some negative figures who sacrifice to the goddess to obtain her support. Fraŋrasiian, Aži-Dahāka, Vaēsakaiia, and Vaṇdarəmainiš are the negative figures that sacrifice to Anāhitā but without receiving her support. The fact that these negative figures—specifically Fraŋrasiian and Aži-Dahāka—are said to sacrifice to her is a key point for our discussion. This will be discussed further below and in Chapters Eight and Eleven.

There are similarities between some stanzas of the *Ābān Yašt* (102-127-130) and the *Ard Yašt* or *Aši Yašt* (6–11), which is devoted to the goddess Aši. Boyce states that "Linguistically Arəduuī Sūrā's hymn appears older than Aši's Yt. 17, which is short and badly preserved; and so it has been assumed that, where there are verses in common, it was Aši who was the borrower." She goes on to note, however, that "In a fluid oral literature … such criteria cannot be relied upon."[3]

Skjærvø has proposed a schematic model of how the individual Yašts were structured.[4] Following this model, one may note the wide variety of material contained within the *Ābān Yašt*. Dividing the hymn's content thematically in this way can help us to separate Anāhitā's various functions in order, and thus lead us to analyze her multifunctional characteristics as will be discussed below.

The first section of the hymn (verses 1–5) serves as a kind of introduction to Anāhitā, describing her various functions. Anāhitā is first described as a water goddess with her fertility functions, which include easing childbirth, assuring timely lactation, and purifying men's sperm and the woman's womb. She increases power and wealth, specifically land and cattle.

Subsequent verses describe Anāhitā as a beautiful, powerful deity, who is transformed into a waterfall-river flowing down from a high mountain range (Yt 5.2, 4, 7, 15, 78, 96, 102). These paragraphs contain many visually rich scenes. Elsewhere, she is described as a powerful goddess riding her chariot (Yt 5.11, 13).

The second section of the hymn (Yt 5.21–83) mentions many legendary and mythological figures, positive or negative, who worship Anāhitā and receive or do not receive her honor and her support. The next section (Yt 5.85–88) is about the influence and importance of Anāhitā's role among different groups of people (priests, warriors, and ordinary people, especially young women) and the ways that she should be worshipped by each of them. It also emphasizes her role in protecting the world. Stanzas 104–118 read like a continuation of sections (Yt 5.21–83), mentioning some other mythological figures (positive or negative), including Zaraϑuštra, and their sacrifices to Anāhitā. Skjærvø, in his compositional taxonomy of the Avestan hymns, places these stanzas within his "Legendary section."[5]

The last sections of the *Ābān Yašt* (Yt 5.120–129) deal once again with her physical description, which is given with great precision: she is a powerful deity who rides her chariot by controlling four white horses, representing the rain, wind, clouds, and hail—the most uncontrolled phenomena of nature, all connected to Anāhitā's role as a water goddess. Her beauty is also emphasized, including her clothes, her shoes, and her crown, which are all described with precision and detail. The *Ābān Yašt* combines different divine aspects—likely acquired by the goddess at different stages in her development—re-fashioning her into an important Zoroastrian deity created by Ahura Mazdā.

The Avestan texts have most often been studied by linguists specializing in ancient Iranian languages. My approach, while making extensive and at times critical use of theirs, is different. As a student of mythology (and a visual artist), my attention to linguistic analysis and debates is not treated as an end in itself, but rather as a means to further my own goal of better understanding the origins of Anāhitā as an Indo-European water deity, her transformations over time, and her various portrayals in the evolving historical contexts of Iranian societies. I have a number of specific questions about Anāhitā (which I have raised in the Introduction), which I seek to illuminate through analysis of the texts. Since my questions are primarily mythological rather than linguistic ones, I am less concerned with challenging or proposing alternative explanations to the work of linguists—even if I do so in certain cases—than I am with understanding Anāhitā's place in Iranian mythology.

For example, I have searched the Avestan texts for passages that could shed light on Anāhitā's possible origin as an Indo-European water deity, focusing on her water origin, her healing function, and even her beaver-skin clothing. Such passages can be used to demonstrate similarities with other Indo-European goddesses, as discussed in Chapter Four. At the same time, the description of her crown, which bears similarity to that of Ištar (including an eight-pointed star), suggests Anāhitā's assimilation of features from non-Iranian, Mesopotamian goddess(es), a discussion that will be continued in Chapter Nine. I will also suggest the possibility of linking Anāhitā's cult to that of the "*daēuua*-worshippers" (*Ābān Yašt* 94).

In sum, my approach to the text in this chapter will center upon reconstructing Anāhitā's mythological image and answering the questions that have been put forward in the Introduction.

Anāhitā's Name: A Linguistic Analysis

Anāhitā appears in the Avesta as *Arəduuī Sūrā Anāhitā*, which is a series of three adjectives, grammatically feminine. Thus, her Avestan nomenclature is a grouping of epithets rather than a proper name as such. We should also note that the adjective *anāhitā* is elsewhere applied to some other deities, a point that will be discussed below.

Arəduuī

The first component of this compound name, *arəduuī-*, was rendered as "moist" by Johansson in 1893.[6] The notion of "wetness" was taken up by Bartholomae and has remained popular among many scholars ever since. The epithet *arəduuī-*, accordingly, would literally mean "the moist one." This translation, however, has not been universally accepted. Benveniste suggested that *Arəduuī* was the goddess's original name.[7] Lommel, on the other hand, proposed that the adjective *arəduuī-* was originally applied to Sárasvatī, the sacred river in Vedic mythology who is related to Anāhitā; according to him, the goddess's proper name would have been *Harahwatī.[8] According to this model of transition, Sárasvatī as the sacred river was forgotten but her epithet, *arəduuī-*, remained.[9] As Panaino notes in this regard:

> We may recall that both the warlike and fertility functions of Ištar are present in the Avestan goddess, who, in her turn, possibly had assumed the characteristics of an old Iranian divinity (the Heavenly River, i.e., Ir. *Harahvatī, given to a region rich in rivers, Av. Harax^{v}aitī-, OPers. Hara(h)uvati-, Greek Arachosia); originally *Harahvatī seems to have been the personification of a great mythical river which plunges down from Mt. Harā into the sea Vourukaša and is the source of all the waters of the world), but appears also as a syncretic figure, which perhaps was under the influence of Mesopotamian cults.[10]

Kellens argues that the Vedic adjective "*ārdrá-*," "moist," does not directly correspond to the goddess's second epithet, "**arəduuī-*." He explains that the only phonetical solution is to pose the adjective *arədu-* as a dialectical variant (or not technical) of Avestan *arədra-* (from Scr. *rādh*: Av. *rād*, "to succeed, be successful, accomplish"[11]). He proposes thus that the term should be translated as "the Competent One," or "She Who Succeeds."[12] Oettinger suggests that *arəduuī-* originally derived from the Vedic √*r̥dh-*. In his opinion, the most likely meaning for the word *arəduuī-* would be "efficient," "beneficial," and "the one who impels."[13] Malandra, meanwhile, considers it to be related to the Vedic *pr̥th(i)vī-* ("broad; Earth").[14] Skjærvø suggests that *arəduuī-* is the feminine form of an adjective corresponding to Old Indic term *ūrdhvá-* "tall, lofty."[15] Skjærvø's translation seems most convincing, since this would be consistent with the goddess's characterization as the heavenly river (or waters) symbolized by the Milky Way. It is also consistent with the meaning of her attribute *bərəzaitī-* "high, lofty," and as well describes her as the "heavenly river" descending down from the sky to the earth (Yt 5.85).[16]

Sūrā

The second component of the goddess's name, *sūrā*, has been most often taken to mean "mighty" or "powerful." Skjærvø's definition is "rich in life-giving strength."[17] Thus, the meaning would imply a particular type of strength, specifically, the kind that gives life. Hintze, meanwhile, points to the noun form of *sūra*, meaning "hero," specifically the Indo-Iranian term for the hero who slays a dragon (from the root √*sū*, "to be strong").[18] The meaning "to be strong" derives from "to be endowed with life-force." It seems that the term functions as an adjective for "strong" in Anāhitā's epithet, and as a masculine substantive when it means "hero."

Anāhitā

The third term in the series, *anāhitā*, is perhaps most controversial of all. Boyce, apparently following Pahlavi glosses on the term,[19] defines *anāhitā* as "undefiled" or "immaculate."[20] Kellens, however, points out that "undefiled" or "immaculate" cannot have been the original meaning, which, as suggested by Hertel[21] and later confirmed by Gotō[22] and Oettinger, must have been "unbound [to anything]"; that is, "unrestrained,"[23] like "her original nature as torrential river" or as a "powerful river."[24]

Malandra attempts to resolve the discrepancy between the two meanings, "unsullied" and "unbound," by drawing Vedic parallels with the term *aditi* (the goddess Aditi) from the root ∏*dā/di-* "to bind,"[25] which has the same meaning and morphology as the Avestan *āhiti*. As in the Avestan case, Vedic *aditi* refers to a goddess who is "unbound from defiling transgressions"; hence, the connection between the two senses of *anāhitā*.[26] Oettinger suggests that *āhiti-* is a derivative of *ā-hi-* "bind."[27]

The alternative explanation for the Avestan fem. *anāhitā-* as "boundless" seems more convincing.[28] In Avestan, as in several other Indo-European languages, the prefix "*a-*" or "*an-*" creates a negation. It is followed here by a directional marker preverb "*ā-*" and the verb "*hi-*" which is weak root derived from √*hā-/hi-*, "to bind." To this is appended the suffix "*-ta*," creating a past perfect participle. Thus, *hita-* is a verbal adjective meaning "bound" and in OIr. *ā*√*hai/hi-* meant "to bind."[29] More precisely, adding "*ā-*" to the verbal root *hā-/hi-* means "to bind (on) to." So, its negated form would be thus "not bound onto anything," or "not being tied to."

The goddess, therefore, seems to be the personification of the verbal adjective *anāhitā-*, meaning "not bound onto [to anything]," which is appropriately connected to her nature as (a) lofty powerful river(s). This etymology seems reasonable and *(an)āhitā-* has retained its etymological quantity.[30]

Like *sūrā*, in the Avesta *anāhitā* as an adjective is applied to a number of deities. For example, in Yašt 8.2 Tištriia is said to be "shining with rays far and wide hither from afar, with bond-less (or unsullied) lights" (*dūrāt viiāuuaṇtəm bānubiiō raoxšnəbiiō anāhitaēibiiō*).[31] The term appears even more emphatically in Yt. 10.88, where the sacrifice of Haoma to Miθra is described thus:

(Yt 10.88)
yim yazata haomō
frāšmiš baēšaziiō srīrō
xšaθriiō zairidōiθrō
barəzište paiti barəzahi
haraiθiiō paiti barəzaiiāँ
yaṯ vaocē hūkairīm nąma
anāhitəm anāhitō
anāhitāṯ parō barəsmən
anāhitaiiāṯ parō zaoθraiiāṯ
anāhitaēibiiō parō vāyžibiiō

Haoma, the radiant beautiful healer, the golden eyed majesty, who sacrificed on
   the highest peak of the high (mountain) Haraitī, which is called *Hūkaiiria* by
   name.
He, the unbound (or unsullied) one (sacrificing) to an unbound (or unsullied)
   one (Miθra)
(with) the immaculate barsom
the unbound (or immaculate) libation
the immaculate words.

So What Is Her Proper Name?

If we accept that the three terms discussed above are the goddess's epithets, the question remains, what was the goddess's actual name? It may be noted that the composition of the Young Avesta (including the *Ābān Yašt* where she is mentioned as "*Arəduuī Sūrā Anāhitā*") presumably occurred during an approximate period of time between 1000 and 600 BCE. The fact that, in Achaemenid period, she is mentioned in the royal inscriptions as "Anah^{a}ta" (e.g., Artaxerxes II "404–358 BCE," inscriptions: A^2 Ha and A^2 Sa[32]) shows that at least from that period she was known by her third epithet.

In other Avestan passages, both "*arəduuī*" and "*anāhitā*" describe "water" (*ap-*): *arəduiiā̊ āpō anāhitāiiā̊* (Yt 1.21, 5.0). However, in Yt 1.21, the river *vaŋᵛhī dāitiiā* is also called (*ap-*). This would suggest that (*ap-*) was not a proper name, but rather evokes the concept and nature of the goddess.

Another Scythian goddess, known to the Greeks as Apatouros (from Scythian *ap-* "water" + *toura* "quick, mighty"), was the principal deity of the Bosphorus region from at least the sixth century BCE; like Anāhitā, she was associated with water and fertility.[33] Herodotus equates the Scythian goddess Api with Gaia, the Earth.[34] The linguistic connection to *ap-* may be merely coincidental, but it is also possible that Herodotus was mistaken in his identification and that the Scythian Api was actually the goddess of water. In fact, Lincoln concludes that the goddess Api may be the same goddess mentioned by Herodotus as "the daughter of the river," who created the Scythian people, with Zeus-Papayus as a couple.[35]

Moreover, in common Indo-European fundamental concepts like "water" seem to have pairs of words: one neuter (**wodr*) and one animate, that is, masculine or feminine (**ap-*). The neuter one is thought to have designated the substance as an entity in the world, the animate one the substance as probably a divine or any fundamental force of nature.[36]

The stem **ap-* (*áp-*) originally expressed the concept of "water."[37] The proto-Indo-European languages had several words for "water." The term **wódr̥* was mostly used for "water" in a generic sense (OPers *vār-* rain), while the second term, **h2ep-* (the labial appears sometimes voiced, sometimes voiceless[38]), was used in some languages as "river" and in others more generally as "water." Some examples are Welsh *Avon*, Latin *amnis* "river," Old Prussian *ape* "river," Hittite *hāpa-* "river," Sanskrit *áp* "water," Tocharian A & B *āp* "river," "water." A dialectal variant **h2ekʷ* gives Lat. *Aqua*,[39] and occurs in Dacian and Illyrian *Apos*, French river *Asse*, and Lithuanian *Apse*.[40] The word **h2ep* (*ap-*) as the "living water" or "water on the move"—which apparently includes "river" among its possible meanings—strengthens the theory that the actual concept (though not necessarily her formal name) of the water-river goddess known as *Arəduuī Sūrā Anāhitā* could have been *ap-* "water." Water also is worshipped in the *Yasna Haptaŋhāiti* (Yasna 38).

As has been mentioned previously, there exists another base word for "river/water" and "water-basin" which is **dānu-*[41] (Av. *dānu-* river), which is also applied to a goddess whose concept and/or name is connected to those of many European rivers (discussed in Chapter Four). It is, therefore, possible that another proto-Indo-European word, **h2ep* (*ap-*), "living water" or "water on the move," could also indicate a river/water goddess. Kellens states that based on Yasna 65.1 which reads, *yazāi āpəm arəduuīm sūrąm anāhitąm*, "I sacrifice to the Water, *arəduuī sūrā anāhitā*,"[42] the word *ap-* in the singular was used in connection to Anāhitā, and Skjaervø states that "The deity (Anāhitā) may therefore well be intended also in the *Gāθās* where water is mentioned."[43] The Avesta calls upon devotees to take care of the physical world, of which water is a major component.

In conclusion, one could propose the following as the full reference to the Iranian river goddess: she is "the lofty one, rich in life-giving strength, the unbound: Water." It seems most likely that *ap-* (water) in its general meaning was the actual concept of the water goddess known as *Arəduuī Sūrā Anāhitā*, which were epithets that were applied to her (water).[44]

Anāhitā's Functions

The stanzas from *Ābān Yašt* cited below are organized so as to show the transformation of Anāhitā and her characteristics over time (not according to their actual sequence in the *Ābān Yašt*). We begin, therefore, with the stanzas showing Anāhitā's nature as a water goddess who lives in the Sky. As a crowned goddess associated with the ruling, Anāhitā's priestly features make her worthy of sacrifice. However, since her sacrificers are not all "positive" figures, the connection between Anāhitā and the "*daēuua*-worshippers" also will be demonstrated and discussed.

As a powerful and mighty goddess who is a chariot rider, her warlike characteristics will be observed. Then, as a fertility goddess, there are examples of her as an increaser who creates abundance, who ensures fertility by purifying men's sperm and the woman's womb, and eases childbirth.

We continue our discussion by analyzing Anāhitā's visualizations in the *Ābān Yašt* through descriptions and visualizations of her body, which place as much emphasis on her feminine beauty as on her divine status or her natural descriptions as water/river goddess. The goddess's clothes (clothed in beaver skins), shoes, and her crown, as well as her image in the form of river/waterfall will all be considered.

One of Anāhitā's most noticeable features is that she comes to possess three very different aspects. As a recipient of priestly sacrifices (Yt 5.1, 8, 9, 17–76), she supports the rulers and the priests (Yt 5.86). She also is a mighty deity who supports warriors (Yt 5.13, 86). Finally, she is a fertility goddess with purifying and healing functions (Yt 5.2, 87). Her multiple functions are described in the Avesta (Yt 5.86–87) in a less abstract and more anthropomorphic way than for other deities. This suggests that her devotees asked for her support in various aspects of their lives and saw her as closer to themselves.

One of the clearer examples from the *Ābān Yašt* showing Anāhitā's multifunctionality can be seen in these stanzas:

(Yt 5.86–87)
θβąm naracit̰ yōi taxma
jaiδiiā̊ṇte āsu aspīm
xᵛarənaŋhasca uparatātō
θβąm āθrauuanō marəmnō[45]

āθrauuanō θrāiiaonō
mastīm jaiδiiā̊ṇte spānəmca
vərəθraynəmca ahuraδātəm
vanaiṇtīmca uparatātəm.

The warriors shall ask you for possession of rapid horses, (and) superiority of *xᵛarənah*. The memorizing priests (*āθrauuan*), the student priests, shall ask you for knowledge and life-giving wisdom for the Ahura-created victoriousness and conquering superiority.

θβąm kaininō vaδre.yaona[46]
xšaθra huuāpā° jaiδiiā̊ṇte
taxməmca nmānō.paitīm
θβąm carāitiš zizanāitiš
jaiδiiā°ṇte huzāmīm
tūm tā aēibiiō xšaiiamna
nisirinauuāhi arəduuī sūre anāhite.

The nubile maidens shall ask you for good wealth and a strong house lord. The women in labor[47] shall ask you for easy birth delivery. You shall confer those things on them, having the power (to do so), O Arduuī Sūrā Anāhitā.

Different social categories are indicated in this passage. The wishes directed to Anāhitā begin with the warriors, then continue with the priests, and finally women present their wishes connected to fertility. In these two stanzas, three categories of people are asking her support connected to their needs: The warrior men (*naracit̰*, together with the adjective *taxma*, "brave"), the priests, and the maidens/women make her capable to support all of the three levels of Iranian society. These two stanzas richly demonstrate Anāhitā's multifunctional nature which includes victory, knowledge, and fertility.

A Water/River Deity Who Lives in the Sky

The *Ābān Yašt* speaks of all the waters that Ahura Mazdā created, specifically mentioning seven rivers flowing to seven countries. Although Anāhitā might have originally been the goddess of a particular river, it seems that at some point she became the goddess of all of the rivers (Yt 5.5). Anāhitā has control and power over water, as it is described when she creates a dry bed over the river "good *Vītaŋhaitī* "[48] (Yt 5.78).

Another noteworthy feature is that, as a river, Anāhitā flows equally during the summer and winter.

> (Yt 5.5)
> *aiṇ́hā̊sca mē aēuuaŋhā̊ āpō*
> *apayžārō vī.jasāiti*
> *vīspāiš aoi karšuuaṇ yāiš hapta:*
> *aiṇ́hā̊sca mē aēuuaŋhā̊ āpō*
> *hamaϑa auua baraiti*
> *hą̇minəmca zaiianəmca*
> *hā mē āpō yaoždaδāiti*
> *hā aršnąm xšudrā̊*
> *hā xšaϑrinąm garəβąnā̊*
> *hā xšaϑrinąm paēma.*

And (now) the flow of this single water of mine, shall go out to all the seven continents, and (the flow) of this single water of mine flows down in the same way both in summer and in winter. She purifies the waters, the semen of the males, the wombs of the females, (and) the milk of the females (for me).[49]

According to Herodotus, among the Scythian rivers there was a river called the "Ister," which is described in terms similar to those used for Anāhitā, always flowing with equal volume in summer and winter alike:

> The Ister, which is the greatest of all the rivers which we know, flows always with equal volume in summer and winter alike. It is the first towards the West of all the Scythian rivers, and it has become the greatest of all rivers because other rivers flow into it.[50]

Herodotus, then, carefully describes how this river has equal water in the summer and winter, which, significantly, is precisely how Anāhitā is described in the Avesta. According to Herodotus, the mountain snows melt during the summer and this is how Ister always has water. His description also shows that this river had been centralized as the greatest river and the source of the water, which is an additional commonality with Anāhitā.

The Ister, according to Herodotus, passed through all of Europe in its way to the sea:

> for the Ister flows in fact through the whole of Europe, beginning in the land of the Keltoi, who after the Kynesians dwell furthest towards the sun-setting of all the peoples of Europe; and thus flowing through all Europe it falls into the sea by the side of Scythia.[51]

"Ister" is the ancient Greek name for the river Danube. In the section on Indo-European river goddesses, we discussed the common etymology of the Don, the Danube, and other rivers related to the IE *danu*. The connection is even more remarkable when we note that Anāhitā shares a number of aspects of Herodotus's description of the Danube. Moreover, the region through which the Ister passes (according to Herodotus) is a place with cold winters, reminding us of Anāhitā's clothing, which seems most likely to have belonged to a cold climate. This is not to say that the Danube was the original river of the goddess. Rather, we merely intend to note some connections showing that our goddess might have inherited some very old traditions connected to her Indo-European roots.[52]

That Anāhitā is symbolized by the Milky Way[53] could emerge from the following text stating that she lives "above the stars." Since Anāhitā is, in fact, originally a river, it is not difficult to connect her with the Milky Way as a "celestial river."

(Yt 5.85)
yahmiia ahurō mazdā°
huuapō niuuaēδaiiaṯ
āiδi paiti auua.jasa
arəduuī sūre anāhite
haca auuaṯbiiō stərəbiiō
aoi ząm ahuraδātąm:
ϑβąm yazāṇte auruuāŋhō
ahurāŋhō daiŋhupataiiō
puϑrāŋhō daiŋhupaitinąm.

The beneficent Ahura Mazdā invited her, come down, descend, O Arəduuī Sūrā Anāhitā, from yonder stars, to the Ahura-created earth. The fleet lords will sacrifice to you, landlords (and) sons of landlords.

Āsmān[54] (sky/Heaven) is the highest level of the four-sphere material world in Zoroastrian cosmology, in which water is the second creation.[55] Closest to the earth is the level of the stars, where Anāhitā as the heavenly river lives. Similar to her, the Vedic goddess Sárasvatī (she, too, being a mighty river) also originates in heaven from whence she flows down to the earth.[56]

And again:

(Yt 5.88)
āaṯ frašusaṯ zaraϑuštra
arəduuī sūra anāhita
haca auuaṯbiiō stərəbiiō
aoi zạm ahuraδātạm:
āaṯ aoxta arəduuī sūra anāhita.
Then she went forth, O Zaraϑuštra, Arəduuī Sūrā Anāhitā,
from yonder stars,
to the Ahura-created earth
Then she spoke, Arəduuī Sūrā Anāhitā.

The text clearly states that Ahura Mazdā has made a path for Anāhitā from the sky to the earth, passing by the sun.

(Yt 5.90)
paiti dim pərəsaṯ Zaraϑuštrō
arəduuīm sūrạm anāhitạm:
arəduuī sūre anāhite
kana ϑβạm yasna yazāne
kana yasna frāiiazāne
yasə tauua mazdā°kərənaoṯ tacarə
aṇtarə.arəδəm upairi huuarəxšaētəm
yasə ϑβā nōiṯ aiβi družāṇte
ažišca[57] arəϑnāišca[58] vaβžakāišca[59]
varənuuāišca varənauua.vīšāišca.
Zaraϑuštra asked her, Arəduuī Sūrā Anāhitā:
O Arəduuī Sūrā Anāhitā
With what sacrifice shall I worship you?
With what sacrifice shall I send you forth in sacrifice?
In order that Ahura Mazdā may make you a course, not in this side (but a course)
above the radiant sun, so that they shall not belie you, the serpents and the
   *scorpions, and the wasps, and the spiders, and the poisonous spiders.

Hukairiia or the "Mountain of Good Deeds," according to Avestan cosmology, established a physical link between the earth and the sky.[60] This is how Anāhitā flows down from heaven to the mountain. The image conjured by the text is visually rich.

(Yt 5.96)
yazāi hukairīm barəzō
vīspō vahməm zaranaēnəm
yahmat̰ mē haca frazgaδaite
arəduuī sūra anāhita
hazaŋrāi barəšna vīranąm
masō xšaiiete xvarənaŋhō
yaϑa vīspåˀimåˀāpō
yåˀzəmā paiti fratacinti
yā amauuaiti fratacaiti.

I will sacrifice to Mount Hukairia, honored with hymns by all, golden, from which (she) flows down to me, Areduuī Sūrā Anāhitā, at the height of one thousand men. (She) reigns over large Fortune (*xvarənah*), as (much as) all these waters that flow forth over the earth, (who) forceful, flows forth.

Hukairiia can be identified with the highest summit of Mt. Hara-Barzaiti, from whence Anāhitā flows downward.

(Yt 5.102)
kəm kəmcit̰ aipi nmāne
gātu *saite[61] xᵛaēui starətəm
hubaoiδīm barəziš hauuaṇtəm
ātacaiti zaraϑuštra
arəduuī sūra anāhita
hazaŋrāi barəšna vīranąm
masō xšaiiete xᵛarənaŋhō
yaϑa vīspā imā āpō
yā zəmā paiti fratacinti
yā amauuaiti fratacaiti.

Also, in (each) and every home, there is a couch (for lying) beautifully spread out, well-scented, provided with pillows.

She flows, O Zaraϑuštra, Areduuī Sūrā Anāhitā, at the height of one thousand men, (she) reigns over large Fortune (*xvarənah*), as (much as) as all these waters that flow forth over the earth, (she who), forceful, flows forth.

A parallel can be found in RV 7.95. 1–2, where Sárasvatī is said to flow down from the mountains as well.[62]

The Recipient of Priestly Sacrifices

The *Ābān Yašt* describes Anāhitā as the recipient of many different sacrifices. The offerings made to her clearly include "*haoma* (mixed) with milk, with *barsom*, and with righteous thoughts, speech and deeds" during the sacrifice ceremony.[63] Anāhitā's priestly function,[64] meanwhile, is clearly shown when Ahura Mazdā sacrifices to her beside "the good [river] Dāitiiā" (*vaŋhuyā° dāitiiaiiā*) asking for her support.[65] She also has the ability to resist and overcome the aggressions of impious warriors and demons.[66] And like many river goddesses, healing is one of her principal functions.[67] In the first stanza of the *Ābān Yašt*, we can see a combination of Anāhitā's diverse functions.

(Yt 5.1)
mraoṯ ahurō mazdā° spitamāi zaraϑuštrāi
yazaēša mē hīm spitama zaraϑuštra
yąm arəduuīm sūrąm anāhitąm
pərəϑū frākąm baēšaziiąm
vīdaēuuąm ahurō.ṯkaēšąm
yesńiiąm aŋᵛhe astuuaite
vahmiiąm aŋᵛhe astuuaite
āδū.frāδanąm ašaonīm
vąϑβō.frāδanąm ašaonīm
gaēϑō.frāδanąm ašaonīm
šaētō.frāδanąm ašaonīm
daŋhu.frāδanąm ašaonīm.

Ahura Mazdā said to Zaraϑuštra Spitāma: Sacrifice to her for me, O Zaraϑuštra of the Spitāma, Arduuī Sūrā Anāhitā, who spreads abroad, the healer, opposed of *daēuuas*[68] and follower of Ahura Mazdā's faith. She is worthy of sacrifices and worshipped by the material world. (She, the) righteous (one) who increases the grains.[69] (She, the) righteous (one) who increases the flocks, (She, the) righteous (one) who increases the world (and its being).[70] (She, the) righteous (one) who increases property. (She, the) righteous (one) who increases the settlements and the lands.

As we may notice, in this introductory passage, Anāhitā is described as an increaser, and a healer deity, who follows Ahura Mazdā and is opposed to the *daēuuas*.

In another passage, Ahura Mazdā sacrifices for Anāhitā on the bank of the "good *dāiitiā*" and directly seeks her assistance to send the good religion to Zaraθuštra.

(Yt 5.17)
tąm yazata
yō daδuuā°ahurō mazdā°
airiiene vaējahi
vaŋhuiiā°dāitiiaiiā°
*haomaiiō gauua barəsmana
hizuuō daŋhaŋha mąθraca +vacaca šiiaoθnaca
zaoθrābiiasca aršuxδaēibiiasca vāyžibiiō

He, Ahura Mazdā the creator, sacrificed to her (Arduuī Sūrā Anāhitā) in the *airiiana vaējah* of the Good *Dāiitiā*, with *haoma* mixed with milk and with *barsom*, with the skill of the tongue and with poetic thought, with speech and action and libations, and with correctly spoken words.[71]

(Yt 5.18)
āaṯ hīm jaiδiiaṯ:
auuaṯ āiiaptəm dazdi mē
vaŋuhi səuuište arəduuī sūre anāhite
yaθa azəm hācaiiene
puθrəm yaṯ pourušaspahe
ašauuanəm zaraθuštrəm
anumatōe daēnaiiāi
anuxtōe daēnaiiāi
anu.varštōe daēnaiiāi.

Then he asked her: "Grant me that prosperity, O good, O mighty, Arduuī Sūrā Anāhitā, that I shall induce Pourušaspa's son, righteous Zaraθuštra, to think, to speak, to act, according to inner self towards religion.

One could ask why a creator-god would have needed a goddess to transmit his religion to his prophet? Actually, it would appear that in the *Ābān Yašt* Anāhitā has the role of supreme deity: it is she who grants (or does not grant) the wishes of a long list of sacrificers, a list that includes Ahura Mazdā. The *Ābān*

Yašt tells us that different figures in different locations (usually around rivers, lakes, and mountains) sacrificed to Anāhitā and asked for her support. This list, of Anāhitā's supplicants and their wishes, occupies a considerable portion of the *Ābān Yašt*.[72] The fact that this passage shows Ahura Mazdā as one who sacrifices and makes supplication to Anāhitā is a clear demonstration of the goddess's exceptional importance.

Martial Aspects, Devotees, and Those Who Sacrifice to *Daēuua*s

Anāhitā's various supplicants include warriors who ask her for help in defeating their enemies. Yima, Θraētaona, Kərəsāspa, Kauua.usa (Yt 5.45), Haosrauua (Yt 5.49), and Tusō (Yt 5.53) are examples.

Moreover, the visual image of Anahita evoked by certain passages in the *Ābān Yašt* is distinctly martial, driving her war chariot like a typical Indo-European mythical hero:

> (Yt 5.13)
> *yeŋhe caθβārō vaštāra*
> *spaēta vīspa*
> *hama.gaonā°ŋhō hama.nāfaēni*
> *bərəzanta tauruuaiianta*
> *vīspanąm ʈbišuuatąm ʈbaēšā°*
> *daēuuanam mašiiānąmca*
> *yāθβąm pairikanąmca*
> *sāθrąm kaoiiąm karafnąmca.*

(She) the one with her four white stallions, all of the same color, the same breed, tall, victorious over the hostilities of all the hostiles, the *daēuua*s (false deities) and people, the sorcerers and the *pairikā*s, the false teachers: the *kauui*s, the *karapan*s.

The sāθrąm, from *sāθr-/sāstar-* (root form √*sāh*), means "to name/to learn"; traditionally, they are the "tyrant rulers who are against the Mazdeans." Skjaervø renders the term as "the false teachers," and Malandra as "tyrants."[73] The *kauui*s and *karpan*s, meanwhile, were probably ruler-priests possessing some ancient rituals who opposed Zaraθuštra. The *kauui*s have a Vedic equivalent, *kaví-* meaning a "wise/sage poet." However, the last ruler of *kauui*s from eastern Iran was the *kauui*-Vištāspa- (Goštasp) who accepted Zoroastrianism and helped Zaraθuštra to develop his religion. The other *kauuis* were blamed by the Mazdaean priests, probably because of their insistence on keeping their older gods and rituals. The *kauuis* reappear through titles or epithets associated with many kings in the *Šāh-nāmeh*. The *karpan*s were another category of priests opposed to Zoroastrianism. The texts' gathering together of these various groups and their association with the older gods and goddesses would appear to reflect a substantial opposition in Iranian society to the agenda of the Mazdaean priests.

However, not all of Anāhitā's supplicants are righteous. In the *Yašts*, of all the Zoroastrian divinities, only Anāhitā and Vāiiu[74] are said to receive sacrifices from evildoers (we may list them as the "*daēuuaiiasna*," those who sacrifice to *daēuuas* or *daēuua*-worshippers, that is, worshippers of the old deities). However, these sacrifices are not accepted.[75]

The fact that some well-known negative characters sacrifice to Anāhitā asking for her support is significant. The Avestan Fraŋrasiian (later Afrāsiāb) and Avestan Aži-Dahāka, the three-headed dragon (later Żaḥḥāk), are examples of such figures.[76] At least some of these characters (Aži-Dahāka as an example) are considered to be mythological. Aži-Dahāka is said to have sacrificed to Arduuī Sūrā Anāhitā in the land of Baβri, and to Vaiiu in his inaccessible (*dužita*) castle, Kuuirinta castle. These two deities, Anāhitā and Vāiiu, are the only ones in the entire Avestan pantheon who count Fraŋrasiian and Aži-Dahāka among their devotees. It seems that both Baβri and Kuuirinta were located in Babylon.[77] Anāhitā did not accept the sacrifices offered by these two negative characters; on the contrary, she accepts Θraētaona's supplication that he gain the power to slay the dragon Aži-Dahāka.[78] We will discuss these two figures, Fraŋrasiian and Aži-Dahāka, in greater detail in Chapter Seven.

Returning to the *Ābān Yašt*, in stanzas 94–95, Zaraθuštra asks Anāhitā a striking question: what would happen if her worship ceremony were to be performed by "those who sacrifice to *daēuuas*" after sunset?

(Yt 5.94)
paiti dīm pərəsaṭ zaraθuštrō
arəduuīm sūrąm anāhitąm
arəduuī sūre anāhite
kəm iδa tē zaoθrāᵒbauuainti
yasə tauua frabarənte
druuantō daēuuaiiasnāŋhō
pasca hū frāšmō.dāitīm.
Zaraθuštra asked her, Arduuī Sūrā Anāhitā, O Arduuī Sūrā Anāhitā,
What become to the *zaoθra* (libations) of you,

Which is sacrificed to you by the lie-possessed *daēuua*-worshippers,
after the sunset?
Anāhitā replies that she would not be there or bless the ceremony.

This dialogue implies the existence of nocturnal ceremonies among the Iranians, rituals which likely predated Zoroastrianism. The implied opposition to such ceremonies presumably reflects the views of the Mazdaean priests trying to assert their own authority, and suggests that at some point significant numbers of Iranians, in fact, did sacrifice to Anāhitā at night, a practice the Avestan priests sought to abolish. The fact that the text's reference to the *daēuua* cult taking place at night[79] could be connected to the depiction of Anāhitā as a heavenly river identified as the Milky Way. Moreover, the fact that at least one of Anāhitā's worshippers, Fraŋrasiian (later Afrāsīāb), referred to in the text as "those who sacrifice to *daēuuas*," performed sacrifices to Anāhitā in his underground cave, which evokes a connection with Miθra. He sacrifices to Anāhitā in his underground fortress:

(Yt 5.41)
tąm yazata
mairiiō[80] tūiriiō fraŋrase
hankaine[81] paiti aiŋ'hā zəmō
satəm aspanąm aršnąm
hazaŋrəm gauuąm
baēuuarə anumaiianąm.

(He) sacrificed to her, the villain Tūranian Fraŋrasiian, in (his) underground fortress (inside) the earth, one hundred stallions, one thousand bulls, ten thousand rams.

The texts' claim that Anāhitā rejects all of the offerings devoted to her by the negative figures also begs consideration. Why do "those who sacrifice to *daēuuas*" figures bother to make offerings to a deity who rejects them, who does not support their wishes, and does not attend their ceremonies performed in her honor? The simple fact that the composer(s) of *Ābān Yašt* mentions these ceremonies shows that they existed and could not be easily ignored by the Zoroastrian priests, following their attempt to enforce Mazda worship.

The Avestan word *daēuua-*, from the same root as the Latin *deus* and the old Indic *deva*, is ultimately derived from the proto-Indo-European **deiu̯ó-*, "god"[82] or Indo-European **deiwos*. In ancient times, the term seems to have only meant "deity," and was given a negative meaning (and we do not know for certain in what context this change occurred) as the false deities only later, presumably after the Indo-Iranian split during the second millennium BCE.[83] The demonization of the *daēuua*s, as Skjærvø notes, is "one of the most striking features of the Old Iranian religion,"[84] and probably happened gradually. In any case, the category of *daēuua* ended up on the enemy side of the Zoroastrian cosmology, in contrast to the *ahura*s. The derivative word in modern Persian, *dīv*, means a kind of monster or demon, and is the root of the Persian word for "crazy" (*dīvāneh*; cf. Arabic *majnūn*, "be-genied," English "bedeviled").

Originally, the *daēuua*s were the old gods (of Indo-Iranian inheritance) who were rejected, either by Zaraϑuštra himself as part of his reform, or/and by priests as an indication of Mazdaean monotheism[85] against the *ahura*s, and their rejection has been historically linked to the prophet's alleged reforms of the old religion. Although it appears that the rejection of the *daēuua*s was a primary focus of the Gathic vision, in the *Gāϑā*s the *daēuua*s are not yet considered "demons" as such but are listed along with a number of other categories, as will be discussed further below.

The combination "*daēuuanam mašiiānąmca*" gives the sense of a "fixed expression," combining "the *daēuua*s and people" and implies that the *daēuua*s were still considered as gods (although the false ones). The expression "*daēuuanam mašiiānąmca*" seems to be an Indo-Iranian tradition since it exists as well in the Vedas as "*devá-/martya*."[86] We will discuss this in more detail in Chapter Ten in connection with the *pairikā*s. But to sum up, the *pairikā*s were female figures with goddess roots, possessing features that may be derived from those attributed to goddesses in ancient times; they are mentioned in the Avesta as demonic creatures. More accurately, they are rejected ancient deities.

In fact, the *daēuua*s probably continued to be worshipped widely (if not necessarily openly) even by people who had accepted the Gathic religion (those who sacrifice to "Mazdā"). Thus, despite the efforts of Mazdaean priests to drive the old deities underground, many of them reemerge in the Younger Avesta, and this may have included some that belonged to the (originally neutral) category of *daēuua*s. If one perceives a rejection of the *daēuua*s in the *Gāϑā*s (and it is not even clear which gods were included in that category), they are not even mentioned in the other Old Avestan text, the *Yasna Haptaŋhāiti* (Sacrifice in Seven Sections). As Herrenschmidt and Kellens have noted:

That they were national gods is confirmed by the fact that they were invoked
by means of the Iranian versions of expressions common in Vedic rhetoric,
for example, *daēuua-/maṣiia-*: *devá-/mártya-*, *vīspa-daēuua-*: *víśva- devá-*, and
daēuuo.zušta-: *devájuṣṭa-*.[87]

Dandamayev even has suggested that the *daivas* mentioned in Xerxes' inscription
were, in fact, Miθra and Anāhitā.[88] Skjaervø argues that the *ahuras* gained in Iran
at the expense of the *daēuuas* because Ahura Mazdā received the role of the
creator god, whereas in India Indra, as an important god who belonged to the
daēuua grouping, made the *asuras* into enemy gods.[89]

Again, it should be emphasized that in the *Gāθās*, neither is it clear which
deities comprised the category of *daēuuas*, nor that they were necessarily
negative; their "demonization" only becomes evident in later texts.[90] As Kellens
observes:

> They (the *daēuua*) were still venerated by the leaders of the larger Iranian nation
> (*dax́iiu-*; *Y.* 32.3, 46.1) and had formerly been worshiped even by the people
> who accepted the religion of the *Gāθās* (*Y.* 32.8); they thus formed part of the
> Mazdaean social and religious system.[91]

Thus, it may be that many rituals performed in honor of Anāhitā by so-called
"*daēuua*-worshippers" or "those who sacrifice to *daēuuas*" were merely the
ancient rituals of Iranians, some (or many) of whom did not follow the religious
prescriptions of the Mazdaean priests.

In his study of Sasanian Zurvanism, Zaehner speaks about "Iranian sorcerers,"
who apparently were connected to the "*daēuua*-worshippers" mentioned in the
Pahlavi texts. Their cult was conducted at nighttime,[92] suggesting that they kept
their ceremonies hidden from the view of the Mazdaean authorities.[93] We do
not know that whether this had always been the case, or what exactly the notion
of "demon" might have meant to them. Again, the most likely explanation is
that the people concerned were merely worshipping their ancient deities in
the traditional way and did not follow the changes the Mazdaean priests were
attempting to impose. If they were coming under pressure from the Mazdaean
priesthood, perhaps they kept their cult hidden in order to protect it. Did the
worship of "*daēuuas*" also represent some kind of movement and reaction
against the formal religion? This intriguing question, unfortunately, is beyond
the scope of the present work.

Chariot-riding Deity, "Rich in Life-Giving Strength"

All the passages in the *Ābān Yašt* emphasize the fact that Anāhitā is a mighty deity. The kind of power that only could have been remained from the older time, when the goddesses, probably human shaped in imagination, were involved in all sides of their worshipper's life. As powerful as she is, however, within the Zoroastrian pantheon, Ahura Mazdā is specifically said to have created her.

(Yt 5.6)
yąm azəm
yō ahurō mazdå°
hizuuārəna uzbaire fradaθāi
nmānaheca vīsaheca zaṇtōušca daiŋ'hōušca
pāθrāica harəθrāica aiβiiāxštrāica
nipātaiiaēca nišaŋharətaiiaēca.

And I, Ahura Mazdā, created her by the impetus of my tongue (speech?), to develop over the home, the village, the tribe and the land, and to protect, guard, care, and watch (them).

Whether stemming from the notion that any deity created by Ahura Mazdā is "worthy of worship,"[94] or because Anāhitā and her cult were too important to be ignored, Ahura Mazdā is said to offer her sacrifice and his respect.

(Yt 5.9)
ahe raiia xᵛarənaŋhaca
tąm yazāi surunuuata yasna
tąm yazāi huiiašta yasna
arəduuīm sūrąm anāhitąm ašaonīm
zaoθrābiiō
ana buiiā°zauuanō.sāsta
ana buiiā°huiiaštatara
arəduuī sūre anāhite
haomaiiō gauua barəsmana
hizuuō daŋhaŋha mąθraca vacaca šiiaoθnaca
zaoθrābiiasca aršuxδaēibiiasca vāyžibiiō.

For her wealth and munificence, I shall sacrifice to her with audible sacrifice. I shall sacrifice to her with well-performed sacrifice, with *zaoθra*,[95] Arduuī Sūrā Anāhitā, sustainer of order, thereby may you present (yourself) by (this) invocation, and may you be better sacrificed, O Arduuī Sūrā Anāhitā, with *haoma* (mixed) with milk, (and) with *barsom*, with the skill of tongue and with *mąθra* (poetic sacred thought), with speech, action, with *zaoθra* (libations) and with words correctly spoken.

Important Indo-European gods typically have vehicles, and Anāhitā is no exception. She holds the reins to her own splendid chariot (5.11), drawn by four white stallions. These four stallions under her control represent the rain, wind, cloud, and hail—appropriate to a water goddess, since these elements are all different forms of water or connected to it in some way, uncontrolled natural phenomena over which people most needed to have control.

(Yt 5.120)
yeŋ́he caθβārō aršāna
hąm.tāšaṯ ahurō mazdā°
vātəmca vārəmca maēyəmca fiiaŋhumca
mīštī[96] zī mē hīm
spitama zaraθuštra
vārəntaēca snaēžiṇtaēca
srascintaēca fiiaŋhuṇtaēca
yeŋ́he auuauuaṯ haēnanąm
nauua.satāiš hazaŋrəmca.

For whom Ahura Mazdā has made four stallions, the wind, the rain, the cloud (or fog), and the hail, for by (their) care, always O Spitama Zaraθuštra, they rain, snow, drip and hail on her for me, who (Anāhitā) has so many armies[97] as nine-hundreds and a thousand.

Anāhitā possesses many palaces, built beside a thousand lakes. Each palace stands upon a thousand columns and has a hundred bright windows. Apart from the aesthetic aspect describing of the goddess's many palaces, the stanza also shows that the she could, in fact, present herself in any location on the earth where there is a lake (or a river, Yt5.2). And, as we have seen in the other stanzas cited, she presents herself as the righteous people are in the process of carrying out the well-performed sacrifice. The word "a thousand" in this stanza (as well as in many other stanzas in *Ābān Yašt*, for example, stanza 96 shows Anāhitā's height, stanza 101, etc.) seems to be more iconic, emphasizing multitude or height, the maximum quantity in imagination of the *Ābān Yašt*'s composer(s).

(Yt 5.101)
yeŋ́he hazaŋrəm vairiianąm
hazaŋrəm apayžāranąm

kascit̰ca aēšąm vairiianąm
kascit̰ca aēšąm apayžāranąm
caϑβarə.satəm aiiarə.baranąm
huuaspāi naire barəmnāi
kaṅhe kaṅhe apayžāire
nmānəm hištaite huδātəm
satō.raocanəm bāmīm
hazaŋrō.stunəm hukərətəm
baēuuarə.fraskəmbəm sūrəm.

(She who) has a thousand bays, and a thousand inlets, and each of these bays and each of these inlets are a forty-days ride for a man riding a good horse. In (each and every) inlet stands a well-made house, radiant with a hundred windows, well made with a thousand columns, strong with ten thousand (supporting) beams.[98]

Thus, Anāhitā also possesses (or generates) a thousand rivers, each as long as "a man can ride in forty days, riding on a good horse."

A Fertility Deity

Anāhitā increases power and wealth, specifically land and cattle. She is, fundamentally, an increaser. She creates abundance, ensures fertility by purifying men's sperm and the woman's womb (Yt 5.5), eases childbirth, and assures timely lactation (Yt 5.1). She helps women to easily give birth to their children, and she brings milk to their breasts in a timely manner.

(Yt 5.2)
yā vīspanąm aršnam xšudrā°yaoždaδāiti
yā vīspanąm hāirišinąm zaθāi garəβąn yaoždaδāiti
yā vīspā°hāirišiš huzāmitō daδāiti
yā vīspanąm hāirišinąm dāitīm raθβīm paēma auua.baraiti.

(She who) purifies the semen of all males and the wombs of all females for birth. (She who) gives easy delivery to all females and brings down their milk in a timely manner and at the proper time.

As has been previously noted, images of Anāhitā in the Avesta are specific; she is easily and vividly transformed from an anthropomorphic goddess into the mighty, flowing waters. The diversity present in her various descriptions, some more realistic and others more abstract, supports the notion that she is a composite deity, comprised of a multiplicity of precedents rather than from a single model. Her strength and power, her beauty and glory, and her fertility and capabilities combine together to make of her a goddess worthy of worship in connection with the full range of human activities. The multiple potencies evoked by her image would have appealed to devotees from all branches of ancient Iranian society, which perhaps helps explain her extraordinary popularity.

Visualizations of Anāhitā in the *Ābān Yašt*

As discussed above, as an originally Indo-Iranian water goddess, Anāhitā possesses some functions in common with other Indo-European water goddesses. Moreover, during the course of her long transformation throughout early Iranian history, she acquired additional functions, which established her role within the Zoroastrian religion as an important deity.

Alongside the many passages that depict Anāhitā as a beautiful, powerful deity, she is artistically transformed into a waterfall-river, which flows down from a high mountain range, *Hara*, with its highest peak *Hukairiia* (the "Mountain of Good Deeds").

In fact, the *Ābān Yašt* also is noteworthy, especially as an oral composition, for presenting an interesting linkage between mythology and art (or creative composition) in some of its verses (Yt 5.4, 78). It displays a mythological description of the goddess and her visualizations, transforming from river to a goddess, which gives us the experience of watching a scenic performance. In fact, these visual spectacles may have played like an additional enactment of the text in the audiences' imagination, accompanied by the priest's recitations. Indeed, one can easily imagine such scenes being reinterpreted by artists in modern times. Although there exist some visual descriptions in some other *Yašts*—the eighth *Yašt* (*Tištar Yašt*- Stanzas 13–34) for example—the *Ābān Yašt* is nevertheless unique among the Avestan texts from this point of view.

In the passage below, where Anāhitā approaches the mythological Vouru-kaša Sea, the scene is rich in unique visualizing imagery:

(Yt 5.4)
yaozənti. vīspe. karanō
zraiiāi. vouru.kaṣaiia
ā vīspō maiδiiō yaozaiti
yaṯ hīš aoi fratacaiti
yaṯ hīš aoi fražgaraiti

arəduuī sūra anāhita:
yeṇhe⁹⁹ hazaṇrəm vairiianąm
hazaṇrəm apayžāranąm:
kascit̠ca aēšąm vairiianąm
kascit̠ca aēšąm apayžāranąm
caθβarə.satəm. aiiarə baranąm
huuaspāi naire barəmnāi.

All the shores of the Vourukaša Sea are in surge, the entire interior rises up in surge, when she flows forth into them (the shores), when she streams along into them, Areduuī Sūrā Anāhitā, who has a thousand bays and a thousand outlets, and each of these bays and each of these outlets, (is) a forty days' ride for a man riding a good horse.

These verses are a good example of the vivid imaginary description of Anāhitā as a river, flowing toward the Vourukaša Sea. From this vivid description one can clearly imagine the scene: towers of swirling water, before which one is immobilized with awe; one can practically feel the spray, hear the ocean's deafening roar.

The *Ābān Yašt* depicts Anāhitā as a powerful spirit helping Ahura Mazdā and some other positive figures, changing into a beautiful woman of superhuman size. Although her description in this *Yašt* emphasizes her femininity, it also has many adjectives emphasizing her strength. One example is that she is said to have "strong arms" (*bāzu.staoiiehi*). Her white arms are said to be the size of a horse's thigh, perhaps evoking the ancient concept of imagining the deities as being superhuman in size.

(Yt 5.7)
āat̠ frašūsat̠ zaraθuštra
arəduuī sūra anāhita
haca daθušat̠ mazdå°
srīra vā aṇhən bāzauua
auruṣa aspō.staoiiehīš
frā srīra zuṣ¹⁰⁰ sispata
uruuaiti¹⁰¹ bāzu.staoiiehi
auuat̠ manaṇha mainimna.

And so, O Zaraθuštra, Arduuī Sūrā Anāhitā went forth[102] from the Creator Mazdā. (Her) arms were verily beautiful, white, (and) thicker than (the thighs) of a horse, a beautifully rushing swell. Roaring, with strong arms, thus she thinks in her thought(s).

Below are examples of the descriptions and visualizations of Anāhitā's body, which place as much emphasis on her feminine beauty as on her divine status, or her natural descriptions as water/river.

(Yt 5.78)
upa.tacaṯ arəduuī sūra anāhita
kaininō kəhrpa srīraiiā°
aš.amaiiā°huraoδaiiā°
uskāṯ yāstaiiā°ərəzuuaiϑiiō
raēuuaṯ ciϑrəm āzātaiiā°
zaraniia aoϑra paitišmuxta
yā vīspō.pīsa bāmiia
arəmaēštā°aniiā°āpō kərənaoṯ
fraša aniiā°fratacaṯ
huškəm pəšum raēcaiiaṯ
taro vaŋhīm vītaŋhaitīm.

She flowed, Areduuī Sūrā Anāhitā, in the shape of a beautiful young girl, mightily strong, well-shaped, girded-high, standing tall, of splendid seed, high-born, pure, wearing shoes up to the ankle, with golden laces, radiant, some of the waters she made stand still, others she made flow forward. She conveyed (him) across a dry bed, over the (river) good *Vītaŋhaitī*.

(Yt 5.126)
yā hištaite[103] *frauuaēδəmna*
arəduuī sūra anāhita
kaininō kəhrpa srīraiiā°
ašamaiiā°huraoδaiiā°
uskāṯ yāstaiiā°ərəzuuaiϑiiō
raēuuaṯ ciϑrəm āzātaiiā°
frazušəm aδkəm vaŋhāna[104]
pouru paxštəm zaranaēnəm.

The one (who) stands to be seen, (the one) Areduuī Sūrā Anāhitā, in the shape of a beautiful young woman, very strong, well-shaped, girded high, righteous, noble and high-born, wearing a robe [with long sleeves][105] with rich designs, embroidered with gold.

The goddess's clothes, shoes, and her crown, all are described with precision and detail. Her belt is bound tightly about her waist to better show off her breasts.

(Yt 5.127)
bāδa yaθa.mąm barəsmō.zasta[106]
frā.gaoṣ̌āuuara sīspəmna
caθru.karana zaranaēni
minum baraṯ huuāzāta[107]
arəduuī sūra anāhita
upa tąm srīrąm manaoθrim
hā hē maiδim niiāzata
yaθaca hukərəpta f̌ṣ̌tāna
yaθaca aŋhən niiāzāna[108].

(Indeed), when she (sacrificed to?) me with barsom in her hand, to display (her) four-sided golden earrings, wear a broach, high-born and noble, Arduuī Sūrā Anāhitā, upon her beautiful neck. She would pull tight her waist, both so that (her) breasts would (appear) well-formed and that (the breasts) would be prominent (swell out).

Anāhitā's diadem, on the other hand, tells a somewhat different story. Her diadem, described as "with eight crenulations," is possibly connected to the Mesopotamian solar system, which symbolized the identification of the planet Venus with Ištar/Innana using the icon of an eight-pointed star.[109]

(Yt 5.128)
upairi pusąm baṇdaiiata
arəduuī sūra anāhita
satō.straŋhąm[110] *zaranaēnīm*
ašta.kaoždąm raθa.kairiiąm
drafšakauuaitīm srīrąm
anu.pōiθβaitīm hukərətąm.

On (her head) she binds a diadem, Areduuī Sūrā Anāhitā, with a hundred stars, golden, (with) eight crenulations, (appears) chariot-shaped and with inimitable, splendid, having a prominent rim, well-made.

Again, Anāhitā's clothing, shoes, and diadem are all described with precision, in marked contradistinction to the Avesta's portrayals of most other deities. The fact that Anāhitā is described as wearing a beaver skin is significant, as will be discussed below.

(Yt 5.129)

baβraini[111] vastrāˁvaŋhata
arəduuī sūra anāhita
θrisatanąm[112] baβranąm
catura.zīzanatąm
yaṯ asti baβriš sraēšta
yaθa yaṯ asti gaonōtəma
[baβriš bauuaiti upāpō.]
yaθa.kərətəm θβarštāi zrūne
caramā[113] vaēnaṇtō brāzəṇta
frāna ərəzatəm zaranim.

Garments of beaver fur, she wears, Arduuī Sūrā Anāhitā, (from the fur of) three hundred beavers, give birth to four young,[114] because, the female beaver is most beautiful, because she is most dense-haired,[115] the female beaver lives in the water normally for a determined period of time, (then the) furs shine (in the eyes) of the viewers, in abundance of silver (and) gold.

Although there is some geographical evidence for the existence of the beavers in Iran in the past, this particular aspect of Anāhitā's imagery possibly could date back at least to around 4,000 years ago, prior to the Indo-Iranian split, when proto-Indo-Iranians occupied the southern Ural region as evidenced by remains at Sintašta and elsewhere.[116] Herodotus describes Scythian land as below:

> Their land is all thickly overgrown with forests of all kinds of trees, and in the thickest forest there is a large and deep lake, and round it marshy ground and reeds. In this are caught otters and beavers and certainly other wild animals with square-shaped faces. The fur of these is sewn as a fringe round their coats of skin, and the testicles are made use of by them for curing diseases of the womb.[117]

In any case, whether beaver fur existed in the Avestan lands[118] or harkens back to an even earlier era, references to beaver skins in the *Ābān Yašt* suggest that its composer(s) is quoting a very old oral tradition, which cannot be, for example, from Mesopotamia. Rather, it shows that at least initially, Anāhitā was originally a goddess of the lands with cold climate.[119]

The description of a goddess clothed in beaver skins, like the snow queen (because of her crown) who appears in many legends belong to cold climates, allows us to imagine some things about the climate and natural environment where she was first conceived. Most of all, it suggests someplace cold. This is consistent with the Avesta's description of the original homeland of the Iranians, *Airyanəm vaējō* (Airiiana Vaējah).[120] In the *Yašts*, this cold country is the place where Zaraϑuštra (Y. 9.14) sacrificed to *Arəduuī Sūrā* and the other deities (Yt 5.104; 9.25; 17.45). Likewise, in the *Vīdēvdāt* this land is described as follows:

(Vd 1.3)
dasa auuaϑra māŋ hō zaiiana
duua hąmina
taēca hənti sarəta āpō
sarəta zəmō
sarəta uruuaraiiā
aδa zimahe maiδim
aδa zimahe zarəδaēm
aδa ziiā scit pairi.pataiti
aδa fraēštəm vōiynanąm

There are ten months of winter there and two of summer and (even) those are (too) cold for water, for earth, for plants. It is the middle and the heart of winter, and (when) the winter ends there are many floods.

Airiiana Vaējah (*Ērān-wēz*) is described in similar terms in the *Bundahišn*, with ten months of winter and two months of summer.[121] (Despite this description, the *Bundahišn* claims that *Ērān-wēz* was the best place in which to live (Bd XXXI.1). Thus, it is not difficult to link the climate of the Iranians' former homeland with the clothing style of their water goddess.

Beavers are also mentioned as sacred animals in some Pahlavi texts, either because they lived in water and were related to Anāhitā or perhaps because they were important in the older tradition. Killing beavers was considered to be a serious sin.[122]

Anāhitā's Description

The *Yašts* contain descriptions of various deities, but for the most part they do not evoke any specific visual image. Thus, while Tištriia and Vərəϑaɣna occasionally take on human or animal form (Yt 8 and Yt 14), it is their traits and functions that are emphasized rather than their actual appearance. Vāiiu, the deity of wind and weather, is merely described as being a warrior (Yt 15). Daēnā, the deity of the conscience and anthropomorphized moral concept (whom every person encounters on the *Činuuat* bridge after death, appearing either as a beautiful maiden in the case of a good person or as a smelly, disgusting hag in the case of sinners), does not have a description in the *Yašts*. Rather, her description appears mainly in the *Hāδōxt Nask*, whereas the *Dēn Yašt* (*Yašt* 16), which is named after her, is actually devoted to another female deity, Čistā (this will be discussed in Chapter Six). There exist other goddesses, Spentā-Ārmaiti, for example, who are worshipped but whose visual aspect is never described in the Avesta. There are similarities in some stanzas between the *Ābān Yašt* and the *Yašt* 17 devoted to Aši (the goddess of fortune and reward; Yt 17.6–11), but Aši is never described in as much detail as Anāhitā.

In fact, it is noteworthy that, in contrast to the Greek and Mesopotamian cases, Iranian texts mostly do not portray their deities as having human-style lives. It would seem that Iranians, for the most part, did not conceptualize their deities in human terms to the extent that the Greeks and Mesopotamians did. As Herodotus noted:

> I am aware that the Persians observe the following customs: so far from being in the habit of setting up statues, temples, and altars, they regard those who do so as fools; the reason being, in my opinion, that, unlike the Greeks, they never considered their gods to be of the same nature as man.[123]

The deities in the Avesta are sometimes described in visual terms. However, as mentioned above, it seems that Iranians did not generally interact with their deities on any kind of anthropomorphic level. In cases where the Avesta does provide visual descriptions, they tend more to reflect the conceptual meaning of the deity's function and duty rather than any actual physical reality. For example, when Miθra is described as having ten thousand eyes or a thousand ears (Yt 10.7), the point is to emphasize his particular divine function: his ability to see and hear everything going on in the world, to help human beings when they ask him, or to catch anyone committing any sin. Such visualizations are primarily symbolic. Anāhitā and Miθra are the two very important deities among the young Avestan deities and strongly stand out in their *Yašts*.[124] Anāhitā is described as the ultimate source of all watercourses created by Ahura Mazdā (Yt 5.3, 4, 5, 15, 78, 96, 101). She is thus first and foremost a river, originally a heavenly river symbolized as the Milky Way (Yt 5.85).[125] In earthly terms she descends from the top of the mythical Mount Hukairya ("the mountain of good deeds" Yt 5. 96). The *Ābān Yašt* lists her as a multivalent deity with many functions and conceptualizes different aspects of her divine personality.

The *Ābān Yašt* is distinctive among the *Yašts* in a number of ways. Not only is it one of the longest *Yašts* (consisting of 133 stanzas), but also its evocation of *Arəduuī Sūrā Anāhitā*'s visual characteristics differs fundamentally from those of other deities described in Avestan texts. No other Iranian deity is visualized on the basis of textual descriptions to the extent Anāhitā is, specifically the vivid way that she is portrayed partly as a river and partly as a beautiful super-sized woman (with detailed descriptions of her clothing and jewelry), who transforms into a waterfall-river. In fact, the *Ābān Yašt's* descriptions of various imaginary scenes present some unique interactions and connections between the written text and the visual aspects it evokes (Yt 5.4, 78). As Skjærvø notes, "she is partly described as a river and partly as a richly dressed woman."[126]

Anāhitā's description in the *Ābān Yašt* is rich and specific, enabling one to visualize the goddess almost as much as through visual art (Yt 5.4, 56). Her feminine body is described in rich detail (Yt 5.7, 78, 126, 127). She hears, speaks, rides the chariot (Yt 5.11, 13, 120), and either walks as a goddess or flows as a river (Yt 5.7, 64, and 4, 15). Water is normally in motion, flowing and transforming; therefore, it is not particularly surprising if the water goddess changes from a woman into water/a waterfall (Yt 5.96, 102). She thus also is a shape-shifter, described alternately as a woman and as a river. Her clothes, her body, her palaces, her horse-drawn vehicle, and many other details are elaborately drawn in the *Ābān Yašt*. In some parts of the *Ābān Yašt*, it is as if the composer(s) had a clear physical image of her in his mind as he/they composed the verses (Yt 5. 64, 78, 126–129).

In the *Ābān Yašt* Anāhitā has many functions, but the most significant is that she is first and foremost a water goddess (Yt 5.3, 4, 5, 15, 78, 96, 101). Accordingly (as has been noted previously), many of her functions—including healing, fertility, and wisdom—are shared by her to a greater or lesser extent with the many other Indo-European water goddesses. Moreover, according to the *Ābān Yašt*, all of the waters that Ahura Mazdā created are linked to her (Yt 5.5, 15, 96). Thus, her multifarious functions also connect her to many different groups of deities.

For example, the *Ābān Yašt's* combining of female beauty and splendor on the one hand with strength and power on the other associates Anāhitā with the attributes and characteristics of ruling and spirituality on the one hand, and healing and fertility on the other; she supports warriors, while also supporting life itself and representing the overwhelming force of the Waters. As a shape-shifter, she transforms herself from a river into a beautiful woman and back into a river again, symbolizing her multiple functions.

The *Ābān Yašt* describes Anāhitā as an awe-inspiring deity, superhuman in size, a chariot rider with four natural horses, and strong enough that even Ahura Mazdā occasionally seeks her assistance, hence she has the attribute *ahurō. tkaēša-*, "(she) who follows the Ahura's teaching" (Yt 5.1).

Conclusions

Many Indo-European and proto-Iranian characteristics of *Arəduuī Sūrā Anāhitā*
are clearly present in the *Ābān Yašt*. We may note her three different functions
where three specific categories of people ask for her support, beginning with
the warriors, continuing with the priests, and finally women who present their
wishes connected to fertility (Yt 5.86–87). Anāhitā's multiple functions in the
Avesta are laid out concretely and at times even anthropomorphically, which
suggests that her devotees felt her as more real and immediate than other deities.

Thus, and firstly as a crowned goddess, Anāhitā is associated with the ruling
group of deities. Her importance in this respect, as with other significant Indo-
Iranian deities, is shown by her possessing a vehicle with four stallions who
represent the rain, wind, clouds, and hail the uncontrolled natural phenomena
over which people most needed to have control. She is worthy of sacrifice,
connecting her with the priestly functions among the deities. Indeed, Ahura
Mazdā himself is said to sacrifice to her.

Second, she is also a mighty deity who helps the warriors, assuring them of
victory. The Avestan Anāhitā is notable for her warrior aspect. In fact, the *Ābān
Yašt* mentions many warriors' names and their wishes in the form of legendary
heroes and figures both positive and negative.

Third, Anāhitā is a fertility goddess with healing functions, assisting births,
and giving affluence; she possesses the traits of blessing, abundance, and
prosperity associated her with the "producer" category of deities.[127] The *Ābān
Yašt* clearly lays out this tripartite paradigm by specifying that the priests, the
warriors, and young women wishing to have children must each sacrifice to her
if they wish to be successful.[128]

Another significant feature of Anāhitā is her vivid description in the *Ābān
Yašt* as she changes from a woman into water or a waterfall (Yt 5.96, 102). Her
shape-shifting feature enables one to visualize the goddess almost as vividly as
through visual art (Yt 5.4, 56). Indeed, certain aspects of Anāhitā's description
in the *Ābān Yašt* seem more likely to be based on a vision than on actual
observation, for example, Yt 5.129, which states that her coat is made from the
skins "of thirty beavers of those that bear four young ones"—how would such
a detail be discernable from a statue? The question of how a sculptor might
have indicated such a detail is beyond the scope of this study, but it makes more
sense to assume that the basis for Anāhitā's "beaver skin" clothing can be sought
elsewhere. Certain elements of Anāhitā's description, at least, could be the

product of long oral tradition; for others, the composer(s)' imagination cannot be excluded. Furthermore, it seems this particular aspect of Anāhitā's imagery likely dates back to at least 4,000 years ago and represent a goddess from lands having a cold climate.

Finally, as we have discussed above, Anāhitā may have been worshipped by "those who sacrifice to *daēuuas*," which may connect her to the warrior groups of deities *-daēuuas*. The cults of these "*daēuua*-worshippers" were partly conducted after sunset (Yt 5.94–95). Was this the time that they imagined Anāhitā living "above the stars," by looking at the sky at nighttime, as mentioned in the *Ābān Yašt* (Yt 5.85), or was it because they wanted to keep their ceremonies hidden from the Mazdaean authorities? These are the questions that are difficult to answer with any certainty.

Other Iranian Goddesses: Comparisons with Anāhitā

Anāhitā is not the only goddess to appear in the *Yašts*. In fact, there are a number of other female deities in the Avestan pantheon, each of whom has her own importance. The most important goddesses in the Avestan texts are Spəṇtā Ārmaiti—the abstract concept of "right-mindedness" and the spirit of the earth; the pre-Zoroastrian deity Aši, goddess of "Reward, Fortune"; Daēnā, the Avestan term for an anthropomorphized moral concept but also a hypostasized Goddess; and finally, the Gathic deities of health and immortality, Hauruuatāt and Amərətāt. Among these female divinities, Spəṇtā Ārmaiti, Hauruuatāt, and Amərətāt are the three female Aməša Spəṇtas, "Bounteous Immortals" (Pahlavi *amahrspands, amešāspands*).

In order to fully understand the evolving role of Anāhitā in ancient Iranian religion, it is important to place her within the context of the pantheon as a whole, particularly in terms of her relationship to other goddesses and the division of functions among them. This comparison can serve to identify similarities as well as differences. A comparative study of these goddesses can not only shed light on their possible similarities in how they are personified, but also—and perhaps more importantly—clarify what makes Anāhitā different (and perhaps unique) from the others.

We have already applied a comparative study of Indo-European water goddesses in order to trace Anāhitā's origin and roots. In the present chapter, our focus of comparison will be on other Iranian goddesses' relationships to Anāhitā, and their main functions within the Zoroastrianism pantheon in relation to hers. As was the case when we looked at Indo-European goddesses, these comparisons will give rise to some questions. What, if anything, do Anāhitā and these goddesses have in common, and to what extent? How and when were these similarities transmitted? These questions reflect our interdisciplinary comparative research approach.

Most of the Iranian deities mentioned in the Avesta—where they are emphasized to have been created by Ahura Mazdā—are, in fact, pre-Avestan gods. Some, like Miθra, can be dated at least as far back as the common Indo-Iranian period, that is to say more than 4,000 years ago.

Among these female divinities, Spəṇtā Ārmaiti, Aši, and Daēnā are the most important ones appearing in the Avesta. We will review these deities in terms of how they compare with Anāhitā in various respects. One comparison can be how each deity is characterized and where it is placed within the pantheon in relation to other deities. In order to make these comparisons, we must rely largely on the Avestan and the Pahlavi texts. What exactly do these texts contribute to this study's topic—that is to say, Anāhitā? To answer this question, we will concentrate on specific passages in the Avestan and Pahlavi texts, not just as a collection of material but rather citing and discussing those passages that can illustrate the differences and similarities between these female deities and Anāhitā. Their importance, their described functions and cults in the *Yašts* and the other texts, and their visual aspects in the texts are the main points for this comparison.

As with any comparative research, we are looking for resemblances by analogy and/or possible homologies. The distinctions and differentiations of characteristics and functions between Anāhitā and these other Iranian goddesses can be seen to have evolved over time, especially when comparing their portrayals in the Avesta with those in the later Pahlavi texts; these changing relationships are important to trace in order to understand the transformations of Anāhitā as the principal Iranian goddess. Moreover, in each case, the beauty of the deity is emphasized, sometimes in a similar way to how Anāhitā is described.

Spəṇtā Ārmaiti (Phl. Spandarmad)

Spəṇtā Ārmaiti (Phl. Spandarmad)—representing an abstract concept of "right-mindedness," "life-giving humility,"[1] or literally, according to Skjærvø, "thinking in right measure"[2]—is the spirit of the earth. Alongside Hauruuatāt and Amərətāt, she is one of three female Aməša Spəṇtas mentioned in the Avesta, being a symbol of femininity and motherhood. An Indo-Iranian deity, she appears in the Vedas as Aramati who is also associated with the earth; she can be recognized as well in later Iranian and Armenian literatures.[3] Among the Aməša Spəṇtas, who are said in the texts to have been created by Ahura Mazdā from his own aura to represent his different aspects, she numbers fourth, but she is first among the female ones. While she represents the earth, she is also considered to evoke the luminous cover of the sky.[4] If we accept that Ahura Mazdā was originally the ancient sky god, then Spǝntā Ārmaiti as the earth and his daughter likely formed a pair with him.

Spǝntā Ārmaiti represents the qualities of wisdom, patience, faith, and devotion. She thus has a multifunctional personality. She is the spirit of the earth who sits on the left side of Ahura Mazdā in the sky. The *Gāθās* describe Spǝntā Ārmaiti as the daughter of Ahura Mazdā (Yasna 45: 4), and also, as Skjærvø states, as Ahura Mazdā's spouse or consort.[5] She is mentioned in association with the earth and its settlement by living beings (Y 47:3). Zaraθuštra considers Spǝntā Ārmaiti as a manifestation of Ahura Mazdā, and as a source of achieving goodness, the correct path and cosmic order (*aša*) (Y 33: 12). In the Young Avesta, Spǝntā Ārmaiti is the symbol and guardian of the earth. In the Story of the Jam (Yima) in the *Vīdēvdāt*, she is addressed as the earth itself, when Jam asks her to provide bounty (Vd 2: 10). As a female symbol, Spǝntā Ārmaiti is an object of worship by women. Righteous (*ašavan*) women worship her first when they worship the Amǝša Spǝntas (Y 21.2). Like Anāhitā, Spǝntā Ārmaiti also is a healer (Yt 1.27), and also, she empowers those warriors who fight against demons, instilling them with intense ferocity (Yt 1.27).

Spǝntā Ārmaiti's identification with the earth has been mentioned. In this way, she follows the old Indo-European mythological paradigm of "sky father–earth mother." In Iranian myth, however, Ahurā Mazdā is "the father" of the Iranian pantheon, whereas Vedic mythology preserves the older pairing in which *Dyaus-Pita* is the "Sky Father" who appears in conjunction with *Mata Prithvi*, "Mother Earth." *Dyaus* is etymologically identical to the Greek *Zeus* and the Latin *Ju(piter)*. The goddess has been identified by the Sumerian goddess Nana.[6] Azarpay proposes that Spǝntā Ārmaiti was identified by Nana and, "the syncretic cult of Nanā- Ārmaiti was fairly wide spread [*sic*] throughout the east Iranian world in early medieval times."[7] If we accept this, then it follows that Nana's cult has affected both of these important Iranian goddesses, Ārmaiti and Anāhitā.

Alongside her identification with the earth, Spǝntā Ārmaiti is associated with obedient, enduring, tolerant, and patient femininity, putting her in contrast with Anāhitā whose divine femininity emphasizes her strength. She is associated with the terrestrial sphere, whereas Anāhitā lives above the stars as "the heavenly river" and is symbolized by the Milky Way (Yt 5.85).

Spəṇtā Ārmaiti (Spandarmad) in the Pahlavi Texts

In the Avesta, and unlike Anāhitā, Spəṇtā Ārmaiti does not have any visualized image. There are, on the other hand, some images of Spandarmad in the Pahlavi texts. In the *Wizīdagīhā ī Zādspram* (The Selections of Zādspram), for example, she is embodied and personified as follows (WZ 4: 4–8):

4.4) *paydāgīh ī dēn pad Spandarmad pad ān gāh būd ka Frāsyāb āb az Ērānšahr abāz dāšt. āb abāz ānīdan, kanīg-kirbīhā pad xānag ī Manuščihr ī Ērānšahr dahibed, anērān pāsox-guftār būd, oh paydāgīhist.*

4.5) *u-š paymōxt dāšt rōšnīg paymōzan, kē be frōgīhist ō wispān kustagān hāsr-ē drahnāy ī ast frasang dō homānāg.*

4.6) *u-š pad mayānag bast dāšt zarrēn kustīg, ī xwad būd dēn ī māzdēsnān, čē dēn band ast kē-š awiš paywastag sīh ud se band ī abar sīh ud se wināh, kē-š hamāg wināh aziš baxtag.*

4.7) *kanīgān kē-šan spandārmad bast kustīg dīd, hu-čihr sahistan rāy, pas az ān pad bastan ī kustīg taftīg būd hēnd.*

4.8) *ēn-iz būd mādarīh ī pad dēn ī pad spandārmad be dahīst, pēš az zardxušt bē ō hampursīh madan pad panǰ-sad ud wīst ud hašt sāl. ī-šān gōkān az dēn mādayān nibēg ī pēšēnīgān.*

4.4) The revelation of the religion through Spandarmad was at that time when Frāsyāb kept the water from the country of Iran. To bring the water back, (Spandarmad) in the shape of a maiden appeared in the house (court) of Manuščihr, Iran's king who was responder to foreigners.

4.5) She wore radiant clothing which shone out on all sides for the length of a *hās*ᵃ*r*, which is, like two *frasang*.

4.6) And, tied on her waist, she wore a golden "*kustīg*" (the Zoroastrian's religious belt) which was itself the religion of the Mazdā-worshippers, since the religion is a cord to which are connected thirty-three cords,[8] which are above the thirty-three sins into which all the sins are divided.

4.7) The maidens who saw Spandarmad with a tied *kustīg* in order to appear beautiful were afterwards ardent to tie it themselves.

4.8) And this was the motherhood of the religion, which was created through Spandarmad, in the year 528 before Zarduxšt took counsel, the details of which (are) in the essential religious writings of the ancestors.[9]

The emphasis on Spandarmad's clothing is noteworthy. She wears a *kusti* (the Zoroastrian religious belt) tied around her waist, but in a way that reminds of Anāhitā's belt described in the Avesta (Yt 5.126–7). Moreover, since this is a story about water, one may ask why in the Pahlavi text it is Spandarmad who is charged with solving the problem of bringing the water back that Frāsyāb (Av. Fraŋrasiian-) had kept back, and not Anāhitā as one would expect? It is also striking that this passage offers a rare example where Spandarmad is described anthropomorphically, with an emphasis on her clothing and her beauty similar to how Anāhitā is presented in the much older Avestan text, the *Ābān Yašt*. Is this an indication of Spandarmad's taking over some of Anāhitā's aspects by the Pahlavi period?

Fraŋrasiian- (Pahl. Frāsyāb, Frāsyāg; NP Afrāsiāb), who in the Avesta sacrifices to Anāhitā (although she does not accept his offering), is mostly associated with the causing of drought through the suppression of the waters and the draining of rivers (as will be discussed further in Chapter Seven). Might the connection in the later Pahlavi text between the "demonic" character Frāsyāb and the divine Spandarmad (the earth?) have to do with Frāsyāb's fortress being located underground? (Bd XXXII.13). An additional connection between these two figures can be found in another Pahlavi text, the *Šahrestānīhā-ī Ērān-Šahr*, where Spandarmad is described as a woman whom Frāsyāb (here with the variant Frāsyāg) wants to marry:

(ŠĒ 38)
šahrestān zarang naxust gizistag Frāsyāg ī tūr kard, u-š warzāwand ātaxš karkōy ānōh nišāst, u-š manuščihr andar ō padišxwārgar kard, u-š Spandarmad pad zanīh xwast ud Spandarmad andar ō zamīg gumēxt, šahrestān awērān kard, u-š ātaxš afsārd ud pas kayhusraw Siyāwaxšān šahrestān abāz kard, u-š ātaxš karkōy abāz nišāst ud ardašīr pābagān šahrestān bun pad frazāmēnīd.[10]

Frāsyāg accursed (of) Tūr ('s race), first built the city Zarang, and established the holy *karkōy* fire there, and surrounded Manuščihr in *Padišxwārgar*[11] and wanted to marry Spandarmad and Spandarmad mixed (*gumēxt*) with the earth, and (he) devastated the city and extinguished the fire and then Kaykhosrow the son of Siyāwaxš re-built the city (Zarang) and re-established the *karkōy* fire and Ardešir-e Bābakān finished (building) of the city.

In the Pahlavi text known as *Čīdag Andarz ī Pōryōtkēšān*, human beings recognize Ohrmazd and Spandarmad as their primordial and uncreated father and mother:

(ČAP 2)

... ohrmazd dām hēm nē ahreman dām, u-m paywand ud tōhm az gayōmard, u-m mād Spandarmad u-m pid ohrmazd ...

... I am created by Ohrmazd and not Ahreman, and my pedigree is from Gayōmard, my mother is Spandarmad and my father is Ohrmazd

In Book 7 of the *Dēnkard*, Spandarmad is described by Zaraϑuštra himself:

(Dk 7. 4. 58)

guft-iš zarduxšt kū: "bē-m ān nigerīd kē Spandarmad andar ān ī rōšn rōz ī an-abr, ud ān man sahist Spandarmad hu-ōrōn ud hu-parrōn ud hu-tarist, kū hamāg gyāg nēk būd, pasīh frōd ward kū šnāsēm agar tō hē Spandarmad"?[12]

Zarduxšt said: But I saw Spandarmad on a clear day without clouds, and she appeared to me beautiful from near and far and from across, meaning on all sides (she) was beautiful. Turn around back so, that I can recognise if it is you Spandarmad!

This passage describes Spandarmad as a personification of the earth and is an allusion to the beauty of the earth, consistent with the Zoroastrian view of the world as a fundamentally good place.

The *Bundahišn* also describes Spandarmad as patient and enduring. She is presented as friendly and softly maternal, very different from Anāhitā. Like the earth, Spandarmad receives with tolerance and forbearance any harm humans do to her:

(Bd XXVI. 81–88)

26.81) *Spandarmad xwēš-kārīh parwardārīh ī dāmān ud har(w) xīr pad dāmān bowandag be kardan. u-š gētīg zamīg xwēš.*

26.82) *čiyōn gōwēd kū Spandārmad ī weh ī bowandag-menišn ud kāmag- dōysᵃr ī Ohrmazd-dād ī ahlaw.*

26.83) *u-š wehīh ēn kū wīdwar ud gilag-ōbār ēn kū anāgīh ī ō Spandārmad zamīg rasēd hamāg be gugārēd.*

26.84) *u-š bowandag-menišn ēn kū hamāg anāgīh ī-š padiš kunēnd hunsandīhā padīrēd.*

26.85) *u-š radīh ēd kū hamāg dāmān az ōy zīwēnd.*

26.86) *ahlawān mēnōg pākīh ī zamīg rāy dād ēstēd kū ka-š dēwān pad šab nasrušt abar barēnd ōy yōjdahr be kunēd.*

26.87) *u-š ēn-iz xwēš-kārīh kū har(w) ēbārag-ē(w) az har(w) dahišn-ē(w) xwarrah-ē(w) abāz ō pēš ī Ohrmazd šawēd. pad ušahin gāh ān xwarrah ō star-pāyag āyēd ud Ōš(e)bām be padīrēd. ud pad bāmdād gāh be ō war ī Ūrwes āyēd ahlaw mēnōg padīrēd ud pad rah ī wardayūn āyēd ud har(w) ĵār-ē(w) xwarrah ī xwēš awiš abespārēd.*

26.88) *kē-š zamīg rāmēnēd ayāb bēšēd ēg-iš Spandārmad rāmēnēd ayāb bēšīd bawēd.*[13]

26.81) The proper function of Spandarmad is the nourishment of the creatures (of Ohrmazd), and making every thing perfect for the creation. And the *gētīg* (material) earth is her own.

26.82) (As) is stated: "The good Spandarmad, the perfect-minded, with the desire to observe widely,[14] created by Ohrmazd, the righteous (one).

26.83) Her goodness is this that she is patient and suppresses (lit.: swallows) complaints; it is such that she bears (lit. 'digests') all the harm, which reaches to the earth of Spandarmad.

26.84) And her perfect mindedness is that she accepts with contentment all the harms which (people) do to her.

26.85) And her generosity is that all the creations live because of her.

26.86) The "*mēnōg*" of the righteous beings is created for the purity of the earth, when the "*dēwān*" pollute it with abomination at nighttime, then she purifies it.

26.87) And she also has this proper function that every evening a *xwarrah* from each creation reverts towards Ohrmazd. The *xwarrah* comes at the *ušahin gāh* (the night *gāh*) to the star station, and the *ōš(e)bām* (dawn) accepts it. And at the time of dawn it comes onto the sea of *Ūrwes*, and the "*mēnōg*" of the righteous being accepts it. And she comes in the chariot, and every time gives back to every one his own *xwarrah*.

26.88) Anybody who pleases or distresses the earth shall have pleased or distressed Spandarmad.

The portrayal here of Spandarmad provides an interesting resonance with contemporary environmentalist thinking, which sometimes anthropomorphizes nature's reactions to how people treat her.

Daēnā

Daēnā (Pahlavi *dēn*) is an Avestan term for an anthropomorphized moral concept. *Yašt* 16 of the Avesta, the *Dēn Yašt*, is named after her but is actually devoted to another female deity, Čistā, whose connection to Daēnā is close but not entirely clear.[15] The word *daēnā-* is derived from the root √*dī*, "to see," connected to *Daēnā*'s enabling one's vision-soul to "see." One may say that it is the hypostasis of one's own moral qualities or inner self especially toward religion, and as Hintze points out, "basically refers to the mental view and attitude of a person toward his own life and towards the world around him."[16] Moreover, Hintze explains:

> A peculiarity of the ancient Iranian (and indeed Indo-Iranian) religion is the personification of abstract notions. In this process, the grammatical gender of a noun could turn into natural gender. For instance, the grammatically feminine noun *daēnā-* 'conscience, vision' came to be represented as a maiden.[17]

The Avestan words *māzdaiiasni-* (of a Mazdayasnian) and *āhūiri-* (ahuric) function as adjectives modifying the *daēnā-* in the liturgical parts of *Yasna*.[18] The *daēnā-* or *dēn* contains each person's inner belief, conscience, and insight. The idea appears in the *Vīdēvdāt*, the *Ardā Wīrāz-nāmag*, the *Hāδōxt Nask*, and also in some other texts.[19] According to this belief, at the dawn of the fourth day after death, the soul of the deceased finds itself in the presence of either a beautiful maiden (who is the mobile and seeing soul) and leads it to the heaven, or an ugly disgusting hag (who is the mobile and seeing soul, again) who takes it to the hell, depending on whether the person has led a righteous or sinful life.

With the function and capacity of distinguishing good actions from bad ones, the *daēnā-* is an embodiment of moral conscience, given to humans as a gift from Ahura Mazdā. In the *Gāθās* this capacity is presented as mostly conceptual, rather than having an actual divine form (Y 31: 11). And it changes in accordance with the free choice of the individual (Y 48–5).

Commenting on the Indo-European myth of the marriage between the sky god and his daughter, Cantera explains that in the mythology of the long liturgy, it is the wedding of Ahura Mazdā with the vision, Daēnā,[20] and through the recitation of the *Ahuna Vairia* and the long liturgy (Y 53), Zaraθuštra emulates Ahura Mazdā by marrying his own daughter, thus in turn each Mazdaean priest emulates Zaraθuštra; his soul is thereby united with the Vision-Daēnā and gains access to Ahura Mazdā. Cantera states that since the Vision is also "the capacity for consultation and transmitting the consultation to the ritual community as the contents of the consultation, thus the meaning of *daēnā* could be seen as "tradition" or "corps of the religious texts". Every consultation transmitted to humans in the long liturgy is *daēnā*, according to Cantera.[21]

In the Young Avesta, however, this capacity for moral discernment is hypostatized as a beautiful maiden in the case of a good person's soul after death as discussed above. The soul and Daēnā first exchange some questions and answers, then Daēnā explains that while she is by nature beautiful and worthy of adoration, the soul's good deeds have made her even more so.

The scene where the soul meets Daēnā also occurs in the (Vd 19: 30). Daēnā is accompanied by the goddess Aši, who is said to be her sister. Together, they are the spiritual guardians of women (Y 13.1).

The *daēnā* in the *Haδaoxta-nask* is a beautiful young girl who has just reached the age of fifteen:

(HN 2.9)

āat təm vātəm nāŋhaii uzgərəmbiiō saδaiieiti yō narš ašaonō uruua kudat aēm
  vātō vāiti yim yauua vātəm nāŋhābiia hubaoiδitəməm jigauruua?
aŋhā°dim vātaiiā°frərənta saδaiieiti yā hauua daēna.

kaininō kəhrpa srîraiiā°xšōiθniiā° auruša-bāzuuō amaiiā° huraoδaiiā° +uzarštaiiā°
bərəzaitiiā° ərəduuafšniiā° sraotanuuō āzātaiiā° raēuuasciθraiiā° pąncadasaiiā°
raoδaēšuua kəhrpa auuauuatō sraiiā°yaθa dāmąn sraēštāiš.

Then the righteous soul feels he (she) smells the (aromatic) wind. "where does this wind come from, the most aromatic wind that I have ever smelled with my nose?
the soul imagines that his conscious (*daēna*) comes along (*frərənta*) with this wind.

Displayed in the shape of a beautiful bright maiden with white strong arms and well-shaped and girded high, upright with well-formed outstanding breasts, well-shaped, noble-born and righteous who seems fifteen with the best body among the other creators.

And further:

āaṭ hē paiti-aoxta yā hauua daēna: azəm bā tē ahmi yum humanō huuacō
hušiiaoθana hudaēna yā hauua daēna xvaēpaiθe tanuuō.

then his (her) conscience (*daēna-*) answered him: O young righteous good-thinking, good-doing, good-speaking man, I am your very own conscience.

The dual conceptualization of Daēnā demonstrates that it is one's behavior during life that makes the difference. Good behavior makes one's Daēnā more beautiful and cherished:

(HN 2.30)

aaṯ mąm friθąm haitîm friθō.tarąm srîrąm haitîm srîrō-tarąm bərəxδąm haitîm bərəxδō.tar ąm.

then I already was cherished, you (made) me more, I already was beautiful, you (made) me more, I already was precious, you (made) me more.

Both the good and evil versions of the spirit are accompanied by a wind. In the case of Daēnā, the wind blows from the south. In the case of the disgusting hag, the wind blows from the north. Daēnā is said to have a precise age: she is a fifteen-year-old girl. This detail clearly represents an aspect of ideal beauty in the mind of ancient Iranians, and it is surely not coincidental that in Persian poetry of the Islamic period the *sāqī*, or wine-bearer with whom the poet falls in love, is said to be this age as well.

Daēnā's depictions in the Pahlavi texts are similar to those cited above. She is described with precision in the *Ardā Wīrāz nāmag*, a text that recounts the journey of a Zoroastrian priest, Wīrāz,[22] through heaven and hell in order to demonstrate the validity of Zoroastrian beliefs. Similar journeys to that of Wīrāz exist elsewhere in Zoroastrian literature, including inscriptions of the third-century priest Kirdīr and the legend of Zaraθuštra recorded in *Dēnkard* VII by King Wištāsp.[23] In the case of Kirdīr, it is a matter of a vision of heaven and hell in the course of a soul-journey, which he describes in the Naqš-e Rajab inscription near Persepolis.

In three different Pahlavi books—the *Ardā Wīrāz nāmag*,[24] the *Bundahišn*, and the *Dādestān ī Mēnog ī Xrad*—Daēnā/Dēn is mentioned as a beautiful young maiden. In the *Bundahišn*, she has a beautiful body, white clothes, and is fifteen years old; her image is generated in relation to the nature of the individual's deeds while alive:

(Bd XXX.30.14 and16)

30.14) *did kanīg kirb padīrag rasēd ī hu-kirb ī sped wistarag ī pānzdah sālag kē az hamāg kustag*
nēk kē ruwān padiš šādīhēd.

30.16) *ēdōn awēšān ēk ēk passox gōwēnd <ku> man hēm ahlaw dēn ī tō ān kunišn ī-t warzēd ka tō ān nēkīh kard man tō rāy ēdar būd hēm.*

30.14) Then a maiden-shaped comes to welcome, with good body, white dress, fifteen years old, who looks good from all sides, and the soul feels comfort by (seeing) her.

30.16) And thus they answer, one by one, "O righteous one, it is me, your conscious (*dēn*), I am that deed that you committed. When you did that good manner, I was there (in) you.

And its Dēn who meets the souls of the deceased as they cross over the *Činuuat* Bridge:

(AWN. 4. 9)

u-š ān ī xwēš dēn ud ān ī xwēš kunišn (padīrag āmada) kanīg kirb ī nēk pad dīdan ī *hu-rust kū pad frārōnīh rust ēstād frāz-pestān kū-š pestān abāz nišast ī dil ud gyān dōst[25] *kē-š kirb ēdōn rōšn čiyōn dīd hu-dōšagtar nigerišn abāyišnīgdar.*

And his own religion and his own deeds, in the shape of a well-appearing (*hurust: hu-rust*) maiden came toward him, as a beautiful appearance, that is, raised in rectitude (*frārōnīh*), with prominent (*frāz*) breasts, that is, her breasts swelled upward, and charming to the heart and the soul, the shape of whose body was as bright and luminous, so was so pleasant to see and desirable.

In summary, the description of Daēnā is precise, emphasizing her beauty. Interestingly, many of the adjectives applied to Daēnā are elsewhere applied to Anāhitā. The beautiful maiden appearance of Daēnā could have some connection to the descriptions of *Arduuī Sūrā Anāhitā* in the Ābān Yašt, which, in fact, uses many adjectives similar to the description of her.[26] Thus, as a divine power, the *daēnā-* takes shape according to an individual human's behavior and deeds while alive in the world. We can confirm Daēnā's quality as a shape-shifter, as is the case with Anāhitā. The difference is that Daēnā's changes vacillate between two basic anthropomorphic female forms, one positive/beautiful, and the other negative/disgusting, reflecting the moral quality of the individual. Anāhitā, meanwhile, can either take on the shapes of nature phenomena (rivers, cascades, etc.) or else that of a beautiful, over-sized goddess who moves from the sky to the earth.

Aši

Known as an ancient pre-Zoroastrian divinity[27] and as a Gathic and Young Avestan deity, Aši is the goddess of fortune and abundance who behaves both as a deity and as an abstract concept in the younger Avesta.[28] Her name, an abstract feminine noun in Avestan derived from the Avestan √*ar*- meaning "to reach, arrive" followed by the suffix—*ti*, is an Avestan feminine noun meaning "thing attained, reward, share, portion, recompense," and, as a personification, the goddess of "Reward, Fortune."[29] The term is one of a group of Young Avestan personified abstracts including Rāman ("joy," "peace") and Daēnā ("conscience," "religion"). In the Young Avesta, she is one of the deities who receive the epithet

Vaŋuhī, meaning "the good one," giving the later Pahlavi form Ahrišwang (from *Aši Vaŋuhī*).[30] According to Boyce, Aši also possesses a characteristic epithet of "great-gifted" and fertility function.[31]

Aši was worshiped widely in Iran (mostly in Eastern Iran[32]), possibly originates from the pre-Zoroastrian time,[33] is mentioned in the *Gaϑas*, and has a specific Yašt (Yašt 17 of the Avesta, the *Ard Yašt* or *Aši Yašt*) devoted to her. According to this Yašt, Aši is the daughter of Ahura Mazdā and Spəntā Ārmaiti (showing their pairing). She also has Sraoša, Rašnu, and Miϑra as her brothers, and the Mazdayasnian Religion (Daēna) as her sister (Yt 17.16). She also is the sister of the Aməša Spəntas (Yt 17.2). She is the one who comes with all wisdom of the Sošiants (Yt 17.1–2). If one accepts that the *Gaϑas* are the oldest preserved expression of Zoroastrian thought, it would seem highly significant to note that apart from the Aməša Spəntas, the only other deities they mention (although not clearly as deities) are Sraoša, Fire, and Aši.

Looking at a later period, Grenet has observed that in the Kushan Empire (first to third centuries CE) the Miϑra cult seems to have been paired with that of the goddess Aši (known as *Ardoxšo*); this would suggest that parallel male–female cults existed at that time.[34] On Kušan coins, Ardoxšo (Aši) appears with a cornucopia in hand. She was also worshipped in Manichaeism. In a Manichaean Middle Persian text, the goddess appears as Baγ-ard (written *by 'rd*), the guardian spirit of the border of Khurāsān.[35]

In the *Gāϑās*, Aši is represented as an abstract concept, actually identified with *aša* ("truth"). Schlerath allows that she may have been a fertility goddess in pre-Zoroastrian times, even though she does not appear in the Vedas.[36] It is in the younger Avesta that Aši emerges clearly as a divinity, the subject of her own Yašt. In the Zoroastrian calendar, the twenty-fifth day of the month is dedicated to her.

As a Gathic and Young Avestan figure, Aši must be considered an important deity, providing wealth, happiness, and rest. She is said to be the daughter of Ahura Mazdā and Spəntā Ārmaiti, and the sister of the Aməša Spəntas and of Sraoša, Rašnu, Miϑra, and Daēna. Like other important deities she has a chariot, and also appears driving Miϑra's chariot.

She is worshipped with many adjectives such as "radiant," "honorable," "mighty," "beautiful and tall" (like Anāhitā), "healer" (again like Anāhitā), and successfully fighting enemies (Yt 17 1:1–2). She is a wealth producer. Thus, she produces alimentation, development, peace, and opulence in the Iranian lands. It is not difficult to understand that her description reflects the desires and priorities of her worshippers, as illustrated by the refrain found in her Yašt invoking good fortune through her support (Yt 17.2.7). And wherever she goes, amenity, amicable, and tolerant thoughts will accompany her (Yt 17.2:6).

There exists a whole list of characters, including the Iranian deity Haōma, *Zaraϑuštra*, and the Old Iranian heroes, who sacrifice to Aši. Interestingly, this list is identical with another list found in the *Gōš Yašt* (Yt 9.3–31), devoted to Druuāspā (an Avestan goddess, who, according to her name, "wild solid horses,"[37] was presumably connected to horses). Following Boyce, Skjærvø thinks that "Druuāspā" could originally have been epithet of Aši.[38] The list is also identical with that of Anāhitā's sacrificers provided in the *Ābān Yašt*, except that in the *Ābān Yašt* the list is longer and contains some negative figures, as has been previously mentioned. Since the *Gōš Yašt*'s formulary contains no original material, in all likelihood it was borrowed from these other two *Yašt*s, as Malandra observes.[39]

As the deity of fortune, Aši is characterized as one whose support brings victory in battle (Yt 17.2.12). The *Aši Yašt* mostly describes an ideal society. In the scenes where she is depicted as assisting humankind, wealth is emphasized. The men whom she helps are wealthy. Their country is wealthy. The agriculture in their country is very productive and there is plenty of food for everybody (Yt 17.2.7). The houses are described as strongly made, and in these beautiful bright houses, lucky women wearing square earrings are lying down in their beds waiting for their husbands. This ideal world is full of happy, successful rulers, beautiful young girls, fast and scary horses, large-humped camels, and strong, enduring houses. It is a happy society, which seems incidentally to be highly patriarchal (Yt 17.2:10). As Skjærvø[40] observes:

> Among the old *yašt*s, however, *Ard Yašt* is quite outstanding both for its literary qualities, especially in its sensually graphic description of the homes of Aši's favorites and their wives, who lie awaiting their men's return from battle on sumptuously decorated couches, and for the concern for marital values expressed in it.

In terms of the distribution of their respective characteristics, the Avestan Anāhitā and Aši are closely interrelated, often contrastingly or in complement with each other. There are similarities in some stanzas between the *Ābān Yašt* and the *Yašt* 17 devoted to Aši (Yt 17.6–11), but Aši is not described in as much detail as Anāhitā. Some passages in the *Ābān Yašt* indicate aspects of Anāhitā's power which correspond closely with others addressed to Aši, and there seems to have been "some blurring of identity between these two beautiful, chariot-driving goddesses," as Boyes points out.[41] Indeed, many of the hymns contained in the

Aban Yašt are repeated in the *Aši Yašt*. Like Anāhitā, Aši is mostly concerned with women, but unlike Anāhitā, Aši's "support" reflects men's interests or benefit on their idealistic wives. In other words, when Aši is described as giving her assistance, it is not support given to women in their own life but rather to the men who possess them (Yt 17.10–11).

Both Anāhitā and Aši are fertility goddesses. Also like Anāhitā, Aši is also closely connected to Miθra, appearing in the *Mihr Yašt* as his charioteer (Yt 10.17.68). As in Anāhitā's case, Aši's *Yašt* contains a list of heroes and kings who sacrifice to her asking for her support and are rewarded for it, although unlike Anāhitā's this list is made up uniquely of "good people." Unlike Anāhitā, whose aristocratic female devotees in Anatolia are said by Strabo to have engaged in sacred prostitution prior to marriage, Aši is free of any association with such "immoral" rituals. Quite the contrary, Aši is portrayed as a strong advocate of female morality. She laments about women who abort their children, who cheat on their husbands, and who lie to their husbands about their children's paternity (Yt 17.10.58).

Thus, as a major Iranian goddess, Aši differs from Anāhitā in important respects. These differences are likely connected to socioeconomic transformations in ancient Iranian society, which become increasingly prominent by the Sasanian period. Aši can be seen as the guardian of a "new morality" for women living in a world dominated by Iranian men. Her complaints regarding "immoral" behaviors of women demonstrate that such behaviors existed and were perhaps even prevalent, and that her role was to remove them. She embodies the female characteristics desired by those in control of this society-in-transformation.

In contrast to Anāhitā, Aši appears to fulfill a patriarchal dream as the goddess of "stay-at-home women" who submissively wait for their husbands. Female happiness equates to domestic happiness, as the author of the *Bundahišn* argues:

(Bd 26.99)
Ard mēnōg ī ardāyīh ud wahištīgīh ast ī ka Ahriswang ī weh ast kē Ašišwang gōwēd. xwarrah-abzāyišnīh ī mān čē har(w) čē be ō arzānīgān dahēnd ōy pad abzōn ō ān mān rasēd. pānăgīh ī ganj ī wehān kunēd čē wahišt-iz mān ēwēnag ī gōhr-pēsīd. čiyon gōwēd mān ud·mānišn ī weh čiyon harwisp axw ī astōmand nē pad ēn dēn ī Ohrmazd hēnd.[42]

Aši is the spirit of the righteousness and being from paradise, (she is) the good "Ahriswang," (who also) is called Ašišwang. (She is) the increase of *xwarrah* in the houses. Because whatever is given to the worthy people she shall revert in abundance to that house. She protects the treasure of the good people and the paradise as well (she protects) since it (paradise) also is like a home for the good people and adorned with precious jewels. As it says, "(paradise) is as the house for the good (beings)." Since all the beings in the material world are not following this Religion of Ohrmazd.

Aši, a non–pre-Avestan goddess who begins her rise to divine status in the Avesta, assumes an increasing importance and respect for the Pahlavi priests, who seem to exalt her in an effort to reduce the prominence of the older and originally more powerful Anāhitā and the values she represents.

Hauruuatāt and Amərətāt

Hauruuatāt (MP Hordād, NP Khordād), who is the subject of Yt 4, means "integrity," "wholeness." Amərətāt (MP Amurdād, NP Mordād) literally means "immortality." These two Gathic divinities mostly act in tandem with each other. According to the *Bundahišn* (26.8), they stand on Ahura Mazdā's left, together with Spəṇtā Ārmaiti.[43]

Hauruuatāt is devoted to water. She also ensures the healthy growth of plant life:

(Bd 26. 106–107)

26.106) *Hordād rad ī sālān ud māhān ud rōzān ēn kū harwīn rad. u-š gētīg āb xwēš. čiyōn gōwēd bawišn ud zāyišn ud parwarišn ī hamāg astōmandān gēhān az āb ud zamīg-iz ābādānīh az ōy. ka andar sāl weh šāyēd zī(wi)stan pad rāy ī Hordād.*

26.107) *čiyōn gōwēd kū hamāg (nēkīh ka az abargarān ō gētīg) āyēd Hordād rōz ī nog-rōz āyēd. ast ī gōwēd kū hamāg rōz āyēd bē ān rōz wēš āyēd*

26.106) Hordād is the chieftain of the years, months, and days, as she is the chieftain of all these. And the *gētīg* water is her own. As it says the existence, birth, and nourishment of all corporeal life are due to water, and the fertility of the land too is due to it. If (people) can live well during the year, it is on account of Hordād.

26.107) As it says, "When all happiness comes to the earth from the supernal beings, it comes on the day Hordād, the new year day." There is one who says, "It comes on all the days, but it comes the most on that day."

Humans can either please or offend her, depending on how they treat water: "one who will please or distress the water shall have pleased or distressed Hordād" (Bd 16:106).

Amərətāt is devoted to plants. In the Iranian creation story, as related in the *Selections of Zādspram*, after the first plant is destroyed by demons during the primordial battle Amərətāt or Amurdād regenerates plant life all across the earth. According to the version in the *Bundahišn*, Amurdād is either pleased or angered by humans depending on how they treat plants:

(Bd 26. 116–117)

26.116) *a-margān Amurdād a-margān urwarān rad čē-š gētīg urwar xwēš. ud urwarān waxšēnēd ud ramag ī gōspandān abzāyēnēd hamāg dām az ōy xwarēnd ud zīwēnd. pad i-z fraš(a)grid anōš az Amurdād wirāyēnd.*

26.117) *kē urwar rāmēnēd ayāb bēšēd ēg-iš Amurdād rāmēnēd ayāb bēšīd bawēd.*

26.116) The immortal Amurdād is the chieftain of the innumerable plants. For the *gētīg* plants (are) her own, and she causes the plants to grow and the flocks of animals to increase. For all the creatures eat and live on account of her, and even at the renovation of the universe *fraš(a)gird* they will prepare the nectar out of Amurdād.

26.117) He who will please or distress the plants shall have pleased or distressed Amurdād.

Hauruuatāt and Amərətāt are said to be offended by chatter (MX 2.33), and harmed by women who do not observe the stipulated procedures when menstruating (AWN 72.5).

Some scholars have sought to connect Hauruuatāt and Amərətāt to certain Vedic deities, which would imply a very archaic origin to this pairing. Dumézil, for example, has drawn a functional correspondence between these two Amǝša Spəntas and the Vedic Nāsatyas.[44] Duchesne-Guillemin and Widengren have supported this hypothesis,[45] while others such as Narten[46] and Gnoli[47] have rejected it.[48] Narten, meanwhile, has pointed out that in the *Yasna Haptaŋhāiti*, *dāenā-* and *Fsəratū-* occupy the place of Hauruuatāt and Amərətāt.[49] Some scholars have also raised the possible but problematic connection between Hauruuatāt and Amərətāt and the Vedic Ādityas.[50]

Echoes of Haurvatāt and Amərətāt are found in Gnostic-Manichaean, Christian, and Islamic traditions. They appear as Harwōt and Marwōt in a Sogdian glossary, as Arioch and Marioch in the Book of Enoch, and the demons Hārūt and Mārūt in the Qur'an (2:96). The flowers referred to as *hawrot-mawrot* in Armenian used in the *hambarjman tawn* ceremony are another reflex of this pair.[51] Most significantly for our purposes, however, the Zoroastrian texts provide no visual description of either Hauruuatāt or Amərətāt.

Conclusions

There are many important female deities in the Iranian pantheon, who have
relative importance in relation to each other and to Arduuī Sūrā Anāhitā. The
goal of this chapter has been to help us understand how Arduuī Sūrā Anāhitā's
multipotential characteristics situated her within the context of Iranian goddesses
as a whole, and how the distribution of these characteristics and the importance
accorded to them by successive generations of Mazdaean priests changed the
dynamics of Anāhitā's relationship to the other Iranian goddesses from the
Avestan through to the Pahlavi periods.

Apart from Anāhitā, Spəṇtā Ārmaiti, Hauruuatāt, and Amərətāt, who
are the three female Aməṣa Spəṇtas mentioned in the Avesta, along with two
others, Aši and Daēnā, are the most important Mazdaean goddesses. Among
these, Spəṇtā Ārmaiti, Aši, and Daēnā figure most prominently in the Avesta,
where their beauty is also emphasized. Spəṇtā Ārmaiti is the spirit of the earth.
Her relationship with Ahura Mazdā as her father (-husband) echoes an Indo-
European mythological model in which the male sky god is counterbalanced by
the female goddess of the earth. This earth goddess, of whom Spəṇtā Ārmaiti
is the Iranian example, represents the qualities of kindness, patience, faith, and
devotion. Alongside her identification with the earth, Spəṇtā Ārmaiti's traits are
more maternal and rather soft, in contrast to Anāhitā whose divine femininity
emphasizes her power and her strength. Anāhitā does not have a maternal role,
and is not associated with obedience, tolerance, or patient femininity; neither is
she passive. (She is not, however, sexually active like the Mesopotamian goddess
Ištar.) The Avestan Anāhitā is notable for her warrior aspect, both powerful and
chaste, as Jenny Rose has pointed out.[52]

The Avestan Daēnā is both a goddess and the hypostasis of one's own inner
moral quality. She is the post-mortal embodiment of an individual human's
behavior while alive in the world. Though her functions are entirely different
from those of Anāhitā, the terms in which their respective beauty is described
are similar.

The Gathic and Young Avestan Aši is the goddess of Reward and Fortune with
some additional fertility and wisdom functions. Her importance is demonstrated
through Yašt 17 of the Avesta, which is devoted to her, and the *Ard Yašt* or *Aši
Yašt*, where she also is considered as the daughter of Ahura Mazdā and Spəṇtā
Ārmaiti. She produces alimentation, development, peace, and opulence in
the Iranian lands. It is not difficult to understand how these traits would have

attracted many devotees to her cult. As in the case of Anāhitā, a whole list of characters are said to sacrifice to Aši; this list is longer in the *Ābān Yašt* than in the *Aši Yašt*, yet the former also includes some negative figures which suggests some tension between the cults of the two goddesses.

As mentioned above, scholars have assumed that where there are verses in both texts (the *Ābān Yašt* and the *Aši Yašt*) it was the latter that borrowed from the former. Some of these borrowings reflect similarities between these two beautiful, chariot-driving goddesses, suggesting that notions of divine female beauty originated with Anāhitā and then were partially transposed onto other goddesses. In terms of their actual qualities, however, the two goddesses are virtual opposites. Both goddesses are concerned primarily with women, but the values promoted by Aši—obedience and submission—are those of patriarchy, in contrast to Anāhitā's strong and independent character. Aši is portrayed as a strong advocate of female morality, fulfilling a patriarchal dream as the goddess of "stay-at-home women." Within the ongoing evolution of the Iranian pantheon she can be seen as the guardian of a new domestic morality, while Anāhitā's martial role is increasingly emphasized as demonstrated by the Sāsānian rulers sending the severed heads of their enemies to her temple.

Figure 1 A female Paleolithic figurine, known as the "Venus of Willendorf," found in Austria, dated to 28,000–25,000 BCE. Image courtesy of Wikicommons.

Figure 2 Ištar, the Mesopotamian goddess, 1800–1750 BCE, Southern Iraq. British Museum collection. Image courtesy of Wikicommons.

Figure 3 The Romano-Celtic water goddess, Coventina. Clayton Museum, Chesters Roman Fort, Hadrian's Wall. Several stone altars have been found in Carrawburgh, near Hadrian's Wall in Northumberland. Image courtesy of Wikicommons.

Figure 4 Sequana Statue, the river goddess of the Seine. Musée Archéologique in Dijon, France. Image courtesy of Wikicommons.

Figure 5 Head and left hand from a bronze cult statue of a goddess known as "Satala Aphrodite," also attributed to Anāhita. First century BC, found at the ancient Satala, Turkey. British Museum collection. Image courtesy of Wikicommons.

Figure 6 The rock engraving commemorating the investiture of Xosrow II (r. 590–628 CE) at Ṭāq-e Bostān, near Kermānšāh. From left to right: Anāhita, Xosrow II, Ahura Mazdā.

Figure 7 Anāhita crowning the Sasanian monarch Narseh I (r. 293–302 CE) in the rock engraving at Naqš-e Rostam in Fārs.

Figure 8 Detail of Anāhita at Naqš-e Rostam.

Figure 9 Persepolis, the ceremonial capital of the Achaemenids.

Figure 10 Zoroastrian temple, Yazd, Iran.

Figure 11 Pīr-ē sabz (the most important Zoroastrian holy site, known as "Pīr-ē ček-ček" among non-Zoroastrians).

Figure 12 Anāhita temple at Bīšāpūr in Fars. It is an open-air temple, with channels where running water from the nearby river could be controlled through the opening or blocking of water conduits. Photo by Richard Foltz.

Anāhitā: A Composite Goddess

Indo-Iranian Characteristics of Anāhitā

Though a number of modern scholars have sought to characterize Anāhitā as either an "imported," non-Iranian goddess, or at best as a hybrid product of cultural syncretism, it has been the contention of this study that she should be seen primarily as an Iranian manifestation of an ancient Indo-European water-river goddess, who acquired additional features and functions in different places and times throughout history. Her specifically Indo-European characteristics have been discussed in Chapter Four.

Anāhitā is the best-known Iranian goddess, due at least in part to her frequent mentions in ancient Greek sources. As De Jong explains:

> After the period of the Old Persian inscriptions [i.e., of Artaxerxes II] and the presumed date of composition of Berossus' *Babyloniaca*, Anāhitā has captured the West to such an extent that she came to be regarded as the most important Persian divinity. Her cult has been amply described by Classical authors, is attested in many descriptions and her statue is represented on the coins of several Anatolian cities. Anāhitā (in her Armenian name *Anahit*) was certainly the most popular divinity in Armenia, the patron divinity of a country which named an entire province after her [Anaitica, another name for Acilisene on the Upper Euphrates].[1]

De Jong has noted that while the frequent mentions of Anāhitā in Greek and Armenian sources attest to her popularity especially in western Iran, the Aməša Spəntas do not seem to have received much attention from those foreign commentators living in closest proximity to Iranians. On the other hand, "the enormous popularity of Anāhitā in Western Iran may be assured, but can be shown to have produced little doctrinal reflection in priestly circles." De Jong concludes from this that "The [Iranian] pantheon thus appears to have varied locally and in different periods,"[2] an observation with which one can only concur.

As a composite goddess, Anāhitā's principal characteristics appear to have been absorbed, on the one hand, from those of a river–lake–stream goddess or goddesses found in many Indo-European societies, and from Mesopotamian goddesses associated with both war and fertility, on the other. In accordance with this model, it may be assumed that certain basic elements of her role and personality date as far back as the common Indo-European period, since many major European rivers and lakes had a goddess-spirit. While throughout much of the historical period, during the time of her greatest importance in Iranian society, Anāhitā possessed many functions reflecting a broad range of influences, it is possible to trace a line of continuity connecting her back to an archaic proto-Indo-European belief in a river goddess.

Anāhitā's Absorption of Non-Iranian Features

As has been pointed out, deities and their associated myths and rituals in any tradition transform themselves over time, and always represent a composite drawn from a range of sources. Anāhitā, in her best-known version from the time of the Iranian empires, is no exception: she is a goddess whose features, functions, and rituals represent a blend of Iranian and non-Iranian roots.

The Bactria–Margiana Archaeological Complex

The Bactria–Margiana Archaeological Complex, also known as BMAC, refers to an ensemble of archaeological remains attributed to the so-called Oxus or Amu Darya Civilization, which existed in Central Asia roughly between 2300 and 1700 BCE. This civilization first was discovered through archeological sites in Afghanistan, Uzbekistan, and Turkmenistan, and included some ancient cities with buildings and tombs filled with treasures. More discoveries followed, and many other archeological remains were found in eastern Iran and Pakistan, which were very similar to the first discoveries.

From the time of the Bronze Age (*c.* 7000 BCE), a civilization developed throughout this region which had many connections with the peoples of Mesopotamia and Elam. The progressive arrival of Indo-European tribes into the area from around 2400 BCE led to cultural exchanges and mutual influences between the newcomers and the existing inhabitants. The resulting BMAC culture, which was centered along the Oxus river valley, thrived in Central Asia for more than half a millennium.

Michael Witzel has highlighted the relationship between the non-IE and Indo-Iranian elements in BMAC culture, as depicted in seals and other art forms. For example, he sees a local non-IE influence on the Avestan version of the widely attested Indo-European dragon-slaying myth, discussed later, where the hero (Vərəθrayna) overcomes the dragon of drought (Aži/Ahi). Specifically, Witzel perceives a transformation of the IE myth into one evoking the releasing waters of the late spring snow melt in Afghanistan (Avestan version) or in the northwestern Indian subcontinent (*Ṛg Veda* version). According to Witzel, the prominence of the BMAC goddess of waters and fertility influenced, at least to some extent, the character of the Avestan river goddess Anāhitā and that of the Vedic Sárasvatī, setting them apart in some ways from the other Indo-European river goddesses discussed in Chapter Four.[3]

Elamite and Mesopotamian Features

By around 2000 BCE, Susa had become the capital of Elam and its most important city. Parallel with this development, its local deity In-Šushin-ak (lit., "the god of Susa") grew in importance. This trend mirrored the rising importance of Marduk during the growth phase of Babylon.

In-Šušin-ak thus became one of the three important deities in the Elamite pantheon. In-Šušin-ak, Humban, and Kiririša together constituted a divine triad, bearing a striking resemblance to that found later in Iran among Ahura Mazdā, Miθra, and Anāhitā. The similarity is probably not accidental. In both cases, we may note the curious fact that while in neighboring Mesopotamia the functions of various deities were becoming subsumed under a single supreme god, among both the Elamites and the Iranians, a divine triad—consisting of two gods and one goddess—was maintained.

Panaino suggests that the descriptions of Anāhitā's jewelry and other ornaments in the *Ābān Yašt* are an example of the influence of the Babylonian Ištar on Anāhitā:

> The image of Anāhitā in Yt 5, 128, wearing "above (the head) a diadem (studded) with one hundred stars, golden, having eight towers, made like a chariot body, adorned with ribbons, beautiful (and) well-made," immediately recalls that of Ištar with her high hat and the eight-pointed star behind.[4]

The Triad of Deities: A Mesopotamian Inheritance?

During the second half of the first millennium BCE, Marduk, the great god of Babylon, and Ištar, the principal Mesopotamian goddess, became a mythological couple. In Babylonian religion, Marduk first became prominent during the late nineteenth century BCE; by the time of Nebuchadnezzar I (1125–1104 BCE), he is named as the "King of the gods" and is portrayed as the original creator deity in the *Enuma Elish* ("Epic of Creation").[5]

Reflecting the political rise of Babylon as the center of Mesopotamian power, Marduk and Ištar were elevated in relation to other regional deities, who became subordinated to their influence and had many of their functions transferred to them. For example, Marduk absorbed many of the functions—including justice and judgment—formerly associated with Šamaš, the Mesopotamian sun god. A similar phenomenon occurred in Elam, with Humban being raised to the status of creator god and In-Šušin-ak, the principal deity of Susa, and the goddess Kiririša joining him to form a divine triangulate within the Elamite pantheon.[6]

When comparing the divine couple of Marduk and Ištar with the Iranian pairing of Miθra and *Arəduuī Sūrā Anāhitā*, some interesting similarities emerge. In fact, in the *Yašts* and in some documents from the Achaemenid period, the functions and powers of Miθra and *Arəduuī Sūrā Anāhitā* are very similar to those of Marduk and Ištar.[7] Although, according to the Younger Avesta, the former pair were not a couple but "co-creations of Ahura Mazdā." The pair of Miθra and *Arəduuī Sūrā Anāhitā* among the other deities was very important.

Whereas in Indo-European religion the functions of various deities tend to be associated with social groups, within the new triangulate Ahura Mazdā–*Arəduuī Sūrā Anāhitā*–Miθra—which is established no later than the early fourth century BCE—important functions connected with all three groups are absorbed: dominion, war, and fertility. The devotional liturgies to Miθra and Anāhitā contained in the Younger Avesta demonstrate their continued religious importance in society—which most likely predated the rise of Mazdaism—while simultaneously subordinating them to Ahura Mazdā who is said in the Yašts to have created them.

The Ahura Mazdā–Anāhitā–Miθra triad is first documented in the inscriptions of Artaxerxes II (r. 404–358 BCE), at a time when a large portion of the population under Persian rule was still culturally Elamite. It is thus very likely that the Elamite triad Humban–In-Šušin-ak–Kiririša and/or the Mesopotamian pairing of Marduk with Ištar served as a model for the Iranian one, reflecting

Artaxerxes' attempt to increase his political base by incorporating the local (non-Iranian) cults of a justice deity and a fertility/war goddess, identified in Iranian terms as Miθra and Anāhitā.[8]

In Central Asia as well, where Anāhitā was considered by some to be the goddess of the Oxus River, a variation of this triad existed: Anāhitā as the goddess, Ahura Mazdā as the father-god, and Miθra as the son.[9] This does not mean in mythological terms that Anāhitā and Ahura Mazdā "married" or produced a child together; rather, the "family" paradigm expressed the hierarchy of their actual functions and roles. As in the case of western Iran, this triad would seem to be related to that found among the southern Elamites.

The Dragon-Slaying Myth, *Saošiiaṇts*, and Possible Connections to Anāhitā

The myth of an archetypal hero (either deity or human) slaying a dragon/serpent (who is most often blocking access to a body of water, and frequently also holding a maiden captive) is very ancient; based on its prominence in the myths of many Indo-European peoples—including those of Iran, India, Greece, and Rome with parallels among the Balts, the Slavs, the Armenians, and the Hittites—it would strongly seem to date back to the proto-Indo-European period or even earlier.[10] A large number of Indo-European deities—who were perhaps once heroic or royal ancestors who became deified over time in the popular imagination—are placed in this ritualization in the role of the hero who slays the dragon.

For purposes of our discussion, it is pertinent to look at the relationship between the dragon (holding back the waters) and women (representing fertility) in the Indo-Iranian version of the dragon-slaying myth. In Indo-Iranian mythology, dragons were associated with natural phenomena such as drought and chaos. They imprisoned the "good waters" (personified either as women or as clouds) or were the carriers of the "destructive and furious waters" (i.e., uncontrolled water, such as rivers in flood). The good waters could not be released until slain by a deity or a hero.

It may be that the association of dragons with rivers arose from the rivers' serpentine shape. We should also note that in agricultural societies, rivers played an ambivalent role: on the one hand, they brought fertility, the most necessary factor of life, but at the same time (in their dragon shape), rivers could also cause massive destruction through floods. Moreover, they might dry up and abandon humans altogether if there was a lack of rain. Dragons were thus sometimes also symbolized as clouds, due to their connection with rain.

Rituals and their attendant myths, therefore, arose out of the vital dependence of ancient Indo-European peoples on rivers to maintain their way of life. Killing a dragon was one symbolic way of exercising control over the potentially chaotic vicissitudes of flowing water. In performing this task, the dragon-slaying hero ensured fertility. Bahar suggests in this connection that because the waters were so vital and sacred, the dragon-slaying heroes who released it could thereby attain immortality.[11]

In the Vedic version of the myth, it is the god Indra who slays the dragon, Vṛtra, who lurks at the foot of the mountain where he holds back the heavenly waters.[12] Indra slays the dragon by cutting off his three heads.[13] After Indra thus frees the seven rivers, the waters rush out in the shape of cows (representing fertility), running to the sea.

The Vedic dragon Vṛtra is referred to both as *áhi-*, "dragon" (similarly, *až-i* is a three-headed dragon in the Avesta) and as *dāsá-* (Av. *dahāka-*), meaning he is man-like.[14] Tracing the etymology of the former term, in Indo-Iranian, the word *áhi-/aži-* means "snake/dragon."[15] *Aždahā* (or *Eždehā*), the modern Persian word for dragon, is derived from a combination of the two terms, *aži-* and *dahāka-*. The above-cited passage in the *Ṛg Veda* describes the "bound waters" as having Vṛtra as their husband-guardian, thus linking the waters with an imprisoned maiden.[16] After slaying Vṛtra, Indra receives the epithet *vṛtra-hán-* "slayer of Vṛtra," from which the Avestan word Vərəθraγna (the war deity) is also derived. Indra is associated with the divine group of *deva*s, deities of the warriors (and thus seen positively) who are demoted to demonic status in the Avesta.

In the Iranian version, meanwhile, the functions of Indra are divided between Miθra and Vərəθraγna (Bahrām), whose name literally means "slayer of [the dragon] Vṛtra"; in Iran the epithet became the name of the god himself. According to the *Bahrām Yašt*, the *Yašt* devoted to Vərəθaγna, if people do not sacrifice to him, or if they share his sacrifice with non-Mazdāyasnians, then a huge flood (uncontrolled waters) will cover the Iranian lands.[17] It seems that "Vərəθraγna" was at first just an epithet and did not exist independently, although by the Young Avesta he has become a strong deity with warrior characteristics. His ten forms, animal and human, remind us of the ten incarnations of Indra. More interestingly, as a deity Vərəθraγna existed in Armenian pantheon and was, in fact, one of the three principal deities, all having Iranian origins. The other two were Ahura Mazdā-Aramazd and Anāhitā-Anahit; the three deities were called *višapak ʿał/drakontopniktḗs*, "the strangler of dragons."[18]

Dragons are found throughout the Iranian Zoroastrian literature, such as the sea monster Gandarəβa, (Pahlavi Gandarb/Gandarw), a monster with yellow heels (*Zairipāšna-*) who is fought and vanquished by Kərəsāspa (Yt 5.38, 15.28 19.41). Gandarw's name is etymologically equivalent to the Vedic *gandharva*, who is said to be surrounded by the heavenly waters, which flow down at his glance.

The *Zamyād Yašt* also mentions the hero Kərəšāspa (Garšasp) who slays the dragon Aži-Sruuara, also called "Aži Zairita," a horned dragon who swallows horses and men (Yt 19.6.40.). Aži Raoiδita, the red dragon (in contradistinction to the Aži Zairita "yellow dragon"), is, together with the "daēuua-created winter," Aŋra Mainiiu's counter-creation to Ahura Mazdā's creation of Airiiana Vaējah (Vd 1.2.). In Zoroastrian tradition, these dragons are all created by the evil, Aŋra Mainiiu, Ahriman.

Possible Connections between Anāhitā and the Avestan *Saošiiaṇt*

In light of the mythological connection between dragons and rivers, we may consider whether dragon-slaying myths can be further connected to the Iranian river goddess, Arəduuī Sūrā Anāhitā, and probably to the Avestan *saošiiaṇt-*. Let us begin with a linguistic analysis. Sōšiians, the Pahlavi's final savior, has different meaning comparing to the Gathic Avestan *saošiiant-* as the "benefactor." The Gathic *saošiiaṇt-* has a ritual function, or as Kellens states: "le sacrifiant," "celui qui va ou qui veut prosérer," who takes part in the exchange of gifts between (the) god(s) and humans.[19] Hintze, however, posits that the *saošiiaṇt-* were persons who played a central role in early Mazdayasnianism, but not necessarily in the ritual inherited from the Indo-Iranian period.[20] As she explains:

> In the oldest part of the Avesta, the Gathas, *saošiiant-* even used in the singular, denotes a member of a group of people following Zaraϑuštra's religion: the Saošyants fight evil during their lifetime and are characterized by an exemplary good "(religious) view" (Av. *daēnā*).[21]

She argues that in Old Avestan a *saošiiaṇt-* refers to a member of a group of people who follow Zaraϑuštra's religion and fights evil during his lifetime. She states that the concept of a *saošiiaṇt-* as a fighter and a savior who ushers in a new age and brings about the final defeat of Evil was, in fact, developed later in time.[22]

In at least one of the Gathic passages (Y 48.12), the *saošiiaṇt-* is someone who fights against enemies; this aspect is very prominent later in the Young Avesta, where the victorious *saošiiaṇt-* as a single person is called *astuuąt.ərəta* and is mentioned with the epithet *vərəθra-jan-* "victorious" (Yt 13.129 and Yt 19.89), which, in fact, is the Vedic epithet of Indra, *vṛtra-hán-*, as has been previously mentioned. Applying the same epithet to Indra (who slew the dragon *Vṛtra*) may link the Avestan *saošiiaṇt-* to the dragon-slaying myth. Furthermore, there is a possible connection between the Avestan word *saošiiaṇt-* ("benefactor"), which also bears the epithet *vərəθra-jan-* (here, "breaking the defense"), with the myth of the hero slaying a dragon.[23] As we will discuss below, in Zoroastrian eschatology, there is a connection between the *saošiiaṇt*s and the river and lake belonging or connected to Anāhitā.

According to stanza 89 in the Zamyād Yašt, this victorious *saošiiaṇt-* is the hero who will bring about the final defeat of Evil. He is expected to be born out of Lake Kąsaoiia, and will overcome the devil by removing falsehood from the world with a special weapon—again similar to Indra, who slew the dragon with his special weapon. In order to accomplish this feat, and to bring about the renovation of the world (Av. *frašō.kərəti-*), the victorious *saošiiaṇt-* will have the power and the support of the *xvarənah-* (the mighty gleaming glory).

Moreover, the word *saošiiaṇt-* contains the verbal root *sū-*, "to be strong (to swell)," from the root √*sū*. *saošiiaṇt-*, therefore, is the participle, and *sūra-* the noun. The Avestan noun *sūra-*, from which the second of Anāhitā's epithets derives, is the Indo-Iranian term for the hero who slays a dragon.[24] Hintze notes that in the *Ṛg Veda*, *śūra-* (heroic) is also an epithet for Indra.[25] She notes that in Indo-Iranian myths, this noun, *sūra*, seems to have referred to the hero who kills the dragon.[26] Since *sūra-* as part of the name (or epithet) of Anāhitā means "strong" and also functions as a masculine substantive meaning "hero," one can posit a connection between the dragon (whose connection with water is mainly that it prevents the water of the rivers from flowing) and/or the heavenly water, and Anāhitā as the heavenly waters associated with the rivers. If we accept that the myth of slaying dragon is connected to the warrior groups of deities (*daēuuas*), then Anāhitā's function could originally be connected to the *daēuuas*[27] as well.

The relevant stanzas of the Zamyād Yašt (66–68, containing the detailed delineation of eschatological events in the Avesta) also provide the location of the *Saošiiaṇt* as the future ruler, which is where the river Haētumant (as well as the other rivers) flows to the Lake Kąsaoiia and where there is mountain in the middle of the lake:

(Yt 19.66)
yaṯ upaṇhacaiti.

yō auuaδāt̯ fraxšaiieite
yaϑa zraiiō yat̯ kąsaēm haētumatəm
yaϑa gairiš yō ušaδā°
yim aiβitō paoiriš āpō
hąm gairišācō jasəṇtō

(The *xvarənah-*), which belongs to (the one) who will rule from the area where Lake Kąsaoiia is fed by the (river) Haētumant, where the Mount *Ušaδā* (is), where from (the mountains) around many water sources come together and flow downward.

(Yt 19.67)
auui təm auui.haṇtacaiti
auui təm auui.hąm.vazaite
xᵛāstraca huuaspaca fradaϑa
xᵛarənaŋuhaitica yā srīra
uštauuaitica yā sūra
uruuaδca pouru.vāstra
ərəzica zarənumatica:
auui təm auui.haṇtacaiti
auui təm auui.hąmv.azaite
haē ... raēuuā°xᵛarənaŋuhā°
spaētiniš varəmiš sispimnō
əmnō paoirīš vōiynā

Into this (lake) come and flow together the (rivers) *Xᵛāstraca, Huuaspaca* (and) *Fradaϑa* and beautiful *Xᵛarənaŋuhaiti*, mighty *Uštauuaiti*, and *Uruua* rich in the pastures, *ərəzi* and *zarənumati*. Into this (lake) come and flow together, the plenteous (and with the) *xvarənah-* (the river) *Haētumant*, swelling with (its) white surges and sending down many floods.

(Yt 19.68)
hacaiti dim aspahe aojō
hacaiti uštrahe aojō
hacaiti vīrahe aojō
hacaiti kauuaēm xᵛarənō
astica ahmi ašāum zaraϑuštra
auuauuat̯ kauuaēm xᵛarənō
+yaϑa yat̯ iδa anairiiā°daŋ́huš
hakat̯ usca us.frāuuaiiōit̯

(The river Haētumant) is dedicated (with) the strength of a horse, the strength of a camel, the strength of a hero, and the *xvarənah-* (the mighty gleaming glory) of the Kauui-dynasty is endowed to it. O Righteous Zaraθuštra, in it (there) is so much *xvarənah-* (the mighty gleaming glory) of the Kauui-dynasty that could completely sweep away all the non-Aryan lands at once.

Stanza 68 refers to the river Haētumant in a way that is linguistically masculine (especially with the word *vīrahe-* which Humbach translated as "hero"[28]). As the reference is to a river (specifically Haētumant), one might ask why the term is not feminine? Hintze has also translated the passage using masculine terms (Strength of a hero accompanied (him), etc.) in her study of the Zamyād Yašt.[29] Privately, she admits other possibilities, however.[30] While in stanza 68 the pronoun *dim* which could be either masculine or feminine, in the preceding stanza the pronoun is *təm* which is masculine. One possible explanation is that both the *təm* of stanza 67 and the *dim* of stanza 68 refer to the lake Kąsaoiia mentioned in stanza 66. If so, the masculine form would be used instead of the neuter, as *zraiiah-* is a neuter noun. Alternatively, the pronouns could refer to *gairiš yō usaδā°* in stanza 66. In that case, the pronouns would have the correct gender, as *gairi-* "mountain" is masculine.

At any rate, these stanzas describe the area full of power of "water" (i.e., of the rivers which come from the mountain and flow to the lake), thus, there is a lot of power in that water and in that area in general.

It would thus seem that by the Younger Avestan period the ancient myth of the deity/hero slaying a dragon had found a new interpretation. It may be speculated that perhaps the Zoroastrian priests of the time transferred the dragon-slaying role (which was retained as a key concept) to the *Saošiiant,* now the new hero, rising and stepping forth from the lake (connecting him to Anāhitā), who will defeat Aŋra Mainiiu (who takes the place of the dragon) and his army and thus bring about the renovation of the world.

The Dragon-Slaying Myth in Iran

Returning now to the dragon-slaying myth, the Zamyād Yašt mentions a hero, Kərəsāspa (Garšasp), who slays the dragon Aži-Sruuara, also called "Aži Zairita," a horned dragon who swallows horses and men.[31] There is another dragon who is mentioned only in the *Nērangestān*, in the context of making an offering to water, whose name is Aži Višāpa (N 48). We should take note of the fact that the last part of this dragon's name has the suffix *āpa,* "water." Skjaervø suggests that the meaning of the dragon's name is the dragon "of foul waters," or the dragon "which fouls the waters."[32] Russell notes in this regard that "in modern Armenia, the steles with snakes and other figures carved on them are called *višap* 'dragon' by the Armenians."[33]

In the Iranian version of the dragon-slaying myth, there are women or clouds (cows, in the Indian version) who are imprisoned by the dragon and are freed when the hero slays the dragon. In different versions of this myth, rain clouds, cows, and women have been alternately identified with the waters.[34]

In the Iranian tradition, in fact, not just Bahram/Vərəθrayna, but a wide range of Iranian heroes—including Rostam, Sām, Θraētaona (Frēdōn), Kərəsāspa (Garšasp), Goštasp, Esfandiār, and in the historical period Ardešīr Bābakān, Bahrām Gōr, and Bahrām Čōbīn—are said to have killed dragons, and thereby established themselves as champions of freedom, women, water, and fertility.

In the Vedic tradition, the dragon-slaying myth was symbolically connected with the new year and the end of the season of drought (i.e., the coming of the monsoon in late spring). Skjaervø notes that in ancient Iran there is no trace of a connection between the killing of the dragon and Nowrūz.[35] However, in the story of Āḏar Barzīnin in the *Bahman-nāmeh*, the hero recognizes black clouds as a dragon who comes out of a mountain every year during the springtime.[36]

In the *Bahman-nāmeh* story, the dragon rapes the daughter of the local king—whose name, interestingly, is Bēvarasp, an epithet of Żaḥḥāk. Subsequently, the hero slays the dragon with arrows and then bathes in a spring. This story connects several symbolic elements with which we have been dealing: a dragon, clouds, an imprisoned/abused woman, and a spring.[37] Similar tales of a hero slaying a dragon in order to rescue a girl (usually a princess) abound in Iranian folklore. Indeed, the slaying of a dragon is found so frequently in heroic tales that it would almost appear to be an indispensable rite of passage defining one's heroic status.

One can also see a direct relationship between the dragon who imprisons the water and creates drought, and the water itself which is personified as an "imprisoned" female needing to be rescued. In many Iranian folkloric tales, a dragon guards the river/spring/well and prevents people having access to the water they need; or, the dragon holds a woman captive. In some cases, the dragon accepts a girl as a sacrifice in order to allow the people to have a little water. In most cases, however, the killing of the dragon by the hero results in the freedom of the captive girl.

A more recent iconographic transformation can be seen in the Iranian appropriation of dragon imagery from China, following the Mongol conquests of the thirteenth century. Ignoring the fact that in Chinese culture dragons are a symbol of blessing and power, later Iranian paintings such as Mirzā Ali's "Goshtasp Slays the Dragon of Mt. Sakila" depict dragons in a Chinese visual style, but with an Iranian meaning which is the *opposite* of the Chinese.[38]

It may be speculated that the association in the Indo-European mind between rivers and dragons arose from the serpentine shape of most rivers. The dragon came to symbolize all the harmful forms a river could take: drying up (the water "imprisoned"), which caused drought, or overflowing its banks, which caused destructive floods. Like many peoples, the ancient Indo-Europeans were utterly dependent on rivers, upon the banks of which they built their settlements and eventually their civilizations. These rivers were ambivalent neighbors; they could ensure fertility and enable life or wash it away in a torrent.

Aži-Dahāka and Fraŋrasiian

It has been noted that the only named negative characters who sacrifice to Anāhitā asking for her support are Aži (Ahi)-Dahāka and Fraŋrasiian (NP Afrāsiāb). Aži (*Ahi*)-Dahāka (MP Azī Dahāg; NP *Aždahā*) as the dragon and the Arabic Żaḥḥāk as the mythological person, *aži-* (Vedic *ahi-*), is the most common name for a dragon-snake in Indo-Iranian. As we have discussed before, Aži-Dahāka thus could be translated to "the dragon with the human face (and body)," according to Schwartz.[39] Dahāka could have connection with Vedic *dāsa-* and *dasyu-*, meaning "enemies, strangers," and referring to the enemies of Indra, the most important god in Vedas who belong to the group of *deva*s.

It is, therefore, worth looking more deeply into the details of these two characters (Aži (Ahi)-Dahāka and Fraŋrasiian) and their possible connections to water and the water goddess. They both share dragon features: the first, Aži-Dahāka, is himself a dragon, and the second, Fraŋrasiian, *behaves* like a dragon by drying up the rivers in Sīstān. What should we understand by this connection? Of course, both are "demonic" characters, and Anāhitā does not accept their sacrifices. Based on the dragon–river relationship, we may note that both are also referred to as "foreign kings" in Pahlavi texts and the *Šāh-namēh*, which may connect them to the rejected group who worshipped the *daēuua*s. Might we surmise that Anāhitā too was worshipped by "*daēuua*-worshippers," that is, people who did not follow the religious prescriptions of the Mazdaean priests?

Aži-Dahāka in the Avesta is a huge monster-dragon with three heads and six eyes, who wishes to bring drought and destruction. He prays to Arduuī Sūrā Anāhitā and Vaiiu asking to have the power to empty the world of people.

Skjaervø specifies that "it is not clear whether he was originally considered as a human in dragon-shape or a dragon in man-shape,"[40] but the same may be said for other dragons as well since they show both attributes.

According to the *Zamyād Yašt*, it is Θraētaona (Frēdōn), Aži- Dahāka's chief opponent, who slays the dragon.[41] The verb that describes the act of killing a dragon is *jan-*. In the *Ābān Yašt*, Θraētaona sacrifices to Anāhitā, asking her to help him to defeat Aži-Dahāka and to obtain the dragon's two captured wives, Saŋhauuāci and Arənauuāci.[42] These two women are described in terms of fertility: both as natural phenomena and in terms of the seasonal freeing of the waters. In later Iranian texts Aži-Dahāka is not slain, but is imprisoned by Frēdōn on Mt. Damāvand.

Aži-Dahāka in the *Šāh-nameh* is Żaḥḥāk, who appears as a foreign (Arab) tyrant with snakes growing out of his shoulders; he carries the epithet Bēwarasp ("owner of ten-thousand horses"), which is given in the Pahlavi texts.[43] Reflecting the fact that in Zoroastrian texts snakes are considered demonic, he is under the influence of Ahriman. Żaḥḥāk thus belongs to the demonic world, and is related to *dīvs* (demonic monsters). According to the *Šāh-namēh* the *dīvs*, perhaps as part of his army, are members of his court. As in the Avesta, he imprisons two daughters of Jamšīd as his wives. Because of their captivity, the world becomes less fertile. As it was mentioned, Frēdōn (Θraētaona) frees the wives and chains Żaḥḥāk to Mount Damāvand.[44]

Skjærvø notes that Żaḥḥāk (Dahāg) is portrayed as the propagator of "bad religion," in opposition to the "good" Mazdayasnian religion; and is also said to be connected with Judaism, and to be of Arab origin.[45] The dragon-man Żaḥḥāk is specifically associated with a river in the *Bundahišn*'s chapter on rivers, where he is said to have asked a favor from Ahriman and the demons by the river Sped in Azerbaijan.[46]

Fraŋrasiian (NP Afrāsīāb) is another demonic character in the Avesta, the name of whose morphophonemics is not clear. However, the *-ŋras-* part of his name could be derived from the old Indo-Iranian *sras-* and come from **slŋk*, "to strike."[47] Hence, his name could be translated as "to strike forth." This concept is reasonable if we accept that he was originally a dragon who captured the water; our discussion below will confirm this idea.

The epithet *mairiia-* ("deceitful, villainous"), which is an adjective and also a noun, is a demonic term for man, specifically a young man, opposed to the Ahuric word *nar-*. Wikander states that the word comes originally from an Indo-Iranian expression and referred to a group of warriors with "Aryan male fellowship" who sometimes disguised themselves as wolves. These warriors highly revered "dragon slayers," such as Θraētaona, in their rituals, and at the same time they did not accept the standard morality of their society but engaged in wild behavior and had promiscuous intercourse with women referred to as *jahī-* or *jahikā-*.[48] The term *jahikā-*, which is often understood to have the meaning of "whore," seems not to refer to actual prostitutes per se but was simply applied in a derogatory way to women who did not recognize the Avestan culture being promoted by the priestly authors of the Mazdaean texts.[49] In Yt 17.57–58, the *jahikā-* is used to describe (and by the goddess Aši, to criticize) women who either do not bear their husband a son or bear him the son of another man; obviously one can envision real-life situations in which such actions would not necessarily be blameworthy, and in any case the issue is not technically prostitution. Vd 18.60 provides another case more directly connected to religious ritual, where the *jahī-* is reproached for "mixing the sperm of those who are experts in the rite with those who are not, and those who offer the sacrifice to demons with those who don't, of those who are condemned and those who aren't." The problem here seems not to be the *jahī-*'s sexuality as such, but rather the standard priestly aversion to mixing things that should not be mixed. In Y. 9.32, the issue is again not the *jahī-*'s sexuality but rather her use of sorcery. Her fault, Kellens concludes, is not sexual licentiousness but simply lack of (or different?) culture.[50]

Ancient Indo-Iranian warrior rituals included orgiastic sacrificial feasts, and were characterized by a positive attitude toward what were called "the dark forces of life"; this apparently included the gods Rudra and Indra in India and the god Vaiiu in Iran.[51] It is reasonable to surmise that these warriors also sacrificed to Anāhitā, since according to the Zoroastrian texts she and the god Vaiiu are the only deities who received (but did not accept) sacrifices from negative characters. Moreover, stanzas 94–95 clearly refer to the ceremonial sacrifices made to her by "*daēuua-*worshippers" after sunset. All of this evidence could indicate that she was indeed connected to warriors and the warrior group of deities.

The new morality and ritual system promoted by the Mazdaean priests banished and rejected the *mairiia*s and their rituals as well, yet the Avestan demonic word *mairiia-* survived in Pahlavi as *mērag* with the meaning of "husband, young man" showing that at least in some parts of Iran their memory was not conceived in negative terms.

The description of Fraŋrasiian, in the *Ābān Yašt* as well as in the other *Yašts*, as discussed above, provides a possible connection between him and these warriors whose group, the *mairiia*s, became his epithet. Later, in the *Šāh-nameh* Afrāsiāb becomes Iran's most notorious enemy. The first question about this figure concerns his origin. He is said to be from Turān, portrayed as a non-Iranian region in *Šāh-nameh*, although its inhabitants all seem to have Iranian names. Turān was located in the northeast, beyond Xorāsān and the Āmū-Daryā (the Oxus river). The Āmū-Daryā served as the traditional boundary between Iran and Turān.

In the *Yašts* the "Danū-Turānians" are mentioned as enemies of the Iranians.[52] In fact, the Turānians were almost certainly of Iranian origin, possibly Sakas who had different rituals and were condemned by the Zoroastrian priests, yet their Iranian roots were strong. Tellingly, even Afrāsiāb is said in the *Bundahišn* to be a seventh-generation descendant of Frēidūn, demonstrating his Iranian roots.[53]

As noted above, dragons can prevent the rivers from flowing, or dry them up, and this is precisely the act committed by Afrāsiāb, who dries up the rivers in Sīstān.[54] In Iranian mythology, Afrāsiāb is mostly associated with the suppression of waters, draining of rivers, and causing of drought;[55] along with Bēvarasp (Żaḥḥāk), and Alexander, he is among the three most hated figures in the Zoroastrian texts.[56] His suppression of the waters clearly connects him with dragon behavior. Perhaps this connection explains his name change from Fraŋrasiian to Afrāsiāb, the latter containing the word *āb* ("water").

Elsewhere in the same text, there is further evidence connecting Afrāsiāb to the waters; he is said to have diverted a thousand springs, including the river Hēlmand, the source of the river Vataēnī, along with six navigable waters as far as the sea of *kayānsē* in Sīstān;[57] It is somewhat strange to mention these things in the context of a demonic figure whom the *Šāh-nameh* considers Iran's worst enemy. As Yarshater suggests, "it appears that either he was originally an adverse deity who like the Indian Vṛtra (the dragon) withheld rain and personified the natural phenomenon of drought, or else he absorbed the features of such a deity."[58]

Conclusions

In this chapter, the Indo-Iranian characteristics of Anāhitā, as well as her absorption of Non-Iranian features, have been discussed. Anāhitā should be seen primarily as an Iranian manifestation of an ancient Indo-European water-river goddess (as discussed in Chapter Four), who acquired additional features and functions in different places and times throughout history.

As a composite goddess, Anāhitā's principal characteristics appear to have been inherited from those of a river–lake–stream goddess or goddesses found in many Indo-European societies. Moreover, she has absorbed many other features from Elamite and Mesopotamian goddesses such as Inanna and/or Ištar. The descriptions of Anāhitā's jewelry and other ornaments in the *Ābān Yašt* show the influence of the Babylonian Ištar on Anāhitā.

The divine couple of Marduk and Ištar and the Iranian pairing of Miθra and Arəduuī Sūrā Anāhitā also display some interesting similarities. In fact, in the *Yašt*s as well as in inscriptions from the Achaemenid period, the religious status of Miθra and Arəduuī Sūrā Anāhitā is similar to that of Marduk and Ištar for the Babylonians.

The Ahura Mazdā/Arəduuī Sūrā Anāhitā/Miθra triangulate is first documented in the inscriptions of Artaxerxes II, at a time when a large portion of the population under Persian Empire was still culturally Elamite. It is thus very likely that the Elamite triangulate Humban/In-Šušin-ak/Kiririša (and to some extent perhaps also the Mesopotamian pairing of Marduk with Ištar) served as a model for the Iranian king to increase his political base by incorporating the local (non-Iranian) cults of a justice deity and a fertility/war goddess, identified in Iranian terms as Anāhitā and Miθra.

Further east in the Central Asian context through which the Iranian tribes migrated, the prominence of the BMAC goddess of waters and fertility influenced to some extent the character of the eventual Avestan river goddess Anāhitā as well as that of the Vedic Sárasvatī, setting them apart in some ways from other river goddesses of Europe who shared their ultimate origin.

This chapter has also highlighted possible connections between Anāhitā and the ancient Indo-European dragon-slaying myth. Dragons were symbol of drought and chaos; they imprisoned the "good waters" or were the carriers of the "destructive and furious waters" (i.e., uncontrolled water, such as rivers in flood). The good waters could not be released until slain by a deity or hero. There was thus a relationship in the Indo-Iranian version of the dragon-slaying myth between dragons who hold back the waters and women who represent fertility. The fact that dragon-slaying indirectly ensured fertility suggests an additional dimension to its relationship to Anāhitā.

The *Ābān Yašt* richly evokes Anāhitā's control and power over water (Yt 5.78). She is in fact the very conceptualization of water (Yt 5.96). At the same time, descriptions of her chariot-riding victories (Yt 5.13) and her support for warriors who sacrifice to her—including Yima, Θraētaona, Kərəsāspa, Kauua. usa (Yt 5.45), Haosrauua (Yt 5.49), and Tusō (Yt 5.53)—reflect her martial aspect. Moreover, at least two of these warriors, Θraētaona and Kərəsāspa, occupy the role of the "hero who slays the dragon," linking Anāhitā to that well-known myth. The goddess is so vital to the interests of the warrior class that even "demonic" warrior figures sacrifice to her, although according to the Avestan priestly authors she rejects those sacrifices.

In the Vedic version of the dragon-slaying myth, it is the warrior god Indra who slays the dragon, frees the rivers, and in doing so receives the same epithet *śūra-* (heroic) as Anāhitā. This epithet, *sūra-*, seems specifically to have referred to the hero who kills the dragon, as Hintze states.[59] It is interesting that the two named "demonic" characters who sacrifice to Anāhitā asking her support to defeat their enemies are Aži-Dahāka and Fraŋrasiian. The first is, in fact, himself a dragon, while the second *behaves* like a dragon by drying up the rivers. One may conclude that at least one aspect of the Avestan editorial effect on the ancient myth was to attempt to divorce the power of the river goddess from the *daēuua-* group of deities with whom she appears to have been originally associated; later evidence from the Sasanian period indicates that this priestly effort was not entirely successful.

It is not difficult to see the connection between the hero who slays the dragon and Anāhitā: the good waters could not be released until slain by a deity or hero. Interestingly, in Armenia, Anāhitā-Anahit is one of the three deities who were called *višapak ʿaḷ/drakontopniktḗs* "the strangler of dragons."[60]

The *Saošiiaṇt*s as well are connected to Anāhitā, since they will be born out of a lake which is Anāhitā's domain. The victorious *Saošiiaṇt* in his form as an individual entity, Astuuaṭ.ərəta, bears the epithet *vərəθra-jan-* "victorious" (Yt 13.129/Yt 19.89), which is the same as the Vedic epithet bestowed on Indra, *vr̥tra-hán-*. Thus, the Avestan *Saošiiaṇt*, Astuuaṭ.ərəta, may have had a dragon-slaying role. Moreover, the word *saošiiaṇt-* contains the verbal root as does the noun *sūra-* "heroic" an epithet for Indra, which is also an epithet for Anāhitā. The Avestan noun *sūra*, from which the second of Anāhitā's epithets derives, is the Indo-Iranian term for the hero who slays a dragon. If we note that *Saošiiaṇt* will rise from the lake *Kąsaoiia* (Zamyād Yašt 15.92–94), gazing with his "insightful eyes of intelligence," we may also consider that he absorbs wisdom from the goddess of the lake, providing yet another connection with water and Anāhitā.

Anāhitā in the Historical Period

The Achaemenid Period

The earliest material evidence specifically relating to Anāhitā may date from the Median Period. The Medes were an Iranian people who conquered the Assyrian Empire during the late seventh century BCE and established the first independent Iranian kingdom in Western Asia. Though a paucity of evidence has not allowed us to form a detailed picture of their culture, we do know that their Achaemenid successors inherited many of their royal rituals. The rock tomb attributed by Diakonov to the Median ruler Uvaxštra I (Cyaxares I)[1] at Qyzqapan, near Sulaymaniyah in Iraqi Kurdistan, has divine symbols carved upon the entryway; these may represent the triad of Ahura Mazdā, Anāhitā, and Miθra attested later during the Achaemenid period.[2]

It would seem that sometime during the Achaemenid period an attempt was made by the Mazdaean clergy to co-opt the cult of Anāhitā by bringing her into the Zoroastrian pantheon, albeit in a subordinate role to Ahura Mazdā. According to both the Avesta and the royal inscriptions of three successive Iranian empires, Anāhitā (along with Miθra) was the most powerful deity created by the supreme being Ahura Mazdā.

Evidence for the cult of Anāhitā exists across three successive Iranian empires: the Achaemenids, the Parthians (Arsacids), and the Sasanians. In the earliest Achaemenid inscriptions, the existence of deities other than Ahura Mazdā is acknowledged, but their names are not given. Nevertheless, goddess worship is evident during the time of the first Achaemenid king, Cyrus II ("the Great," r. 559 to 530 BCE). His Greek biographer, Xenophon, like Herodotus, describes Cyrus as sacrificing in the first instance to an important goddess, whom he equates with the Greek Hestia:

> And Cyrus when he entered sacrificed to Hestia, the goddess of the Hearth, and to Zeus the Lord, and to any other gods named by the Persian priests.

… But Cyrus himself went home and prayed to the gods of his father's house, to Hestia and Zeus, and to all who had watched over his race.[3]

In fact, the ancient Greek writers variously identified Anāhitā with several different Greek goddesses, including Aphrodite (Urania), Athena, and Artemis. The earliest written trace of Anāhitā is found in Herodotus, who mentions a goddess whose cult, according to him, had only recently been introduced into the Iranian Pantheon.[4] He wrongly names this celestial goddess as "Mitra" (Miθra), who we know is a god and not a goddess.[5] Rather, both from his description and by comparison with the Arabian goddess al-Lāt and Assyrian goddess Mylitta, as well as his equating the deity with the Celestial Goddess, it would seem that the figure in question is actually Anāhitā.[6] Herodotus states that the Iranians sacrificed to a heavenly goddess,[7] whom later Greek writers called "Aphrodite-Anaïtis."

It may be noted in this regard that although the Indo-Iranian pantheon was dominated by male deities, the Sakas had an important mother-goddess, as evidenced by the Herodotus's list of Saka deities (as discussed in Chapter Three: the list begins with "Hestia," the Greek equivalent for the chief Saka goddess). Herodotus's account suggests that in his time Saka society may have accorded a broader public place to women than in later periods of Iranian history, which is a common feature of nomadic steppe societies.

The Sakas, like other Indo-Iranian peoples of Central and West Asia, blended their culture with that of the earlier native peoples of the region, exchanging influences in both directions. In the case of Mesopotamia, we know that goddesses of the native peoples were more powerful and central to the pantheon than those of the Indo-Iranians, and the same may have been true of the pre-Iranian inhabitants of Central Asia (the BMAC peoples, for example). This could explain why the Sakas had an important mother-goddess, while other Iranian groups such as the Persians apparently did not.

The oldest known Iranian shrine in Anatolia, at Zela in Cappadocia, built in the sixth century BCE, was devoted to Anāhitā and a deity referred to as "Omanos."[8] Iranian settlers in Anatolia maintained their cultural traditions, including Anāhitā worship, for many centuries thereafter. As Boyce observes: "if a Greek inscription discovered in Asia Minor from Roman times has been rightly interpreted … this appears to be dedicated to "the great goddess Anaïtis of high Harā."[9] Greek inscriptions from the Roman imperial period have been found in the same region, including one that gives her the epithet *Barzoxara* "high Harā."[10] In Lydia further west, another region with a large Iranian population, nearly one-quarter of the dedications so far discovered are to Anāhitā.[11]

Later inscriptions from the time of Artaxerxes II (r. *c.* 404 to 358 BCE) at Hamedan (A² Ha) and Susa (A² Sa, on four columns of the Apadāna palace), specifically invoke Miθra and Anāhitā, demonstrating that these two deities were worshipped alongside Mazda. The Greek historian Xenophon describes a glorious royal ceremony with three chariots that was performed every year during the time of Cyrus the Great. Following the performance of the sacrifice a chariot with a white horse, representing that of Ahura Mazdā (Zeus), chariots representing those of the sun, Miθra (Helios), and with purple trappings followed by a fire altar—possibly for Anāhitā (Hestia)—then passed before the king and the aristocrats of his court.[12]

This ritual may demonstrate an attempt by the Mazdāean clergy to co-opt the existing cults of Anāhitā and Miθra by bringing them into the Zoroastrian pantheon, albeit in a subordinate role to Ahura Mazdā. Boyce claims that in ancient Iran the color purple was associated with the warrior class,[13] but even if this is correct, it could reflect a connection between Anāhitā and the warriors as we have discussed in Chapter Five, particularly as regards her epithet *sūra-*. Recall that this epithet is related to the word *sura-*, which in Hintze's view means "hero," specifically the Indo-Iranian term for the hero who slays a dragon and was discussed before.[14] Silverman suggests that the martial aspects of Anāhitā may explain the purple trappings.[15] As noted above, another example of Anāhitā's association with the warrior groups is the old Indo-European ritual of sending the severed heads of enemies to her temple in Eṣṭaxr which were regularly dedicated.[16]

Notwithstanding the vigorous promotion of the Mazdā cult by the Magian clergy and its adoption by certain individual Achaemenid rulers, by the late Achaemenid period, Anāhitā was recognized as one of the three most important deities in western Iran alongside Mazdā and Miθra. Berossus (*c.* 345 to 270 BCE), a Hellenistic-era Babylonian scribe, mentions the erection of many statues of Anāhitā (whom he calls Aphrodite Anaïtis) by Artaxerxes (Old Persian Artaxšaçā) II in different cities throughout the empire, specifically Babylon, Susa, Ecbatana, Persepolis, Bactra, Damascus, and Sardis.[17]

The erection of cult statues appears to have represented a major innovation in Iranian religious practice, since they had been previously noted precisely for *not* creating physical representations of their gods. The building of Anāhitā statues, which began in Artaxerxes' time, has thus usually been attributed to foreign influence. Some scholars, including Meyer, Cumont, and Boyce, see a Semitic origin for this practice, while others, such as Windischmann and Wikander, attribute it to the Greeks.[18]

In either case, it may be that the departure from ancient Iranian religious norms represented a conscious attempt on the part of the Achaemenids to accommodate and co-opt those of their highly cosmopolitan subject population, among many of whom a goddess cult may have been strong. Whether or not this innovation generated controversy and debate among competing priestly groups active at the royal court, we do not know. Artaxerxes appears to have made the Anāhitā temple at Persepolis the premier religious site in the Empire. Her statue there was later replaced by a fire, probably shortly before the establishment of the Sasanian Empire six centuries later.

Chaumont notes that the royal cult of Anāhitā under Artaxerxes II and later Achaemenid rulers emphasized her martial aspect. Plutarch mentions that Artaxerxes II was crowned in the temple of a "warrior goddess," presumably Anāhitā, whom he equates with Athena: "Here (in Pasargadae) there is a sanctuary of a warlike goddess whom one might conjecture to be Athena."[19] Plutarch also mentions of another temple devoted to "the Artemis of Ecbatana who bears the name of Anaïtis," who possibly also was Anāhitā.[20] These nominally different goddesses all demonstrate the multifunctional characteristics of Anāhitā; "Athena" reflecting her warrior aspect connected with the royal investiture, while "Artemis" evoking her purity.[21]

Thus, both the Greek and Persian evidence would suggest that unlike his predecessor Darius I who clearly considered Ahura Mazdā to be his patron deity, Artaxerxes II considered himself first and foremost a devotee of Anāhitā. As suggested above, in Xerxes' (Xšayāršā) inscription it is possible that the "punished rebellions" mentioned by the king actually refer to people from parts of Iran where the *daiva*s were still worshipped. These *daiva*s may have included Anāhitā and Miθra.[22]

De Breucker sees the erection of cult statues of Anāhitā as a deliberate attempt by the Mazdaean clergy to bring non-Iranian subjects into the fold and more closely tie them to the Achaemenid regime.[23] Anāhitā's acquisition of martial functions, which would seem to indicate an innovation within the existing cult of the Iranian water goddess, may have resulted from this process. The most likely explanation is that she took over this role from local non-Iranian goddesses.

Indeed, Anāhitā's iconography, in the different spatio-temporal contexts in which it appears, seems to lack any unifying features. During the Achaemenid period, she is depicted in royal regalia. Shenkar mentions a well-known Achaemenian seal, which is possibly intended to represent Anāhitā's physical appearance.[24] In the Parthian period, she is mainly depicted as an armed warrior-goddess, whereas in Sasanian times her original role as heavenly river is more often evoked, holding a pitcher from which water pours. In all cases, her appearance seems to reflect local artistic traditions more than any essential recurring iconographic features.[25] This diversity of representation supports the contention that Anāhitā's diverse manifestations in different places and times reflect her taking over the roles and symbols of whichever preexisting local goddess had previously been most important. As Kuhrt notes, while acknowledging the difficulty in sifting through Anāhitā's identification with other, non-Iranian goddesses during the Achaemenid period, "The one thing that seems plausible is that the figure of Anahita was flexible enough to be merged with other female deities. And this must have worked differently in different places and been transmogrified over time."[26]

According to Strabo, the Armenians shared in the religion of the Persians and the Medes, and particularly honored "Anaïtis" (Anāhitā).[27] An Anāhitā temple at the Armenian town of Erez (modern Erzincan in eastern Turkey) contained a solid gold statue which was looted by the Romans in 36 BCE.[28] The ancient practice of sacred prostitution before marriage was practiced there, reflecting a survival of Mesopotamian ritual in an Armenian environment. Other Anahita temples in Armenia existed at T'il, Aštišat (where she was paired with Vahagn/Vərəθrayna), and at the capital, Artašat (where she was paired with Tir).

The Parthian and Sasanian Periods

Incorporating influences from Greek goddesses such as Aphrodite and Artemis and their associated rituals, the Anāhitā cult became even more widespread during the Seleucid and the Parthian periods. Hellenized Iranian settlers in Anatolia and Mesopotamia retained many Iranian rites—in which Anāhitā's cult was especially prominent—even while blending them with local traditions. Her "warrior" aspect persisted through the Parthian period, and she was recognized as "the Persian Artemis/Diana."[29]

Anāhitā's cult remained strong in Lydia and Cappadocia, where she was worshipped as Anaïtis, Anaïtis-Artemis, or "Persian Artemis." Her image predominated on Lydian coins. The geographer Pausanias (c. 100–180 CE) uncomprehendingly describes her cult rituals, presided over by Iranian priests chanting before a fire in a language he did not understand.[30]

Ghirshman believed that during the Parthian period Anāhitā's cult surpassed that of Mazdā in western Iran and Armenia.[31] Within the Parthian heartlands, Ecbatana, the greatest city during the Median period, retained a temple of

Anāhitā where sacrifices were regularly offered. This temple was apparently very rich: according to Polybius, in 209 BCE the Seleucid ruler Antiochus III took 4,000 talents of precious metals from it.[32] Isidore of Charax mentions two Anāhitā temples on the banks of the Euphrates in Mesopotamia, one at Basileia (OP *apadāna*), and the other at Beonan.[33] Susa likewise had a place of worship, described by Pliny as a "great temple to Diana" (*Dianae templum augustissimum*), perhaps continuing the local Elamite goddess tradition, and which the resident Iranian population likely identified with Anāhitā.[34]

In terms of religion, the Parthian period is unique in Iran's history, in that there does not appear to have been any official state cult and all religions—not just local expressions but also foreign ones such as Judaism, Buddhism, and Christianity, as well as Babylonian cult in the west and Indic ones in the east— were practiced freely. Descendants of Greek settlers from the Seleucid period continued to follow their traditional rites, which were sometimes conflated with local Iranian ones. Already at the tomb of Seleucid ruler Antiochus I (r. 281 to 261 BCE), Zeus was identified with Ahura Mazdā, Apollo with Miθra, and Vərəθrayna with Herakles. During the Parthian period this tendency continued. There is evidence of a substantial Herakles cult in western Iran, the statue and inscription at Bisotun being merely the best-known example. Further evidence is found at Karafto in northern Kurdistan,[35] Seleucia-on-the-Tigris,[36] and Sang-e Tarvak and Tang-e Butan in Khuzestan.[37]

The Parthians' attitude of religious tolerance allowed for a considerable degree of syncretism and mutual influence between different communities. The deities of one group were often identified with those of another; for example, Ba'al and Zeus were both equated with Ahura Mazdā, Šamaš and Helios with Miθra, and Ištar and Aphrodite with Anāhitā. Anāhitā and her goddess analogues were certainly widely venerated throughout the Parthian Empire, and Ghirshman has identified goddess images on several ossuaries with her.[38]

There are many references in Greek and Roman sources to the Iranian reverence for water. Herodotus reports that "into a river they neither make water nor spit, neither do they wash their hands in it, nor allow any other to do these things, but they reverence rivers very greatly." He also describes the Iranians' cultic practices, which differed considerably from those of the Greeks:

> These are the customs, so far as I know, which the Persians practise: Images and temples and altars they do not account it lawful to erect, nay they even charge with folly those who do these things; and this, as it seems to me, because they do not account the gods to be in the likeness of men, as do the Hellenes. But it is their wont to perform sacrifices to Zeus going up to the most lofty of the

mountains, and the whole circle of the heavens they call Zeus: and they sacrifice to the Sun and the Moon and the Earth, to Fire and to Water and to the Winds.[39]

Strabo (*c.* 63 BCE to 24 CE) corroborates this: "Iranians do not bathe in water, do not throw a cadaver or corpse into it. All in all they do not throw anything unclean in it." Yet he also mentions that bloody sacrifices were offered to the waters, echoing the severed head sacrifices of the Celts and others (including later the Sasanians) mentioned in Chapter Four:

> But it is to fire and water especially that they offer sacrifice … They sacrifice to water by going to a lake, river, or fountain; having dug a pit, they slaughter the victim over it, taking care that none of the pure water near be sprinkled with blood, and thus be polluted. They then lay the flesh in order upon myrtle or laurel branches; the Magi touch it with slender twigs, and make incantations, pouring oil mixed with milk and honey, not into the fire, nor into the water, but upon the earth. They continue their incantations for a long time, holding in the hands a bundle of slender myrtle rods.[40]

The pairing of fire and water cults seems to have ancient precedents in Indo-Iranian religion. Fire temples were sacred to both Ahura Mazdā and Anāhitā.[41] Strabo's descriptions of Iranian shrines, including Anāhitā temples, likewise demonstrate that her cult also involved fire:

> The Persians have also certain large shrines, called Pyrætheia. In the middle of these is an altar, on which is a great quantity of ashes, where the Magi maintain an unextinguished fire. They enter daily, and continue their incantation for nearly an hour, holding before the fire a bundle of rods, and wear round their heads high turbans of felt, reaching down on each side so as to cover the lips and the sides of the cheeks. The same customs are observed in the temples of Anaitis and of Omanus.[42]

The Parthian king of Armenia, Tīrdād, who was himself a priest, when traveling to Rome to receive his crown from the Emperor Nero, refused to travel by the sea so as not to pollute the water.[43] Although these sources do not mention Anāhitā specifically, her connection with water and rivers makes these references relevant to her discussion.

Anāhitā was worshipped in Eṣṭaxr (near Persepolis) possibly in her aspect of war-goddess,[44] just as she had been at Pasargadae in the Achaemenid period. Around the end of the second century CE, the temple of Anāhitā at Eṣṭaxr was under the custodianship of a certain Sāsān, the eponymous ancestor of the Sasanian dynasty.

Anāhitā as Patron Deity of the Sasanian Royal House

The Sasanian family who established Iran's last great pre-Islamic dynasty (224–651 CE) were originally custodians of a major Anāhitā temple at Eṣṭaxr in Pārs province, and the goddess remained the dynasty's patron deity.[45] The Sāsānian king Ardešīr I (r. 224–242 CE) showed his devotion to Anāhitā, to whom—paralleling a tradition found throughout ancient Europe—he offered the severed heads of his enemies.[46] This cult was continued by his son Šāpūr I, who sent the heads of twelve Christian martyrs to be exposed in the Anāhitā temple at Eṣṭaxr.[47]

Anāhitā, Ahura Mazdā, and Miθra are the main deities found on Sasanian rock reliefs. Of the three, Anāhitā and Ahura Mazdā are shown as proffering the divine ring of glory (probably *xvarənah-*[48] or the *xwarrah ī kayān*) to the Sasanian kings.

Perhaps the best-known historical image of Anāhitā is her representation in the rock engraving at Naqš-e Rostam in Fārs, where she is depicted crowning the Sasanian monarch Narseh I (r. 293–302 CE)[49]—in fact, the symbolic object is a ribboned ring—a possible parallel to the earlier instance mentioned by Plutarch. In the inscription at Paikuli (in modern Iraqi Kurdistan) carved for Narseh in 283 CE, the king of the kings invokes Ōhrmazd, "Anāhīd, the lady," and "all the gods (NPi. 9.19?)."[50] At an earlier Sasanian site she appears alongside Ahura Mazdā in stone reliefs commemorating Šapur I (242–272 CE). She also figures in an engraving commemorating the investiture of Xosrow II (r. 590–628 CE) at Ṭāq-e Bostān, near Kermānšāh, an important rock relief from the Sasanian period and also rare because it is located outside of Fārs, their origin provenance, while being close to their capital at Ctesiphon.

Throughout the Sasanian period there were many temples devoted to Anāhitā, as the patron deity of the ruling dynasty, and she was venerated through a number of rituals and celebrations. She was worshipped as an important goddess in the whole period of Sassanian with ups and downs. Also, she seems to have faded out after the period of the King Narseh; she rose up again into importance under the last Sasanian kings from Xosrow II to Yazdgard III.[51]

The two best-known temples of Anāhitā, indeed, are those located at Bīšāpūr in Fars and at Kangavar, near Hamedan. The Bīšāpūr temple was discovered by the archeologist Ali-Akbar Sarfaraz in 1968. It is an open-air temple, with channels where running water from the nearby river used in ceremonies was brought via *qanāt*s and could be controlled through the opening or blocking of water conduits. In the square central courtyard, worshippers could see their images reflected in the water, reminding us that even today Zoroastrians perform the *āb-zohr* ceremony beside a body of water, pouring their libation into usually a spring, river, or pool at the center of a garden. The Kangavar temple has been identified with the "temple of Artemis," mentioned by Isadore of Charax.[52]

The archeological complex at Taxt-e Soleimān in the northwest of Iran also includes both a fire temple and a temple dedicated to Anāhitā.[53] The fact that all these sites possessed locations for worshipping both fire and water suggests a pairing of their rituals—and, by extension, a pairing of the deities associated with them.

Shenkar summarizes Anāhitā's iconography in Sasanian period:

> In the Sasanian Empire, Anāhitā was always represented investing the king and had three variants of her crown and three attributes: a barsom, a diadem, and an ewer. The Kushano-Sasanian Anāhitā had two types of crown and a spear, a diadem and a bow as her attributes. If the goddess in the Northern Chapel of Temple II at Panjikent also represents Anāhitā, to her attributes in Eastern Iran we may also add a banner and a sistrum.[54]

(The Panjikent painting mentioned by Shenkar will be discussed.)

Anāhitā's royal iconography underwent significant changes by the later Sasanian period. In a rock engraving attributed to Xosrow II (r. 591–628 CE), Matthew Canepa detects an emerging Roman influence:

> The diadems that appear on Xosrow II's monuments preserve the long fabric ties from the traditional Sasanian diadems; however, the portion that encircles the head is composed of inlaid metal plaques joined with round jewel or precious metal segments. The closest analogue to this portion of the diadem is the Roman diadem ...[55]

By Sasanian times, if not earlier, Anāhitā was identified with the planet Venus, probably reflecting an association between Aphrodite, Venus, and Ištar. Panaino observes:[56]

> It is also possible that from Indo-Iranian times Sárasvatī and Anāhitā were associated with the Milky Way, but, if so, such a link was no longer operative in the later Mazdean context when Anāhitā/Anāhīd was connected with the planet Venus.

What effect this identification had on her cult in Iran, however, is unclear. Given the likelihood that the cult surrounding Ištar, which connected her to the planet Venus, became conflated with that of Anāhīta, it is not surprising that by the

Sasanian period she was associated with this planet as well. This association would seem to be an intrusion, however, since in the Mazdaean belief system based on the Pahlavi sources, planets, in contrast to stars, mostly were seen as demonic. Panaino states that the planets assumed a negative role in Pahlavi sources while this "hostile function" in the Avesta was played by *yātus* and *pairikas*.[57]

Apart from the rock carvings of Naqš-e Rostam and Ṭāq-e Bostān, many artistic works have been considered as possibly representing Anāhitā, but in no case is this identification absolute. As Bier notes, "neither the images in art nor the architectural monuments correspond precisely to descriptions in literature, and none of the numerous (contested) attributions to her of images and sanctuaries rests upon firm ground."[58] Anāhitā has been argued to appear on an Achaemenid cylinder seal,[59] on some reliefs from the Parthian period,[60] on two ossuaries, one found near Bīšāpūr and the other Sogdian,[61] and in some Sasanian silver utensils. Some scholars believe that the colonnaded or serrated crowns on Sasanian coins belong to Anāhitā.[62] A manor house in Hājīābād (Fars) contained an Anahita temple which included statues of her.[63]

Sacred Place Names

Many popular religious sites and sanctuaries in different parts of Iran have *doxtar*, *Bībī*, or *Bānū* as part of their name, suggesting a possible connection to Anāhitā. The sanctuaries such as Bībī Šahrbānū, near Ray, Pīr-ē sabz (the most important Zoroastrian holy site, known as Pīr-ē ček-ček among non-Zoroastrians), Pīr-ē-harišt, and many other places have legends about a Sasanian princess (usually known as the daughter of Yazdigerd III) who was chased by Arabs and saved by the mountain. At Pīr-ē sabz, also known as Pīr-ē ček-ček (NP ček/čekeh, "drop/drip"), water drips from the cliff above into a pool in the prayer room; the popular name for the shrine refers to the constant dripping of water. In the case of Bībī Šahrbānū, there also is a *daxmeh* (tower of silence) near the site, which demonstrates its Zoroastrian roots. In Bāstānī-Pārīzī's view, the archeological evidence and written sources (as well as folkloric legends) connected with sacred sites having *doxtar*, *bībī*, or *bānū* as part of their name indicate the former location of a temple and/or a cult of Anāhitā;[64] Mary Boyce came to the same conclusion.[65]

As mentioned in Chapter Two, in 2001 an interesting discovery was made in two copper mines at in the western central Iranian plateau, where a cave containing a small lake was used as a sacred site with ritual activities covering the period from 800 BCE until the eighth century CE.[66] Archaeologists found thousands of objects which had all been deposited into the water. These offerings were almost certainly made to a water deity, presumably Anāhitā. The objects included ceramics, jewelry, a Parthian coin, a Sasanian coin, and even an Islamic coin dating to the eighth century CE, showing that the offerings to the waters continued over a long period. The sacrificial items also included a weapon, a single bronze two-winged arrowhead, but most of the offerings were feminine accessories.[67] These offerings remind us the tradition of offering ritual to many Indo-European river/lake goddesses with objects thrown to the water as offerings. Among these one may mention Sequana, goddess of the river Seine in France. A considerable number of objects, as offerings in a religious or a ritual context, were found at the source of the Seine (see Chapter Three).

As Jennifer Rose observes in this regard:

> The similarity of provenance as part of a dedicatory group of offerings placed in water, raises the possibility that such action was not confined to a central Iranian cult, but could evidence a more widespread ritual activity, possibly a lay offering to the waters mirroring the ancient priestly libation, known as *āb-zōhr*. ... Sacred sites from many religious traditions comprise a cave with a water source, which are said to evoke the womb and amniotic fluid respectively, thus connecting any ritual activity with fertility or rebirth.[68]

The Panjikent Paintings

Certain frescos among the wall paintings adorning the Sogdian-era temples at Panjikent, Tajikistan, are related to very old rituals. A painting in Temple II depicts a scene of mourning around a dead young prince, whom Guitty Azarpay has identified as the legendary Iranian hero Siāvaš (Av. Siiāvaršan).[69] Azarpay describes a female figure (haloed, with a lotus-shaped crown) in the painting as clearly being a river goddess (Anāhitā) but "her exact identity remains tentative."[70] If these identifications are correct, what we have in this scene is a fascinating example of convergence of deities between east and west, Semitic and Indo-European, Siāvaš being merely a Central Asian reflex of the Mesopotamian Dumuzi.

Anāhitā and Siāvaš are thus both connected with two of the central characters in Mesopotamian mythology, Anāhitā with Inanna-Ištar, and Siāvaš with the beautiful young man, son or lover of Inanna-Ištar, known as

Dumuzi and other names. Inanna, the Sumerian name for the goddess and Ištar is Akkadian name for her. She was associated with battle and war as well as with sexual desire. The sixth tablet of the Babylonian Epic Gilgameš speaks about Ištar's lust toward Gilgameš and also lists her many lovers (this subject will be further discussed).

Inanna's lover was Dumuzi. (As a goddess was associated with sexual desire, she never had a permanent lover.) There are various Sumerian poems about her love for Dumuzi,[71] even though she was responsible for his untimely death. It is worth noting that Inanna/Ištar was associated with the planet of Venus, just as Anāhitā is in the Pahlavi texts.

During the centuries leading up to the Arab conquests, the goddess Nana/Nanai, as she was locally known, was apparently the principal Sogdian deity. She was the patron goddess of the city of Panjikent, where she was referred to as "the Lady."[72] Further south in Bactria, she was the principal protector of the Kušān king Kaniškā, where, as Skjaervø notes, she probably replaced Anāhitā.[73] Skjaervø adds that the phonetic (acoustic) similarity of the names "Nanai and Anāhitā" may have played a role in this identification. Anāhitā absorbed many of Nanai's characteristics and was syncretized with her widely. As with the Achaemenids centuries earlier, the transformation of the Mesopotamian Nanai into the Iranian Anāhitā appears to have been due to a conscious effort on the part of the Sasanians, who took over the eastern regions during the third and fourth centuries: a Bactrian coin from the time of Hormizd II bears an image of Artemis the Hunter but with the Pahlavi inscription "Lady Anāhid," whereas the coinage of the previous Kušān ruler used similar iconography but identified the figure as "the goddess Nana."[74]

The Mesopotamian vegetation god and his goddess lover, his death and descent into the underworld, symbolized winter, while his revival and return to the world signaled the coming of spring. (We will discuss this matter further under the subsection Sūdābeh and Rūdābeh: Two Sides of Female Power.) Nevertheless, such mourning rituals, which involve much crying and sometimes self-flagellation and recur every year, seem to have been borrowed from the Sumerian, Semitic, and Mediterranean cultures with which Iranians came into contact, along with the myths and mythical characters (specifically Ištar and Dumuzi) associated with those rituals. One of the main components of the annual ritual cycle connected with this myth was mourning and lamentations over the death of the divine son/lover, who was considered to have died the death of a martyr.

Returning to the mourning scene in Temple 2 at Panjikent, if indeed the goddess figure is Anāhitā, then we may recall that by Sogdian times her cult had been deeply influenced by rituals associated with Ištar and other Mesopotamian goddesses. It is thus not unreasonable to interpret this scene as an Iranian version of the Ištar and Dumuzi story. Grenet and Marshak, while confirming that the Panjikent mourning scene derives from the Mesopotamian myth, argue that the dead figure is actually a girl, whom they propose derives from Dumuzi's sister Geštinanna. In this latter feature, the two authors see a Greek layer as well, with the dead girl as an echo of Persephone; the goddess Demeter is also present at the mourning.[75]

Anāhitā in the Pahlavi Texts

One of the intriguing questions about the transformations of Anāhitā over time has to do with the difference between her portrayal in the Avesta and references to her in the Pahlavi texts. The Avestan *Ābān Yašt*, together with a range of other sources from the Achaemenid period into Sasanian times a millennium later, demonstrates her central importance in the religious life of Iranians. The Pahlavi texts, on the other hand, speak rather little of her, and when they do their mentions are often ambiguous. There are some problems, however, regarding these valuable sources: (1) most texts are late redactions of the Islamic period, containing several strata, which reach from the Old Iranian to the Islamic period, hence extracting a "Sasanian" version is problematic and often hypothetical, if not sustained by older material; (2) they reflect theological or scholastic views, which might have differed considerably from popular beliefs in the Sasanian period.

Therefore, several questions arise regarding the role of Anāhitā in the Pahlavi texts. Does her treatment in the Pahlavi texts represent some kind of reluctant, perhaps even awkward priestly concession to accommodate (but also subordinate) an overwhelmingly popular goddess figure within the society or her believers? Or should it be read more as evidence of an ongoing tension between the dominant Mazdaean priestly cult and its various rivals for religious authority within Iranian society?

Shaked notes that:

> Although she was integrated fairly early on into the Zoroastrian body
> of scriptures, Anāhīd stands out as an incongruous part of Zoroastrian
> worship, and in fact very little of the official priestly ritual of later times
> is directed towards her. Her prominence in Sasanian life seems to be in
> defiance of the canonical religion, as can be deduced from the fact that
> she sinks into a kind of oblivion once we have to rely mainly on the
> Pahlavi books for our information about what is the "correct"
> Zoroastrian religion.[1]

Anāhitā is referred to as both *Anāhīd* and *Ardwī-sūr* in the Pahlavi texts. This bifurcation of her earlier Avestan epithets will be discussed further below. Skjærvø suggests that the Pahlavi rendering of the Avestan word *anāhitā-* can be read either as *awinast*, "unsullied," or as *aniwast*, "unattached." He notes that the "unattachedness" of heavenly entities in the material world (including the heavenly river, Anāhitā) is well attested in Zoroastrianism, and thus the heavenly river like the sky does not require any "ties" to keep her suspended in the heavenly sphere without falling down.[2]

(GBd X.10.6)
čiyōn gōwēd kū Hugar ī buland az hamāg sūrāg ī zarrēn kē padiš frāz ǰahēd Ardwīsūr ī awinast/aniwast hazār wīr bālāy.

It is said that the high *Hugar* (is the one) that from all of its golden holes, the unpolluted (or unattached) *Ardwī-sūr* descends from the height of a thousand men.[3]

In this paragraph *awinast* "unsullied, unpolluted," a rendering of *anāhitā-*, can also be read *aniwast* "unattached" according to Skjærvø, though he inclines somewhat toward the latter definition (*aniwast* being the *negated* past participle of *niwend-* (*niwenn-*) with the negative prefix *a-*, "tie (something) to (something)".[4] In this sense, the reading *aniwast* would evoke Anāhitā's original mythological status as a water/river goddess, as discussed above.

Women in Pahlavi Texts

Anāhitā is rarely (and only briefly) mentioned in the Pahlavi texts, and her role there is not one of great importance. It may be that with the passing of time, goddess-worship became less important (perhaps even less acceptable) in Iranian society, with male deities securing the major divine roles to a growing extent. We may recall that Iranians are descended from Indo-European peoples, whose pantheon was dominated by male deities.

Although many contemporary Zoroastrians claim that their religion promotes gender equality between men and women—a view supported by scholars such as Boyce[5] and De Jong[6]—Choksy has argued that in the Pahlavi texts the prevalent attitude toward women was negative. Zaehner and Widengren attribute this negativity to Zurvanite influence (of which Widengren saw traces even in the Avesta[7]), but Choksy explains it as part of a cosmic dualism where "In specific situations, the feminine was perceived by the Mazdean tradition of ancient and medieval times as negative owing to its having been linked with agents of cosmic disorder."[8]

These same texts, Choksy points out, repeatedly warn male Zoroastrians to protect themselves against the threats posed by both women and demonesses.[9] As he states, "the demonic feminine was more powerful than the divine feminine" and "shaped the day-to-day lives of many Mazda-worshipers, especially women."[10]

Rose points out that the concept of the *ašauuan-* (righteous believers) is applied to both men and women. Referring to the *Ardā Wirāz-nāmag*, she says that both genders will be "held accountable for their action in life." However, Rose also observes that:

> Although such texts present the concept of spiritual parity for both men and women, Zoroastrianism developed historically as a patriarchal religion in which the priesthood is male and the liturgical life of the religion is in men's hand. Zoroastrian women have largely been excluded from holding higher religious positions and becoming priests.[11]

In fact, the Avestan texts seem to convey a very different image of women in the Zoroastrian cult from that in the Pahlavi texts, and negative portrayals of the female are more numerous in the Pahlavi texts that it is hard to deny they must represent strongly rooted social attitudes of the time.[12]

Hintze points out that "a passage in the *Yasna Haptanghaiti* (Y 41.2), carefully analyzed by Narten,[13] suggests that in ancient Zoroastrianism both men and women (*nā vā nāirī vā*) could function as good leaders (*huxšθra-*) in both physical and spiritual life (*ubā- ahu-*)."[14] Yet it seems that it refers more to the time that the Avestan texts were composed, although as Hintze points out, "The appointment of both men and women as spiritual leaders appears to have continued for a long time."[15] Still in Sasanian times, Macuch notes that women had the right to obtain some kind of education, specifically "religious education" such as the knowledge of the *Zand* (Pahlavi version of the Avesta with commentaries), which could be obtained by all men and women.[16] Macuch qualifies, however, that "Women were generally regarded (with only a few exceptions) as dependent persons having either no legal capacity or in certain cases only limited legal capacity." She notes that they were under the guardianship (*sālārīh*) of the male members of their family, that "it would not even have been conceivable" for women to have any kind of education that required them to leave their home without their guardian's permission,[17] and that they would never gain full legal capacity:

Anāhitā

In contrast to the adult man the woman remained under the legal guardianship of a man not only as a minor, but during her whole life. She never gained full legal capacity, since she was as a rule first under the *manus* of her father, brother, uncle or any other relative who became family guardian (*dūdag-sālār*), later under the guardianship of her husband in the marriage "with full matrimonial rights" (*pādixšāy*-wedlock). There were, however, many exceptions to this regulation.[18]

There were, nevertheless, some exceptions to this, For example, when the woman became a widow or entered the so-called "consensus- marriage" (*xwasrāyēn/ gādār*) in which she was her own guardian, she could attain to a certain extent the right to litigate and to enter into legal transactions.[19] Even so—and we must recall that modern notions of "rights" and "freedoms" cannot be applied to the Sasanian period when men and women alike were bound with many restrictions—"the range and limit of a woman's legal capacity was … generally determined by her guardian."[20]

It should be noted, however, that the more or less equal standing between men and women in a *religious* sense must be distinguished from their position within the *legal* system of the Sasanian era, in which women's status is clearly subordinate to that of men.

Hintze argues (in a *religious* sense) that the idea of equality between men and women in terms of their potential to be "righteous Zoroastrians," active both morally and spiritually in the universal fight between good and evil, is "deeply rooted" in Zoroastrian thought as expressed in the Avesta and the Pahlavi texts.[21]

As has been mentioned, in the *Bundahišn* ("Primal Creation, the establishment in the beginning"[22]), male deities are more prominent than the female ones. The often misogynistic tone of this late (i.e., ninth century) Pahlavi text would appear to indicate an atmosphere of "emerging patriarchy" in Iranian society. As the writer of the *Bundahišn* clearly states:

(GBd X1V *A*.1)

guft-iš Ohrmazd ka-š zan brēhēnīd kū dād-iz-m hē tō kē-t jehān sardag petyārag. u-m nazdīk ī kūn dahăn-ē(w) dād hē kē-t māyišn ēdōn sahēd čiyōn pad dahăn mizag ī xwarišnān šīrēntom. az man tō ayārīh čē-t mard aziš zāyēd. man-iz āzārē kē Ohrmazd hēm. bē agar-im windād hād jāmag kē mard aziš kunēm ā-m nē dād hād hagriz kē-t ān ī jeh sardag petyārag. bē-m xwāst andar āb ud zamīg ud urwar ud gōspand ud bālist ī garān ān-iz ī zofr rōstāg nē windād jāmag kē mard ī ahlaw aziš bawēd jud zan kē jeh petyārag.

When *Ohrmazd* created woman, he said: I created you while your nature is from Jeh the wicked prostitute. I created a mouth near your buttocks so that coupling would be like the sweetest dishes in the mouth, and you have my support, because man would be born from you. (Nevertheless) You (women) annoy[23] me too, I who am *Ohrmazd*. But if I had found a vessel/container out of which I could make man, I would never have created you because your nature is from Jeh the wicked prostitute. But in water, earth, plants and livestock (lit. sheep) and on the top of the high mountain and in the depths of the villages (I searched) and I did not find a vessel/container out of which the righteous man could be born from but woman, whose nature is from Jeh the wicked prostitute.[24]

This passage would seem to provide a clearly negative statement about women. In the Pahlavi literature, "Jeh" (*Jahikā*) is the name of Ahriman's (*Aŋra-Mainiiu/Gannāg Mēnōg*) daughter. When one considers that according to Zoroastrian tradition it was Jeh, daughter of Ahriman, who encouraged her father to attack Ohrmazd's creation, finding a generalized negative attitude toward women throughout the *Bundahišn* is not surprising. Moreover, in the *Bundahišn* (Bd IV. 4.5), the origin of women's menstruation (which is strongly considered ritually polluted and unclean) is specifically attributed to Ahriman, and is said to have first accrued to Jeh after her words revived Ahriman and he kissed her on the head:

(GBd. IV.4–5)
u-š ān duš-kunišnīh ōwōn pad gōkān ōšmurd kū Gan(n)āg-Mēnōg be rāmīhist ud az ān stardīh frāz jast ud sar ī Jeh abar busīd. ēn rēmanīh ī daštān xwānēnd pad Jeh paydāg būd.

She (Jeh) described the evil-acts (with) such detail (that) *Aŋra-Mainiiu* relaxed and overcame[25] his stupefaction, and kissed her head. This filth that they call it menstruation (*daštān*), revealed itself through Jeh.[26]

Hence, in the Zoroastrian tradition, women were considered polluted for a period of time every month because of their menstruation, which was seen as the consequence of evil entering into them during their period (precluding the possibility of pregnancy) and thus making them ritually impure (Vd XVI.I–II). Moreover, as has been mentioned above, menstruation was interpreted as being the result of demonic harm wrought upon women rather than as something natural. Does the connection between the lunar cycle and women's menstrual also connect women to darkness? It seems possible that the answer is yes.

One may note the reference to a Zoroastrian myth as an example: according to the Avesta, a figure by the name of Taxma Urupa (Tahmūras) had managed to defeat all of the demonic creatures including *Aŋra-Mainiiu* himself.[27] He succeeded in changing *Aŋra-Mainiiu* into the shape of a horse and rode him for thirty years (Yt 18.28–29). In the *Rivāyāt* version of the story, Ahriman seduces Tahmūras's wife and is able to kill Tahmūras through his wife's weakness. Ahriman gives the wife a gift that causes her to menstruate, which remains in women forever after.

All of this could lead us to speculate regarding the situation of women during the periods in which these texts were composed. The ancient "goddess-centered" influence (which derived in large part from Mesopotamian society) seems to have faded over time, not only among Iranians but also within the culture of their neighbors as well. However, since goddess worship was a strongly rooted belief among the people due to its close connection to fertility and production upon which their survival depended, the sanctity of goddesses (in this case, primarily Anāhitā and Aši) persisted throughout the Sasanian era and even into Islamic times. It seems that the situation of women mostly depended on their social class, as was the case for men as well. Women were dependent on men, but they were by no means at the bottom of the hierarchy; non-Iranians and slaves ranked lower.[28]

In fact, due to the huge importance placed by Zoroastrianism on marriage and the producing of children (especially male children), one could imagine that women might have been seen most importantly as the "vessels/containers" for bearing future righteous men (GBd X1V A.1). However, the fact of their having to live under the control of male guardian reflected male interests concerning their standards. In the ideal Zoroastrian society, both male and female Zoroastrians would fight for the victory of Ohrmazd. This concept can be clearly seen in the Yašt devoted to the important goddess Aši (Yt 17), which emphasizes her characteristic as a strong advocate of female morality. In fact, Aši embodies precisely the feminine characteristics most desired by those in control of this patriarchal society-in-transformation, notably that of obedience. In any case, the negative attitudes toward women and their possible reasons require separate and detailed theological and anthropological studies and analyses that are beyond the scope of this research.

In conclusion, Anāhitā's decreasing visibility in the Pahlavi texts in comparison with the Achaemenid period may actually be an indication that her cult and its rituals enjoyed continuing popularity and thus posed a threat to the agenda of the Mazdaean priests. This hypothesis can be considered in light of the ongoing tensions between the priesthood and the royal house—who, we should remember, descended from the custodians of an important Anāhitā temple— tensions that persisted throughout the entire Sasanian period.

The available Pahlavi sources are all late redactions and consist of several strata. More specifically, they reflect a priestly, "orthodox" viewpoint that does not necessarily correspond with the diverse forms of Zoroastrianism or more correctly, Mazdaism practiced by the Iranian population in the Sasanian and early Islamic periods. Furthermore, it seems that the official Sasanian Mazdaism was also dualistic, which affected their interpretation of the traditional pantheon. The evident popularity and persistence of goddess-centered rituals throughout Iranian history might be an indication of a disparity between the Mazdaean priestly caste and the general population, or perhaps of attitudes among the non-Iranian (e.g., Mesopotamian) substratum of Iranian society, who were inheritors of a religious tradition in which goddesses were more central. Moreover, we should recall that as the patron deity of the Sasanian royal house, she and her associated rituals could be used by the Sasanians as a natural counterweight during periods when individual emperors were seeking to rein in the power of the Mazdaean priests. The iconographic representations of the goddess appeared in the Sasanian rock reliefs (e.g., her representation as crowning the Sasanian monarch Narseh I (r. 293–302 CE) in the rock engraving at Naqš-e Rostam) can be seen in this light. While again a detailed analysis of the reasons for this is beyond the scope of the present work, anthropological and economic changes as well as developments in people's religious beliefs may all have played a role.

Similarities and Transformations between the Avestan *Arəduuī Sūrā Anāhitā* and *Ardwī-sūr Anāhīd* in the Pahlavi Texts

The Pahlavi books do offer some evidence for an ongoing sacrificial cult to Anāhitā. There are, however, some differences and changes in her features and functions compared to the Avesta. Interestingly, her astronomical aspect (originally the celestial "river"; i.e., the Milky Way) shifts toward association with the planet Venus. As Panaino notes: "It is possible that from Indo-Iranian times Sárasvatī and *Arduuī Sūrā Anāhitā* were associated with the Milky Way, but, if so, such a link was no longer operative in the later Mazdaean context, when Anāhitā/Anāhīd was connected with the planet Venus."[29]

One significant change is that sometimes the goddess seems to be mentioned as two separate deities: *Ardwī-sūr* and *Anāhīd*. Sometimes *Ardwī-sūr* is mentioned without *Anāhīd* (e.g., Bd III.19), while elsewhere *Anāhīd* is mentioned as the spirit of the planet Venus (Bd VA.2). In yet other instances, *Ardwī-sūr Anāhīd* (e.g., Bd III.20) is mentioned as a single entity.

When the *Bundahišn* describes the world's lakes and seas, it says they all have their origin with *Ardwī-sūr* (Bd X.1–9). In some other sections, however, she is said to be concerned with the stars and planets. This suggests that her *Ardwī-sūr* designation mostly retains her original features connected to water, whereas her alternate designation of Anāhīd is used primarily in reference to the planet Venus. Mesopotamian dualism could be a factor here as will be discussed further.

Further, in the Bundahišn, *Ardwī-sūr Anāhīd* comes to be transformed from a goddess into a deity with the features of both genders, like a hermaphroditic deity: he or she is the mother—and, interestingly, also the father—of the waters. This issue will be discussed in more detail below.

Anāhīd and *Ardwī-sūr* in the *Bundahišn* both retain many of the earlier Avestan Anāhitā's functions, as we will discuss further. *Ardwī-sūr*, like Anāhitā (Yt 5.4.101), possesses the springs and lakes (Bd X.10.2–10.9, XVI.16.5 and some other verses). Just as in the *Abān Yašt* (Yt 5.96), she descends from the heights of the mountain as a waterfall, as high as a thousand men:

(GBd IX.9.7)
Hugar ī buland ān kē-š āb ī Ardwī-sūr aziš frōd jahēd hazār mard bālāy.

The high *Hugar* (is) the one that the water of *Ardwī-sūr* descends from the height of a thousand men.[30]

(GBd XVII. 17.17)
Hugar ī buland kē āb ī Ardwī-sūr padiš jahēd bālistān rad.

The high *Hugar* where the water of *Ardwī-sūr* descends (from) is the Chieftain of the mountains.[31]

As in the Avesta (Yt 5.2), *Ardwī-sūr Anāhīd* is associated with fertility, which she ensures by purifying men's sperm and women's wombs before and during their pregnancy:

(GBd XXVI.26.91)
u-š (mēnōg ī) hamāg ābīhā Ardwī-sūr āb ī anāhīd mād ī ābān tōhm ī narān ka az xōn pālūd ēstēd ud mādagān-iz ka zāyēnd ud dudīgar ābus bawēnd xwēš-kārīh ī Ardwīsūr.

And the spirit of all the waters, *Ardwī-sūr*, water *Anāhīd*, mother of the waters, (to protect) the male's seed, by purifying it of blood, and also the females while they give birth, and be pregnant again, these are *Ardwī-sūr*'s functions.[32]

The Pahlavi Anāhīd also retains her role as protector identified with the waters. According to the *Bundahišn*, Zaraθuštra's seed (here *xwarrah*) is preserved and kept by Anāhīd in water (Bd III: 3.20), again similar to the Avesta (Yt 18.56.66). Zaraθuštra copulated with his wife Hwōvī three times, and each time his seed penetrated into the earth. *Nēryōsang*, the deity of lighting and (male) power, received Zaraθuštra's seed and sent it on to Anāhīd to be kept and protected by her (Bd 35.61).

Lake Kayānsē (which can most likely be identified with the modern Lake Hāmun in Sīstān),[33] fed by the river Helmand, is mentioned several times in the Avesta. Once it appears together with the name Kąsaoiia-. In Yt 19 (66–69), the *x'arənah-* of the *Kauuis* is connected with the "Helmandic" Kąsaoiia (*Kąsaēm haētumatəm*), where nine rivers flow together. At three appropriate times in the future, a young virgin will swim in the lake and become impregnated by Zaraθuštra's seed, so as to bear him sons. The place where Zaraθuštra's seed resides is shining, like three lights within the lake:

(GBd XXXIII.43–45)
ēn sē pus ī Zardu(x)št čiyon Ušēdar ud Ušēdarmāh ud Sōšyans rāy gōwēd kū Zardu(x)št be ǰuxt ēg-šān xwarrah ī Zardu(x)št andar zrēh ī Kayānsē pad nigāh-dārīh ō ābān xwarrah ī ast Anāhīd yazad abespārd. nūn-iz gōwēd kū sē čirāᵧ andar bun ī zrēh waxšēd ī pad šab hamē wēnēnd.

ēk ēk ka-šan zamānag ī xwad rasēd ēdon bawēd kū kanīg-ē(w) sar šustan rāy ō ān āb ī Kayānsē šawed u-š xwarrah andar ō tan gumēzēd ud ābustan bawēd. awēšān ēk ēk pad zamānag ī xwēš ēdōn zāyēnd.

About these three sons, who are Ušēdar, Ušēdarmāh and Sōšiians, it says that when Zarduxšt copulated, they entrusted his *xwarrah* in the Kayānsē Sea to the *xwarrah* of *Ābān*,[34] who is the deity Anāhīd, to be protected by her. And it is said that even now three lights blaze in the deep of the sea, which can be seen at the night-time. One by one, when their time arrives, a young virgin goes to the Kayānsē water (lake) to wash her head and the *xwarrah* goes to her body and impregnates her. Then they (the saviours) also one by one each will be born in their own period.[35]

Dēnkard 7 provides the names of these three maidens, who all have roots from Zaraθuštra's lineage. According to this text, they are called "Nāmīg-pīd," "Weh-pīd," and "Gōwāg-pīd."[36] The prophet's seed is protected by the 99,999 *frauuašis* (Yt 13.62),[37] the guardian spirits, which, interestingly, are described collectively as female beings[38] (Yt 13.45–49, 67–70) from whom will be born the three *saošiiants* (the beneficent ones) who are Ahura Mazdā's "soldiers" and "messengers."

The coming of the third savior, Sōšiians, will mark the advent of the Resurrection and the end of the world. He comes from an area around the Haētumat river in Sīstān (note the connection with water). His epiphany is the sign of justice. This theme has a strong presence in both the Avesta (Yt 19.92 and Vd 19.5) and in the Pahlavi literature.

The story of the three sons of Zaraϑuštra and their connection to the lake is repeated in other Pahlavi texts. In the *Zand ī Wahman Yasn* also Zaraϑuštra's son, Ušēdar, is said to be born in a Lake:

(ZWY 7.2)

guft-iš ohrmazd kū, spitāmān zarduxšt, ka dēw ī wizard-wars ī xēšm-tōhmag ō paydāgīh āyēd pad kust ī xwarāsān nazdist nīšān ī syā paydāg bawēd. zāyēd ušēdar ī zar-12

He, Ohrmazd, replied: "O *spitāmān Zarduxšt*, when the *dēw* having dishevelled hair, of the seed of *dēw Xēšm* (anger), will show his appearance in Xwarāsān, first a black sign will appear, Ušēdar the (son) of Zarduxšt will be born on the lake *Frazdān*; {that there (was) some one who said that it was on the Sea (lake) *Kayānsē*; that there was some one who said that it was in *Kāwulistān* (Kābolestan)}."[39]

The lake also is called the "Lake of Three Seeds": *war ī sē-tōhmag*.[40] It will be observed that in the ZWY apart from the "Lake of Three Seeds," which, we may recall, belongs to Anāhitā, who protects the seeds—the author mentions an Iranian army from Xorāsān whose banner is made from beaver skin (Anāhitā's clothing in the Avesta) and from the wind (one of Anāhitā's horses in the Avesta):

(ZWY 7.14)

ō pušt ī ērān dehān amar spāh ī *xwarāsānīg abrāstag-drafš hēnd {<hād> kū drafš ī *babr(ag) pōst dārēnd. u-šān wād-drafš < ī> *bandag < ī> spēd}.[41]

In support of the Iranian countries, there will be the innumerable armies of *Xwarāsānīān* with raised banners {that is, they have banners of beaver's skin and wind banners, which will be (of) white cotton}.

In another Pahlavi text, the *Abdīh ud sahīgīh ī sagistān* (The Wonder and Remarkability of Sagastān/Sīstān); the author notes the importance of Sīstān in the Zoroastrian religion according to several different reasons.[42] First, the birth and the appearance of Ušēdar, Ušēdarmāh, and Sōšiiāns, the future prophet's sons, will take place there (which, as we may note, is the location of one *Ardwī-sūr Anāhīd*'s lakes). But, in addition, the text mentions *Ardwī-sūr Anāhīd* (connecting her with water) when Frēdōn (Θraētaona) goes to the "sea" (lake) Frazdān, asking *Ardwī-sūr Anāhīd* for her support:

(AS 4–8)

4) ēk ēn kū paywand ud tōhmag ī kayān dahibedān ī pad ēn kišwar wizend awiš mad. 5) az frazandān ī frēdōn salm kē kišwar ī hrōm ud tūč kē turkestān pad xwadāyīh dāšt, ērij ērān dahibed būd, u-š <ān >bē ōzad. 6) ud az frazandān < ī > ērij bē kanīg-ē ēnyā kas bē nē mānd. 7) ud pas frēdōn ō war frazdān nīd ud pad nihān dāšt dā < n- > ohom paywand ka az ān kanīg pus zād. 8) pas frēdōn ō war ī frazdān šud, u-š az ardwi-sūr anāhīd < ud > abārīg yazdān kē andar sīstān gāh < ud > mehmānīh abartar, āyaft xwāst, pad abāz ārāstan < ī > ērān-šahr ud xwarrah < ī > kayān, āyaft windād abāg abāg manuščihr ud awēšān ērān āfrīn.

One reason is this, that the lineage and family of the *Kauui*-dynasty, i.e., the rulers of this country sustained some damage. Of the children of Θraētaona, Salm (**Sairima*) who had the reign of the Roman (/Western) Empire, Tūč (**Tūraca*) who had the reign of Turkestān, killed Ērij (**Airyaēca*) who was the ruler of the Aryan (land). And of the children of Ērij none remained except a daughter. Then Frēdōn conducted (her) to the lake Frazdān and kept her hidden for ten generations, when a son was born from that daughter. Then Frēdōn went to the Frazdān sea (lake), and from *Ardwī-sūr Anāhīd* and the other deities (who had) higher authority in Sīstān, asked for their favour (*āyaft*) to strengthen Irān (*ērān-šahr)* and the (*xwarrah <ī> kayān*). He obtained the boon, together with Manuš-čiθra and the Aryans. Blessing.[43]

The Frazdān lake also is connected to Anāhitā. According to Avestan geography, the region of the Haētumant had several rivers, including *Xᵛāstrā*, *Hvaspā*, *Fradaθā* (Frazdān), *Xᵛarǝnahvaitī*, *Uštavaitī*, *Urvā*, *Ǝrǝzī*, and *Zarǝnumatī*. In the *Ābān Yašt* there is a paragraph about Kauui Vīštāspa, who is presented as making a sacrifice to *Arǝduuī Sūrā* Anāhitā, near *Fraz-dānu*, the same *Frazdān* as is found in the *Abdīh ud sahīgīh ī sagistān*.[44]

Several Pahlavi texts confirm the importance of the Haētumant and its region in the Zoroastrian tradition. The most important of these, as Gnoli discusses, is the *Abdīh ud sahīgīh ī Sagistān* as was mentioned above, which lists the wonders of Sistān, collecting all of those themes already present in the Avesta.[45] Also, the important role that Lake Frazdān and the rivers in the region of Sīstān have played in Zoroastrian tradition is linked to the special connection between them and the *xwarrah/xᵛarǝnah/(farrah, farr)* of the *Kauuis*, the Kayanids of the national tradition.[46] We see in the *Abdīh ud sahīgīh ī sagistān* that Frēdōn went to the shore of Lake Frazdān to ask the deities' support for *xwarrah <ī> kayān*. There is the *war ī frazdān*, which may be the *gawd-e zira* (the lowest part of an inland drainage basin covering large parts of southern Afghanistan and Iran, known as the "Sīstān Basin").

Again regarding Lake Frazdān, the *Bundahišn* says that when a generous righteous person throws anything into the lake, the lake accepts it. However, if a person is not righteous, the lake throws it out again (GBd XII.12.6–7, see below). This paragraph also evokes other water-goddess cults, showing the continuation of an older version of offering and sacrifices to the water goddesses, which we have discussed before in connection with "the offerings by the worshippers" to the lake/river, which are linked to the water goddess cult (as we have discussed in Chapter Four):

(GBd XII.12.6–7)

War ī Frazdān pad Sagestān. gowēnd kū āzād mard-ē(w) ahlaw kē tis-ē(w) andar awiš abganēd padīrēd ka nē ahlaw abāz ō bērōn abganēd.[47]

The *Frazdān* Lake is in Sīstān. It is said that if a noble, righteous person (man) offers something to it, (then the lake) accepts. If (the person) is not righteous, (the lake) throws it (the offering) out.

According to the *Bundahišn*, the world's nature is water, and the creation had a watery nature at the beginning. Human beings also have a watery nature (Bd XXVIII. 28.2).[48] Finally, one notes a connection between the moon and water (Bd XXVI. 26.24).[49]

In sum, in the Pahlavi literature (and in the Avesta as well), the third savior Sōšiians will rise from the lake, which belongs to Anāhitā who protects the seed of Zaraϑuštra that has been preserved within it. The idea of the lake as feminine is pertinent to our discussion: the prophet's seed is given from the male deity *Nēryōsang* to the female deity, *Arəduuī Sūrā Anāhitā*, who is identified as a lake (Bd XXXIII.43–45 above). As noted above, the Zoroastrian tradition speaks of the coming of three saviors. Apart from the *Bundahišn* and the other previously mentioned Pahlavi texts, in the Avesta in Yt 19.92 and in Vd 19.5, there are references to the birth of the *saošiiant-*/saviour, *astuuaṯ.ərəta-*, from the waters of Lake Kạsaoiia.

All of the passages mentioned above connect Anāhitā to the *saošiiant-*/Sōšiians who bring about the final defeat of Evil and thus could embody the "saviour" concept. As mentioned in Chapter Seven, the Sōšiians figure shares some common roots with the goddess in terms of their names: Sōšiians, from the word *saošiiant-*, contains the verbal root *sū-*, "to be strong (to swell)," as well as *sūra-* which is the noun form and the goddess's epithet. Moreover, in the *Ṛg Veda* (*śūra-* heroic) is an epithet for Indra,[50] or as Hintze notes,[51] the noun *sūra-* seems to have referred to the hero who kills the dragon (as discussed in Chapter Seven).

A Goddess with the Features of Both Genders

As has been previously mentioned, in the *Bundahišn Ardwī-sūr Anāhīd* (here united as one deity) is described as the mother and the father of the waters:

(GBd. III. 20)

Panjom az mēnōgān Spandārmad u-š az dahišn ī gētīg zamīg ō xwēš padīrift u-š dād ō ayārīh ud ham-kārīh Ābān ud Dēn ud Ard ud Mānsarspand ud Aršišwang ud Ardwī-sūr Anāhīd. čiyon ⁺Ābān mēnōg ī yojdahrgar ī zamīg ud ābān tōhmag u-š padiš Māraspand ī Mānsarspand gōwišn ī Ohrmazd. Ard ud Dēn andar xwarrah mān ast kē Aršiswang gōwēd xwarrah ī wahištīg ardāyīh Ardwī-sūr Anāhīd pid ud mād ī ābān pad ēn hamkārīh andar ēbgatīh win(n)ārd ēstēnd ud ēn mēnōgān ham-kār xwarrah pāk dārēnd.

The fifth of the spirits (*mēnōgān*) is Spandārmad. From the material (*gētīg*) creation, she accepted earth as her own and he created for (her) help and collaboration Ābān and Dēn and Ard and Mānsarspand and Aršišwang and *Ardwī-sūr Anāhīd*. As ⁺Ābān, who is the purifying spirit (*mēnōg*) of the earth and the seed of the waters, in which (is) Māraspand, the Mānsarspand, Ohrmazd's (holy) word, Ard and Dēn have their domain in the *xwarrah*, which is called Aršišwang, *xwarrah* of the righteousness of heaven, (and) *Ardwī-sūr Anāhīd* (is) the father and mother of the Waters. In this cooperation during the (period of the onslaught of) Evil they are arranged and these cooperating spirits keep the *xwarrah* pure.[52]

The *xwarrah* should be kept pure, since according to the Zamyād Yašt the Renovation of the world is connected to it (Yt 19.92).[53] Also, in the paragraph above, *Ardwī-sūr Anāhīd* is a purifier among the other deities, yet she alone is mentioned as the father and mother of the Waters who cooperates to keep the *xwarrah* pure.

This process of androgynization, however, also associates *Ardwī-sūr Anāhīd* with Ohrmazd who is described the same way—that is, as both the mother and the father of his creatures:

(GBd. I.58)

Ohrmazd pad dām-dahišnīh mādarīh ud pidarīh ī dahišn ast če ka-š dām pad mēnōg parward ān būd mādarīh ka-š bē ō gētīg dād ān būd pidarīh.

Ohrmazd (has) by (the process of) creation (both) the motherhood and fatherhood of creation because when (he) created them spiritually (in the *mēnog* state), that was motherhood, and when he created them as material (in the *gētīg* state), that was fatherhood.[54]

Ardwī-sūr Anāhīd comes to be transformed from a goddess into a deity with the features of both genders, like a hermaphroditic deity, the mother and the father of the waters. Perhaps one way to explain this apparent folding of both genders into one divine entity is due to the influence of the Mesopotamian goddess Ištar and her hermaphrodism,[55] as will be discussed below.

The Connection between the Goddess and the Planet Venus

Most significant, as it was mentioned before, in the Pahlavi texts Anāhitā sometimes seems to be two separate deities: *Ardwī-sūr*, as the river, and *Anāhīd*, identified with the planet Venus. Since she also is mentioned as one deity with two genders (as noted above), one might ask why she is receiving these very opposite functions. Being influenced by Mesopotamian culture and astrology (Venus: Inanna/Ištar as two different planets, each with its own specific identity) seems to be a more acceptable explanation, as will be discussed further below. Again, however, references to Anāhitā in the *Bundahišn* appear to subsume or conflate figures that may not be identical.

As mentioned before, Anāhitā (*Anāhīd*) is identified with the planet Venus. As a planet, even Anāhitā's precise astronomical position in relation to the sun is given:

(GBd.VA.8)
ud Anāhid pad dō hazār ud hašt sad ud sīh ud ēk lipī[56] az mihr bast ēstēnd.
Anāhid is located at a distance of two thousand, eight hundred, and thirty-one minutes from Mihr (the sun).[57]

The association between Anāhitā and Venus, which becomes highly manifest during the Sasanian period, most likely derives from an earlier syncretism between the cults of Anāhitā and those of Inanna/Ištar and Aphrodite. It is surely significant that Inanna/Ištar, the Mesopotamian goddess of love and war, was also associated with the planet Venus. Because Venus (with whom Ištar was linked) appears both in the morning and the evening, and due to her mythological hermaphrodism,[58] it was perceived as two different but related "stars," the goddess of the evening star being held to be female, and the morning star considered as male.[59] We know that Mesopotamian astrology had a strong influence on Iranian beliefs, Tištar/Tir being another prominent example.[60] And, as has been mentioned previously, Anāhitā possibly was syncretized with the goddess Inanna/Ištar.

The idea of Venus (Inanna/Ištar) as two different planets, each with its own specific identity, perhaps came to be absorbed into the Iranian pantheon, giving two different versions of *Ardwī-sūr Anāhīd*. One was related to the waters—Anāhitā's original identity—and the other related to the planet Venus, *Anāhīd ī abāxtari*, who has a negative spirit, although the planet's light (like the other *abāxtar*s) comes from Ohrmazd. Because of this light, the *abāxtar*s cannot cause too much damage and sin in the world (Bd VA.10). It is interesting to note that Ohrmazd is also the name of the planet Jupiter, which has the same negative features as Anāhitā. Yet these two planets are both less "sinful" than the other *abāxtar*s.[61] As Panaino explains:

> The name of the five planets visible by the naked eye are clearly attested only in Middle Iranian sources, although the knowledge of these astral bodies should be much more ancient; in Pahlavi they are: *Anāhīd* (Venus), *Tīr* (Mercury), *Wahrām* (Mars), *Ohrmazd* (Jupiter), and *Kewān* (Saturn). The later demonization of the planets appears to be in evident contrast with the peculiar fact that some of them have the same names of the most important Mazdean gods. When western Iranians discovered the existence of the planets, they followed the earlier Mesopotamian denominations, exactly as the Greeks did. The Mesopotamian schools of astral divination first distinguished and then denominated the single planets, associating them with some of the highest divinities of the Iranian pantheon. Then their names became so deep-rooted that they could not be changed even when the planets were demonized.[62]

The Negative Connotations of Anāhīd as the Planet Venus

Within the Sasanian dualistic astrological framework, the planets seen as negative are set against the positive forces of the stars, with whom they are locked in constant battle. The planets are actually referred to as *gēg*, that is, "thieves" or "bandits." As Panaino explains:

> In the heavenly conflict between the two celestial armies, the starred one against that of the planets, the stars give—and in their own quality of divine beings (in Avestan *yazatas*) they "give" only in positive manner—while, to the contrary, the planets subtract, diverge, and damage, i.e., they try to rob the positive impact of the lights shed by the luminaries upon the sublunar world.[63]

Somewhat inconsistently, the astrological chapters of the *Bundahišn* do not consider the planets negative but rather "as harmonic parts of the creation."[64]

One explanation for this apparent inconsistency could be that the process of demonization took time and did not happen quickly. During this process, possibly in the intermediate stage, the planets Anāhīd and Ohrmazd were considered less "sinful" and were thus categorized as "beneficent" (*kirbakkar*) (Bn V*B*.12).

The *Bundahišn* also introduces *Anāhīd ī abaxtari* as a new, negative version of Anāhitā, who is the spirit of the planet Venus (Bn V.4). As an example of this negative quality, the astral deity, Sadwēs[65] (Avestan *Satavāesa-*), restrains the planet Venus from engaging in destructive activities: "Sadwēs happened to be of greater vigour than Jupiter and Venus; they disabled Jupiter and Venus from doing harm."[66] *Abāxtar*s are a group of demonic planet-spirits, each of which has a specific opponent among the "good" stars (*axtar*s):

(GBd V*A*.10)
hamāg rāyēnišn ī āwām čiyōn band ō axtarān čiyōn čašm-dīd paydāg wišōbēnd ul frōdēnd ud kast abzōn kunēnd. u-šān rawišn-iz nē čiyōn axtarān če ast ka tēz ast ī dagrand ast ka abāz-rawišn ast ka ēstādag hēnd. u-šān abāxtarān-nāmīh ēd kū nē axtar hēnd. u-šān ēn rōšnīh aziš paydāg ham rōšnīh ī Ohrmazdīg. Handāzag ī wattarān kē paymōzan ī debag paymōxt hēnd. čiyōn rōšnīh andar čašm ī xrafstarān aziš sūdōmandīh u-š ēk ēn kū paymoxtan ī ān rōšnīh rāy[67] wināh kardan kam tuwān ud ēk ēn kū mardōm wēnēnd aziš nē tarsēnd.

All of the order of the cosmos which is connected to the (*axtarān*), they (*Abāxtars*) make it to chaos, as it is clear to see. Make the upward down, increase the diminished. And their movement (also) is not like (*axtarān*), since it (the movement) is sharp, and is slow (long), and is back-motion since (they) are standing. They are named as *Abāxtarān* because they are not *Axtar*. Their luminous appearance is of Ohrmazd's light, like the vulgar ones[68] who wear the brocade. Like the light in the eyes of noxious creatures, there is benefit in this, and one is that they can do little harm, due to wearing the light, and (another) one is that when people see them they are not scared of them.[69]

The Iranian cosmos as a battlefield between Good and Evil can be seen clearly in the following paragraph, where the planets and the stars take a side and each has a corresponding opponent:

(GBd V.5.4)
andar-iz spihr mihr ī tamīg ō xwaršēd māh ī tamīg ō māh ī gōspand-tōhmag[70] mad hēnd. u-šān ō rah ī xwēš bast hēnd pad ham-paymānagīh. abārīg jādūgān parīg abāg harwīn murnjēnīdārān[71] abāxtarān <ō> axtarān. haft abāxtarān spāhbedān/ō haft spāhbedān\axtarān čīyōn Tīr/ī abāxtar < īg>\ō Tištar {Ohrmazd ī abāxtarīg ō Haftōring} Wahrām ī abāxtarīg ō Wanand Anāhīd ī

Abāxtarig ō Sadwēs Kēwān {kē abāxtarigān spāhbedān spāhbed} ō Mēx ī mayān āsmān Gōzihr-iz muš-parīg ī dumbōmand ō xwaršēd ud māh ud stāragān mad hēnd.

Even in the Firmament the dark Mihr came against the Sun, and the dark Moon against the Moon having the seed of the *Gōspands* (Beneficent Animals). They bound them (the sun and the moon) to their own rays for adherence, other sorcerers and witches, with the licentious fatal *Abāxtars* came against the *Axtars*: the seven *Abāxtar* leaders (against) the seven *Axtar* (leaders), such as Tīr (*Abāxtar*-Planet Mercury) against Tištar (*Axtar*-Sirius), the *Ohrmazd ī Abāxtari* (Jupiter) (against) *Haftōring* (the 'Seven Bears'), the *Wahrām ī Abāxtari* (Mars) against *Wanand*, the *Anāhīd ī Abāxtari* (Venus) against *Sadwēs*, *Kēwān* (Saturn) who is the Chieftain of the leaders of the Planetary (against) the wedges of the sky. *Gōzihr*,[72] also the tailed *muš-parīg*[73] (Rat-*pairikā*) came (against) the sun and the moon and the stars.[74]

The passage below could belong to an intermediate stage of the myth's development in which the status of planets gradually changed, since both Ohrmazd and Anāhīd are here seen as "beneficent":

(GBd V*B*. 5b.12)

pad bun ka ēbgat[75] *andar dwārist ōwōn ĵast kū mihr ud māh ī tamīg <ham-> paymānagīh abāg rah ī xwaršēd ud māh rāy wināhgārīh kardan nē tuwānist ud Haftōring ud Sadwēs az Ohrmazd ud Anāhīd freh-nērōgtar ĵast hēnd u-šān Ohrmazd ud Anāhīd az wināh kardan padīrānēnīd. ham čim rāy axtar-āmārān awēšān rāy pad-kirbakkar xwānēnd.*

In the beginning, when evil (*Ahriman-ēbgat*) attacked, it so happened that the dark Mihr and Moon could not do any harm, because of their dependence on the rays of the Sun and the Moon; and *Haftōring* (the Seven Bears) and *Sadwēs* became more powerful than *Ohrmazd* and *Anāhīd* (Jupiter and Venus) (thus) they made *Ohrmazd* and *Anāhīd* incapable of committing sin. This is why the astrologists call them "the beneficents."[76]

Being paired with the Creator god as two "beneficents" shows the importance of the goddess. It is noticeable that in some parts of the *Bundahišn* Ohrmazd and Anāhīd are mentioned together. As we have previously noted, they are also mentioned as "the mother and father" of the "waters" (Anāhīd) and "creation" (Ohrmazd) (Bd I.58, III.20).

In the following verse, however, both Anāhīd and Tīr (Mercury) are portrayed in negative terms:

(GBd V*B*.14)

gōwēd kū Anāhīd āb-čihrag[77] *čē-š hamēstār Sadwēs āb-čihrag ud Tīr wādīg gōwēnd čē-š hamēstār Tištar ud wād ud wārān-kardārān.*

It is said that *Anāhīd* has a watery nature, because her opponent, *Sadwēs*, has a watery nature. And (also) *Tīr* (Mercury) has a windy (nature), because his opponent *Tištar* creates the wind and the rain.[78]

Even so, it is not just *Anāhīd* who has a watery origin. The author(s) of this passage also describe(s) *Ardwī-sūr* as a water spirit, and hence state(s) that their pairing arises from the fact that they are both of a "watery nature" (Bd V*B*, 5b.14). The priestly author(s) of the *Bundahišn* cannot escape or ignore the original watery nature of the goddess. However, they do produce an explanation in order to justify the separation of *Anāhīd* from *Ardwī-sūr*. Malandra has argued that the separation between *Anāhīd* and *Ardwī-sūr* shows that the Avestan Anāhitā is a late combination of two originally distinct goddesses, Anāhīti and *Ardwī-sūrā*.[79] However, the water origin of both *Anāhīd* and *Ardwī-sūr*, as mentioned above, makes it more likely that this separation was, in fact, absorbed under the influence of Ištar and the planet Venus. We should recall that Ištar was associated with the planet Venus, who was considered bisexual, changing her sex according to her position in the sky. Venus also was considered as the "beneficent" as the morning star.[80]

Moreover, the Mazdaean opposition of *aṣa-* versus *druj-* required the Pahlavi-text writers to create an opponent for each of the various Iranian deities in their priestly official version of the ancient myths. Apart from such editorial considerations, the influence of Mesopotamia, Greek, and India and the cultural exchanges between them and Iran also should be borne in mind.

Wisdom and Its Connection to the Water Goddess

As previously discussed, wisdom is one of the functions (among with healing, fertility, and victory) of Indo-European water goddesses, including the Avestan Anāhitā. (The Celtic Brigantia, of whom it was said that she lost her sight in order to gain wisdom, is another example.) Wisdom thus has some connection to both water and femininity. In Iranian religion, the main female deities are all somehow related to nature: Spəntā Ārmaiti—the earth, Haurvatāt and Amərətāt—the plants, water and the growth and fertility of the life, and Anāhitā—the waters (*āb*). The question arises as to why this is the case.

Almost everything in nature has a disciplined cycle—as precise as if there is a wisdom driving it—and women are central to this wisdom. In contrast to men, the ability of females to give birth to children makes them more closely related to nature and the cycle of the life, to the trees and their fruits, and to the annual agricultural harvests. Even the monthly period of women's cycle is like the monthly appearing and disappearing of the moon (and, as we know, connected to it).

In the *Zand ī Wahman Yasn* (the most important apocalyptic work in Zoroastrian literature[81]), Ohrmazd foretells for Zaraθuštra all of the events that will happen to Iran until the end of the world. The book consists of a dialogue between Zaraθuštra and Ohrmazd. Zaraθuštra drinks in the wisdom of all knowledge *xrad ī harwisp-āgāhīh* (the "all-in-encompassing wisdom")—which, significantly, is in the form of water—then goes into a visionary trance enabling him to see the future until the end of the world. (The trope of a seer drinking a hallucinogenic beverage to inter into a trance is widespread, and presumably very ancient; it is seen also in stories about the early Sasanian high-priest Kardēr and in the *Ardā Wīrāz nāmag*.)

Having entered into a trance, Zaraθuštra sees several future time periods. After seven days of being unconscious, when he returns to his normal state Ohrmazd helps him to understand and analyze what he has seen.[82]

Zaraθuštra's asking for *xrad ī harwisp-āgāhīh* (the "all-in-encompassing wisdom") to know about the future resembles a less complete version of the well-known soul-journeys of *Ardā Wīrāz* and Kerdīr, although with a different purpose. The journeys of the latter two are intended to prove the correctness of Zoroastrianism, but in the *Zand ī Wahman Yasn*, Zaraθuštra's request to see the future and his receiving the wisdom of omniscience from Ohrmazd appears more like a consultation between them about future events.

Arguably, the most significant issue in the *Zand ī Wahman Yasn* is not the end times per se as much as it is about wisdom as such and its form. Zaraθuštra is able to see future events by receiving the "wisdom of omniscience," in the form of water, from Ohrmazd, according to the text:

(ZWY 3.5–7)
Ohrmazd pad xrad ī harwisp-āgāhīh dānist kū-š čē menīd, spitāmān zarduxšt ī ahlaw frawahr.

6) *u-š ān ī zarduxšt dast frāz grift. u-š- - ohrmazd, mēnōg <ī> ābzōnīg, dādār ī gēhān <ī> astōmandān ī ahlaw- - u-š xrad ī harwisp-āgāhīh pad āb kirb abar dast ī zarduxšt kard u-š guft kū, "frāz xwar."*

7) *ud zarduxšt aziš frāz xward. u-š xrad ī harwisp-āgāhīh pad zarduxšt andar gumēxt.*

Ohrmazd through the all-in-encompassing wisdom (*xrad ī harwisp-āgāhīh*) knew that what the Spitāmān Zarduxšt, with righteous *frawahr*, thought. He took hold of Zarduxšt's hand, He, Ohrmazd, with the increasing and bountiful (*ābzōnīg*) spirit (*mēnōg*), Creator of the material existence, He laid the all-in-encompassing wisdom, in the shape (*kirb*) of water, on the hand of Zarduxšt, and He (Ohrmazd) said: "drink (it)." Zarduxšt drank it and the all-encompassing wisdom of Ohrmazd was mixed with Zarduxšt.[83]

It may be noted that the word used here for "form-shape" is *kirb*, which, in fact, means "body." This is a combination of *xrad*, the wisdom, which is a moral concept and belongs to Ohrmazd, and something related to nature: the water (*āb*), which connects this wisdom to the water, which as we know is linked with Anāhitā. And this latter point is significant.

Thus, while moral-cultural concepts mostly belong to the male deities, it seems that in this case having water stand as the form of the "wisdom of omniscience" would connect this *xrad* to nature—and hence, to the female—remembering that Ohrmazd is also described as both the mother and the father of his creatures as has already been mentioned: " ... *Ohrmazd pad dām-dahīšnīh mādarīh ud pidarīh ī dahišn ast* ... "[84] Apparently, the maternal characteristic was considered necessary for the creation and the creator, since as it was mentioned before, Anāhīd is also called "mother and father" of the water.

According to the *Dēnkard*, when the creator made the two kinds of *xrad*, he made the *gōšōsrūd-xrad* (Av. *gaošō.srūta-xratu-*, "wisdom acquired through hearing") as male, and the *āsn-xrad* (Av. *āsna-xratu-* "inborn (or innate) wisdom") as female. And knowledge is born from the combination of innate wisdom (*āsn-xrad*) (and) the acquired wisdom (*gōšōsrūd-xrad*). Through their *xwēdōdah* (consanguinal marriage), all of human's knowledge is born:

(Dk 3.80):
hamāg-iz dānišn ī mardōmān az xwēdōdah bawīhēd čē dānišn zāyīhēd az hamīh ī āsn-xrad gōšōsrūd-xrad. āsn-xrad mādag gōšōsrūd -xrad nar ud ēd rāy čē har 2 az dādār āfurišn xwāh ud brād hēnd.[85]

All human knowledge comes from the *xwēdōdah*, because knowledge is born from the combination of innate wisdom (*āsn-xrad*) (and) the acquired wisdom (*gōšōsrūd-xrad*). The innate wisdom (*āsn-xrad*) (is) female, acquired wisdom (*gōšōsrūd-xrad*) is male, and this (is) because both are ever since the creation of the Creator sister and brother.

Thus, the *āsn-xrad* is "female" wisdom, and the *gōšōsrūd-xrad* is "male" wisdom (as has been previously mentioned, the *Bundahišn* attributes Anāhitā both the male and female genders: *Ardwī-sūr ī Anāhīd, pid ud mād ī Ābān*).[86] It seems that although there is no gender connection in the Avesta in regard to this, there is one in the Pahlavi texts, which Macuch suggests recognizing as "gender symbolism," that is, mind and body, nature and culture, etc.[87]

Macuch states:[88]

> In this assignment of the two types of reason to the sexes we can easily recognize a procedure that in philosophy and literature is denoted by the term "gender symbolism." This concept is based on the idea that, in all dichotomies of human perception, in basic dualism such as nature and culture, mind and body, feeling and reason, emotion and rationality, private and public, beauty and ugliness, etc., the duality of the sexes is implicitly thought of. These basic dualisms can vary considerably in different cultures, but one can observe that they are simultaneously connoted with classifications of femininity and masculinity in a manner that reflect social structures exactly, so that they can be recognized immediately by a person socialized in that specific culture.

The two wisdoms also complete each other; one cannot learn the acquired wisdom without having the innate wisdom, and one cannot use his innate wisdom without learning the acquired wisdom, according to the *Bundahišn*:

(GBd XXVI.17)
> *āsn-xrad ud gōšōsrūd-xrad nazdist abar Wahman paydāg bawēd. kē-š ēn har(w) dō ast ō ān ī påhlom axwān rasēd. ka-š ēn har(w) dō nest ō ān ī wattar axwān rasēd. ka āsn-xrad nēst gōšōsrūd-xrad nē hammōxtēd. kē-š āsn-xrad ast ud gōšōsrūd-xrad nest āsn-xrad ō kār nē dānēd burdan.*

The innate wisdom (*āsn-xrad*) and the acquired wisdom (*gōšōsrūd-xrad*) first come to Wahman. One who has both of these wisdoms could have the best life force. One who does not have these two (wisdoms) would have the worst life force.[89] Without the innate wisdom, the acquired wisdom could not be learned. One who has the innate wisdom and does not have the acquired wisdom cannot use the innate wisdom.[90]

Piras suggests that the Pahlavi commentators on this passage may have missed a key aspect of the Avestan notion of *āsna-* as an adjective. *āsna-xratu* reflects a particular situation and *āsna* which he proposes (through etymological analyses)[91] may mean "rising [with the dawn]" or the "rising *xratu-*. Piras states:

> Actually, this connotation of the substantive *xratu-* with the qualification of *asna-* 'innate' (or natural in the Pahlavi texts, or 'congenital' to the soul according to Piras[92]) fails to take in the specific nature of the Avestan *xratu-* in the *MihrYašt* or *ArdYašt*, where the context is better defined in terms of a mythological scenario centred on the moment of sunrise.[93]

Piras quotes two verses of paragraph 92 of the Zamyād Yašt, about how *Saošiiant* looks to the creation with *xratu-* (after rising from the lake Kąsaoiia):

(Yt 19. 92)
āaṭ astuuaṭ.ərətō fraxštāite
haca apaṭ kąsaoiitāṭ
aštō mazdā°ahurahe
vīspa.tauruuaiiā°puθrō
vaēδəm vaējō yim vārəθraynəm
yim baraṭ taxmō θraētaonō
yaṭ ažiš dahākō jaini.[94]

When Astuuaṭ-ərəta (Saošiiant), Ahura Mazdā's messenger, son of Vīspa. tauruuaiiā, shall rise up from the lake *kąsaoiia-*, he will have a victorious mace, (the same mace that) the brave Θraētaona bore when the dragon Dahāka was slain.

(Yt 19.94)
hō diδāṭ xratəuš dōiθrābiiō
vīspa dāmąn paiti vaēnāṭ
+pasca išō dušciθraiiaiiā°
hō vīspəm ahūm astuuaṇtəm
ižaiiā°vaēnāṭ dōiθrābiia
darəsca daθaṭ amərəxšiiaṇtīm
vīspąm yąm astuuaitīm gaēθąm.[95]

He (Saošiiant) shall gaze upon all of the creatures with (his insightful) eyes of intelligence to the one with demon nature; then attack. He shall gaze with the eyes that render strength at the whole of material life, with eyes that shall deliver immortality to the material world.

It seems that this particular type of "*xratu*-sight" is "thus characteristic of *Saošiiant* rising up from the lake *kąsaoiia-*."[96] The expression *xratəuš dōiθrābiia* is connected to *āsna-xratu-*, according to Piras,[97] which is the kind of wisdom as a source of visionary insight and mental enlightenment. We may add that in the verses mentioned above (Yt 19.92–94), a connection may be noticed between wisdom as one of Anāhitā's functions and "this particular type of *xratu-*." Moreover, if we note that *Saošiiant* is rising from the lake *kąsaoiia-*, and the first thing that he does is to gaze with his "insight eyes of intelligence" upon creation, we may consider that wisdom is absorbed from the lake *kąsaoiia-* from whence he rises and thus may be linked with water and Anāhitā.

The word *xratu-*, usually translated as "wisdom," has been widely analyzed[98] in terms of its philology and its Indo-Iranian historical-cultural background for its meaning and translation, among which "mental," and/or "magic-spiritual" may be mentioned.[99] As already noted above (and in contrast to the Avesta) in several Pahlavi texts, the *āsn-xrad* "innate or inborn wisdom" is connoted with "female" wisdom and its functions are related to the body and nature. The *gōšōsrūd-xrad*, "wisdom acquired through hearing," on the other hand, is "male" wisdom, which is more involved with morality, rationality, and abstract moral concepts. Both wisdoms, together, seem to lead humans toward a righteous life.

Macuch observes that:

> In this assignment of the two types of reason to the sexes we can easily recognize a procedure that in philosophy and literature is denoted by the term "gender symbolism. This concept is based on the idea that in all dichotomies of human perception, in basic dualisms such as nature and culture, mind and body, feeling and reason, emotion and rationality, private and public, beauty and ugliness, etc., the duality of the sexes is implicitly thought of. These basic dualisms can vary considerably in different cultures, but one can observe that they are simultaneously connoted with classifications of femininity and masculinity in a manner that reflect social structures exactly, so that they can be recognized immediately by a person socialized in that specific culture.[100]

In the Pahlavi *andarz*-text, *Ayādgār ī Wuzurg-mihr* (the memorial of Wuzurg-mihr),[101] the two wisdoms' duty is to protect humans. The author of this Pahlavi text made the functions of these two "*xrad*" very clear. According to this text, the *āsn-xrad*'s function is mostly related to protecting the body from committing sins associating the body with the female and emotionality (AW 45) while the *gōšōsrūd-xrad* is more involved with morality of the mind associating the mind with the male and rationality (AW 46) and to enabling one to know the righteous path:

(AW 43)

Dādār ohrmazd pad abāz dāštan ī ān and druz ayārīh ī mardōm rāy čand čiš ī nigāhdār ī mēnōg dād: āsn-xrad ud gōšōsrūd-xrad ud xēm ud ummēd ud hunsandīh ud dēn ud ham-pursagīh dānāg.

The creator Ohrmazd in order to keep away these several demons and to help people created several things to take care of the spirit *(mēnōg)*: inborn wisdom (*āsn-xrad*) and wisdom acquired through hearing (*gōšōsrūd-xrad*), and character, and hope, and satisfaction, and religion, and consultation of the wise.[102]

(AW 45)

xwēš-kārīh ī āsn-xrad tan az bīm kunišnīh wināh nigerišnīg ī ud ranj abē-barīh pādan ud frasāwandīh ī xīr gētīg, frazām tan pad daxšag dāštan ud az xīr fraš-girdīgīh ī xwēš nē kāstan ud pad ān wadgarīh ī xwēš nē abzūdan.

The function of innate wisdom is to protect the body from the horror of committing intentional sins and to keep it from the useless[103] pain and ephemeral nature of the material world, and remembering the final end of the body (thus) do not reduce its (the body's) share of eternity (after the Restoration) and do not add to its (the body's) sin (evil-doing).[104]

(AW 46)
xwēš-kārīh ī gōšōsrūd-xrad pand ud ristag ī frārōn bē šnāxtan ud padiš ēstādan, čiš ī pēš bē widerīd bē nigērīdan ud ān ī pas aziš āgāh būdan, čiš ī būdan nē šāyad nē wurrōyistan ud kār ī frazāmēnīdan nē šāyad andar nē griftan.

The function of the wisdom acquired through hearing (*gōšōsrūd-xrad*) is to distinguish the path of goodness and (how) to follow it, and look at what has been done in the past and be aware of what (will be done) in the future. And to that which could not last should not be chosen, and the deed which could not be completed (perfectly) should not be started.[105]

Conclusions

Although mentions of Anāhitā in the post-Sasanian Pahlavi priestly texts are not particularly prominent or detailed, her appearance in a wide range of contexts connected with the Sasanian period, especially in archaeology, suggests that she remained a prominent deity during the Sāsānian period, at least for the Sasanian royal house and possibly among large parts of the Iranian population as well. Her important role as "king-maker" in certain Sāsānian rock reliefs and the fact that the Sāsānian ruler Ardešīr sent the severed heads of defeated enemies to her temple at Eṣṭaxr are two important facts attesting to her importance for the royal house.[106] Indeed, the ambivalence shown to her in the Pahlavi texts may reflect that there were some underlying tensions connected with Anāhitā's cult, the post-Sasanian texts perhaps reflecting the unelaborated recollection of a competition over religious authority at court and/or a refusal on the part of some Iranians to completely follow the directives of the court priests (as the proclamations of Kirdir obliquely show).

The portrayal of Anāhitā in the Pahlavi texts is a complex phenomenon and indeed not easily deciphered. She ultimately appears there as two separate deities, with both positive and negative portrayals: *Ardwī-sūr*, as the river, and *Anāhīd*, identified with the planet Venus. Moreover, as discussed above, *Ardwī-sūr Anāhīd* is said to be both the mother and the father of the waters. The fact that she is sometimes transformed into a goddess with the features of both genders (like a hermaphroditic deity) may arise from this fact. Interestingly, the concept of "wisdom" in the Pahlavi texts was divided according to the two genders (like *Ardwī-sūr Anāhīd* herself). The *āsn-xrad* "innate wisdom" is connoted with the female wisdom, and its function seems to be related to the body, nature, and natural cycles.

The aspects which are portrayed negatively by the Pahlavi authors seem to be mainly those which can be associated with the Mesopotamian elements of her evolving character, notably the goddess Inanna/Ištar. The Mesopotamian goddess, like the Pahlavi Anāhīd, was linked to the planet Venus, whose dual appearances as both morning and evening star mythologically symbolize her hermaphroditism.[107] Thus, Anāhīd's ambivalent treatment in the Pahlavi texts may be connected with the (foreign) influence of Mesopotamian astrology into the historical evolution of her character, dividing the deity into two different identities opposed to each other. These divisions included the important deities as well, even the Creator god Ohrmazd.

The case of Anāhitā would seem to be an example of the kind of influence Mesopotamian culture and ritual, including astronomy, had on Iranians and their pantheon. More specifically, this Mesopotamian influence provided Anāhitā with two opposing identities, both genders, along with their respective functions. Existing in two distinct versions, *Ardwī-sūr/Anāhīd* came to be divided in the Pahlavi texts into two different identities: one who was related to the waters—Anāhitā's original, positive identity—and another more linked to the planet Venus, *Anāhīd ī abāxtari*, a negative spirit. Even so, the original "water origin" of both *Ardwī-sūr* and *Anāhīd* was never lost.

As has been discussed in previous chapters, there are several distinct functions and concepts to be found among the various Indo-European water goddesses, one of which is their connection with wisdom and knowledge. Sárasvatī,[108] Dānu, and Brigantia are merely the best-known examples of this. The Armenian Anahit also was known for her knowledge, even being described as "the mother of all knowledge."[109] Similarly, the Avestan *Ābān Yašt* contains a prayer offered to *Arəduuī Sūrā Anāhitā* for her insight and her knowledge (5.86). Wisdom and knowledge would thus appear to be connected to the healing function of water goddesses. This could be due to women's knowledge of medicinal plants, which on more than one occasion in history resulted in their being accused of witchcraft.

In the Scandinavian tradition and belief system as well, "the sacred water of the goddesses brought inspiration and knowledge to those who drank from it. It was said that Odin cast one of his eyes at a spring as an offering to gain a 'drink' which would give him the knowledge and more specifically the reveal of the future."[110] Scandinavian mythology speaks of "the sacred water [which] brought inspiration and knowledge to those who drank from it"; Odin is said to have gained knowledge of the future by drinking sacred water.[111] Similarly, in chapter seven of the Zoroastrian apocalyptic work *Zand ī Wahman Yasn*, when Zaraϑuštra drinks the "wisdom of all knowledge"—which, significantly, is in the form of "water"—he goes into a visionary trance enabling him to see the future. Since the concept of "knowledge" is seen to be connected to sacred water, then it would seem that the custodian of this sacred water, who is a goddess, would by extension be connected to knowledge as well.

Myths from a number of different cultures involving water feature a sacred child who is entrusted as a water-keeper. The Hebrew Moses falls into this category, as does the Assyrian king Sargon, and, according to the *Bundahišn*, the Iranian monarch Kawād. In Iranian mythology, Zaraϑuštra's sperm (i.e., his "children") are entrusted to the water (a hypostasis of Anāhitā). Behind this notion would seem to be the idea that water serves as a kind of sacred womb to the world. If we accept that the earth was considered as female (Spəntā Ārmaiti), then lakes and wells could metaphorically be considered as the vagina and womb of the earth, and thus sacred. The idea of sacred lakes devoted to female deities has been discussed before. The fact that almost all of the water-connected goddesses have childbirth/fertility/healing functions is reflected in myths about the water-keeping child. Certain deities connected with elements of nature exist in all archaic human cultures. Among these the sky, the earth, and water are the most common; the first is most often worshipped as a male deity, and the latter two most often as goddesses. Anāhitā, as it is mentioned before, is associated with knowledge and wisdom.

It is not surprising then, that in the renovation of the world, *Saošiiant* will be rising up from the lake *kąsaoiia-* (Zamyād Yašt.19.94), with the expression "*xratəuš dōiϑrābiia.*" This particular type of wisdom "*xratu-*sight," which is characteristic of *Saošiiant*, connects him, therefore, to the lake and water and to Anāhitā.

Traces of Anāhitā in Islamic Iran

This chapter surveys and identifies possible survivals of Anāhitā in the literature and rituals of Islamic Iran, focusing on the attributes of female figures in literary works such as the *Šāh-nāmeh,* the *Dārāb-nāmeh,* and other sources and their possible connection to Iranian goddesses and the Avestan *pairikās.* Although it is not possible to know with certainty whether or to what extent such continuity existed (or continues to exist) within Iranian society, these connections between the pre-Islamic and Islamic periods are intriguing and, in many cases, appear highly likely. Our approach will be to analyze—albeit with caution—a number of female literary figures and popular rituals using the frameworks of comparative mythology and gender studies.

With the progressive Islamization of Iran from the seventh century onward, Anāhitā disappears as a distinct object of popular devotion. However, as is generally the case when any society adopts a new religion, many traces of earlier beliefs and practices remain under new guises. The goddess worship practiced by Iranians in pre-Islamic times, within which Anāhitā was the principal figure, became subsumed under popular rituals, especially those having to do with water, or reverence for supernatural creatures such as the *pairikās,* or the survival of shrines and other sacred places, many of which belie their goddess origins by containing the words *doxtar* ("girl, daughter"), *bībī,* or *bānū* ("lady").

In popular Iranian folklore, even some ostensibly Islamic figures, notably the prophet Muhammad's daughter Fatima, contain some echo of Anāhitā. For example, Iranians say that Fatima's dowry (*kābīn, mehriyeh*) was water. It is written in Shi'ite religious texts that "Four rivers are Fatima's dowry: Euphrates, Nile, Nahrawaan, and Balkh."[1] In some mourning ceremonies and grief rituals in Shi'ite Iran during the 'Ashura ceremonies,[2] the "*Rowzeh-khan,*" the person who speaks about the oppression and injustice happened to the Imam and his family before being martyred, sometimes says that the enemies didn't let the thirsty family of the Prophet drink water from the Euphrates river although the water was the rightful dowry of the Imam's mother, Fatima.[3]

There are many other elements in Iranian popular rituals that preserve a connection between women and water. Persian literature as well preserves numerous details that may reflect lost myths about divine or semidivine female figures.

Traces of Goddesses in the *Šāh-nāmeh*

Many of the characters in the Persian national epic, the *Šāh-nāmeh* ("Book of Kings") of Ferdowsī, a tenth-century epic poem which celebrates the glories of Iran's pre-Islamic past, are also found in the Avesta and in the *Rg Veda*.[4] Following the separation between Indo-Iranians into Iran and India during the second millennium BCE, most of their gods lost their prior mythological status, but their influence remained, with many being reconceived as heroes. (The same is true of other Indo-European mythologies, including the Greek, Roman Germanic, etc.) In other words, these originally divine figures were reimagined as humans, but possessing special, superhuman features.

Zoroastrian symbolism is also deeply evoked in art from the Islamic period, such as the painting known as "The Court of Gayumars," from the illustrated *Šāh-nāmeh* commissioned by *Šāh* Tahmasp in the early 1620s.[5] Gayumars or Kiyumars (Av. *gayō marətan*), described in Yašt 13 of the Avesta as the "Primal Man," was created after sky water, earth, the first plant, and the first cow. The seventeenth-century Muslim painter Sultan Muhammad's depiction of "The Court of Gayumars" shows a garden scene of inter-species harmony and primordial bliss prior to its disruption by the evil deity Ahriman, a well-known image from Zoroastrian mythology.

In fact, while various *Šāh-nāmeh*s were the most commonly commissioned book by all the Muslim dynasties who ruled Iran, Ferdowsī's epic work is an unparalleled celebration of pre-Islamic Iranian culture, championing recognizably ancient proto-Indo-European patriarchal and martial values, throughout which Mazdaism is the (hidden) formal religious framework. Many of the "heroes" in the *Šāh-nāmeh* are originally Indo-European or other deities. As such, Zoroastrian as well as common Indo-European mythological motifs and symbols are predominant, though Mesopotamian, Byzantine, Indian, and other influences are present as well. Another example is Żaḥḥāk, portrayed as a man-dragon in both the Avesta and the Vedas, who in the *Šāh-nāmeh* is transformed into a tyrannical king with snakes coming out of his shoulders. Żaḥḥāk is depicted in this way in virtually every illustrated manuscript of the *Šāh-nāmeh*.[6]

Although the *Šāh-nāmeh* was written during the Islamic period, its female characters are very strong-minded and behave with a self-determination that might seem inappropriate in the patriarchal context of tenth-century society. A number of these women actively try to meet their beloved and even "promise" to offer themselves to their lovers. They send messages in order to arrange secret meetings, and even go to their beloved's bed during the night. Sometimes, notably in the case of Gord Āfarīd, they take on the role of a mighty warrior. Even so, these assertive women can be strangely obedient to their male masters, which sends us some mixed signals. Can "good" women be bold as well as obedient? Why are these characters sometimes able to freely choose their lovers, while at other times they appear to have little or no autonomy at all?

Seeking the mythological roots of these female behaviors would seem to point us back to a goddess-centered belief system (possibly with Mesopotamian roots), distinct from Indo-European mythology, of which Indo-Iranian is a branch. The Indo-European pantheon, while it contains many goddesses, nevertheless, accords the most important roles to male deities.

While a detailed analysis of women in the *Šāh-nāmeh* is beyond the scope of this study,[7] it will be helpful to highlight some examples of its relevance to our discussion. In terms of the *Šāh-nāmeh*'s numerous heroic female figures, one may draw a parallel with the fact that such characters are common in the myths of Sakas and other pastoral nomadic peoples of Central Asia as well, including the Mongols and the pre-Islamic Turks. It also may be noted in this regard that the epic is made up largely of stories and legends from eastern Iran, where a number of Saka tribes had settled (e.g., Sistan/Sakastan). Since many characters in the *Šāh-nāmeh* can be interpreted as mythological figures who became transformed into human heroes (e.g., Av. Yima/Jam or Jam-šīd, Av. *gayō marətan*/Gayumars), it should not surprise us to find strong, self-assertive women in the *Šāh-nāmeh*.

The Connection to Mesopotamian Myth

Before evaluating the example of two female figures in the *Šāh-nāmeh*, we will begin by considering the possible origin of their stories in Mesopotamian mythology. The Sumerian version of the martyr/regeneration myth, referred to as "The Descent of Inanna," is the most detailed, and shows clearly that the vegetation god Dumuzi regularly died and rose again, ensuring seasonal fertility. The basic theme bears a striking similarity to the Greek myth of Persephone, daughter of the goddess Demeter, which may in part be derived from it.[8] A similar and possibly related Sumerian myth is that of the goddess Ninlil (who was identified by Mylitta)[9], who was later identified with the Mesopotamian Ištar (who, in turn, came to be identified with Anāhitā). Her original name was "Sud" before being married to the god Enlil, and it is he who changes her name to "Ninlil." The story begins with advice from a wise old woman to the young Ninlil:

> Ninlil was advised by Nun-bar-ce-gunu: "The river is holy, woman! The river is holy – do not bathe in it! ... The Great Mountain, Father Enlil – his eye is bright, he will look at you! ... his eye is bright; he will look at you! Straight away he will want to have intercourse, he will want to kiss! He will be happy to pour lusty semen into the womb, and then he will leave you to it!"[10]

But, of course, Sud (Ninlil) does not accept the advice, and bathes in the holy river. Seeing the beautiful young Sud (Ninlil) bathing naked, Enlil desires her and then rapes her. This sinful act angers the entire Sumerian pantheon (fifty great gods and seven lesser gods), who banish Enlil to the underworld. Afterward, however, Sud (Ninlil) follows him there voluntarily. She gives birth to several children, including Suen or Sin, the deity of the moon (with whom Ninlil became pregnant when first raped by Enlil) and Nergal, the deity of the death (to whom Ninlil gives birth in underworld). Sin and Nergal became two of the most important deities in the Mesopotamian pantheon. The myth is significant for our discussion in that it connects Sud/Ninlil (who also was identified by Ištar) to water, specifically the sacred river—this, as we shall see, provides a natural link to the river goddesses of the Indo-Europeans which may have resonated with early Iranian migrants into Mesopotamia.

The Mesopotamian myth of Ištar and Dumuzi emphasizes the sexual aspect of the story, stating that all sexual activity on the earth—animal and human—came to a halt when Ištar descended to the underworld:

> As soon as Ištar went down to kurnugi (underworld),
> No bull mounted a cow, no donkey impregnated a jenny,
> No young man impregnated a girl in the street,
> The young man slept in his private room,
> The girl slept in the company of her friends.[11]

One may note that it is by allowing "the lover of her youth, Dumuzi to become a prisoner during a part of the year that Ištar obtains her own freedom from the underworld; in this sense, the goddess would seem to take precedence over the god. In this myth, Ištar is captured underground, and obtains her freedom by allowing Dumuzi" to become a prisoner during a part of the year and come back to earth annually. When the goddess goes down to the underworld, all of the sexual activities in the world stop.

Following the death of the vegetation god, life activities are seen to cease: in other words, the sexual frustration of the goddess results in an end to fertility in the world. The appropriate human response to this life-threatening disaster was to engage in a massive mourning ceremony for the martyred god. The spilling of their tears was to have had a dual effect, both commiserating with the bereaved goddess and, through a kind of sympathetic magic, to get the "sky to cry" as well, thereby bringing the dormant crops back to life. In fact, this annual mourning ritual appears to have been the single most important collective religious event in the agriculturally dependent Mesopotamian society, following the repeating cycles of nature.

It may be summarized that in the Sumerian/Mesopotamian myth of martyrdom and regeneration—upon which the later Iranian story of Siāvaš is presumably based—the central conflict is between a goddess and a vegetation god who dies or is killed and is then reborn each year, symbolizing the annual regeneration of plant life so important in an agricultural society. The story culminates in the sacrificial death of the latter, symbolizing the end of the rain and the withering of plants with the onset of the Mesopotamian winter. We may recall that such myths, in fact, represent an interpretation of the annual cycle of nature and its affect on human societies. We will see reflections of this in the *Šāh-nāmeh*, discussed in the following section.

Sūdābeh and Rūdābeh: Two Sides of Female Power

Many female characters in the *Šāh-nāmeh* are striking for their extraordinary independence and self-assertion, qualities not typically associated with women in the medieval Islamic society in which Ferdowsī lived (like Sūdābeh, Rūdābeh, Manīžeh, Tahmīneh, and Katāyun) and/or are considered possibly as *pairikā*s or goddesses.[12] This may be an indication that such female figures have superhuman roots, possessing features that may be derived from those attributed to goddesses in ancient mythology. The characters of Sūdābeh and Rūdābeh, who can be seen as representing opposing archetypes of feminine power, are analyzed in terms of their possible derivations from female divinities in Iranian and Mesopotamian mythology. We will focus here on these two female figures in the *Šāh-nāmeh* whose features show possible extensive surviving goddess descriptions and, therefore, possibly constitute reflections of the ancient goddesses some of whom became part of Anāhitā's features.

At first glance, Sūdābeh and Rūdābeh appear to have two very different personalities and roles, one positive and the other negative, but they also show some similarities, like two sides of the same coin. They both have foreign roots, in that their fathers are characterized by Ferdowsī as not "Iranian." In Rūdābeh's case, she is descendant of Żaḥḥāk, the ancient man-dragon whom we discussed before. Ferdowsī actually describes Rūdābeh as demon-born (*dēw-zād*).

Rūdābeh's father, Mehrāb, despite his Iranian name, is king of Kābūl, which, according to Ferdowsī, lies beyond the pale of Iranian lands. Mehrāb's name derives, in fact, from two words: the god Mehr or Miθra and *āb* (water); it thus embodies a pairing that we have noted throughout our study. Moreover, the name is clearly connected to the term "Mehrāb/Mehrābe," which refers to a Miθraic temple in Persian.

Ferdowsī does not consider Sūdābeh's father as Iranian either, although he is from Hāmāvarān (understood to be Yemen, or possibly Egypt), where he is also a king. Some sources, on the other hand, propose the possibility of another origin for Sūdābeh's father. According to Tabari and Ibn-Balkhi, Sūdābeh's father is Afrāsīāb (Av. Fraŋrasyan, MP Frāsiyāv), the king of Turān, based in Samarkand.[13] It is striking that the term *āb*, "water," occurs as an element in all four elements of these father–daughter pairs: Sūdābeh- Afrāsīāb and Rūdābeh- Mehrāb. Unfortunately, the origins of all these names are unclear and we can only speculate about their symbolic meanings and their relationship to each other, though their mutual connection to water cannot be accidental.

Both fathers share a reluctance to give their daughters to the Iranian king. Wary of Iranian power, they resort to ruse to prevent this happening. The daughters, for their part, have very strong personalities and, once they are in love, they know what they want and fight for it.

Sūdābeh and Rūdābeh are both attributed with superhuman lifespans, like numerous other characters in the *Šāh-nāmeh* who have divine or mythic roots. They are connected as well by sorcery, being referred to as *jadū-zan* ("witch"). Both are said to be possessed of extraordinary beauty. All these features suggest an echo of surviving goddess myths and their attendant rituals.

The extraordinary beauty of these two women, moreover, is described in nearly identical terms, which are exactly those applied to other beautiful women in the *Šāh-nāmeh* as well: they are elegant and splendid, tall and beautiful, with dark long hair and black eyes. Does this description represent the ideal of feminine beauty for the Iranians of Ferdowsi's time, or does it harken back to an earlier period? In fact, while the physical characteristics of Iranian women in the tenth century are somewhat difficult to reconcile with this model, in many details, it closely resembles descriptions of goddesses in the Avesta.

In terms of personality, both Sūdābeh and Rūdābeh are determined and resolved. They both will stop at nothing to obtain the person whom they love. Ethically, however, the two women are polar opposites, representing opposing female models. Rūdābeh's love, being ethically sound, brings a positive result: She marries her beloved and gives birth to Rostam, the most important hero in the whole of the *Šāh-nāmeh*. Rūdābeh thus initiates a blessed family line. Although she is described as a demon-born witch, her life-giving role is nevertheless connected in a positive way with fertility. Sūdābeh, by contrast, through her unethical lust for her stepson, generates bad luck for her beloved; this ultimately results in her own death and his as well. She thus represents the opposing, negative aspect of the goddess, a bringer of death.

The myth of paired goddesses with opposing functions is frequently found in other Indo-European myths. The Vedic Aditi and Diti and the Scandinavian Freyja and Frigg are but two examples. Freyja and Frigg would seem at first glance to have little in common: Frigg is the one with positive features as a good wife with clear maternal role, while the other, known as Freyja and under other names as well, is a negative character, free in her sexual behavior, lustful in love, and yet, paradoxically, also related to childbirth.[14] In keeping with her overall negative character, Freyja was also associated with war and death, involved with magic and possibly male sacrifice.[15]

At the same time, like their Iranian counterparts Sūdābeh and Rūdābeh, Freyja and Frigg share certain characteristics—even their names may stem from a common root. Their identities continue to be a matter of debate among scholars: were they once a single goddess who came to be divided into two opposing aspects, or were they always distinct?[16]

Sūdābeh

Etymologically, Sūdābeh's name could mean "owner of illuminating or beneficial (from *sū*-) - water."[17] Kellens draws attention to √*sū*- (Vedic *śū*-) as the root of the word *Saošiiant*-, which means "to strengthen,"[18] but there is no evidence showing the connection between this and the beginning of Sūdābeh's name.[19] Justi presumes that Sūdābeh's name was Arabic and was modified to accord with Rūdābeh, but this hypothesis raises more questions than it answers.[20] It has been suggested that she may herself have originally been connected to a water goddess.[21] It seems more likely that the name is a recent invention, built to correspond with Rūdābeh, which is explicitly constructed with the words "river" and "water." Whatever the origin of her name, Sūdābeh's story bears considerable similarity to the Mesopotamian and Sumerian Inanna-Ištar myths, and is thus most likely extra-Iranian in origin.

Returning to the *Šāh-nāmeh* version, Sūdābeh is the beautiful wife of king Kay-Kāvus, a character who (as Kauui-Usan) is mentioned in the Avesta among those who perform sacrifices to Arduuī Sūrā Anāhitā (Yt 5.45). Sūdābeh also is stepmother of Siāvaš (Kay-Kāvus's son), or perhaps originally his mother. In Khaleghi-Motlagh's opinion, in the original version of the myth she was the mother who fell in love with her own son (which would have been unsurprising according to Zoroastrian custom), but since an incestuous alliance was no longer considered socially acceptable in the Islamic society of Ferdowsī's time the mother figure was transformed into a stepmother.[22]

In any event, Sūdābeh desires Siāvaš and attempts to seduce him, but he refuses her advances and avoids betraying his father. After a long narrative during which Siāvaš strives to prove his innocence in the face of Sūdābeh's lies, he is finally exiled to Turan, where he is unjustly murdered by order of the Turanian king, Afrāsiāb,[23] Iran's most notorious enemy in the *Šāh-nāmeh*. After his murder, a plant (referred to as *xun-e Siāvošān*, or later, *par-Siāvošān*) grows up through the nourishment of his blood, demonstrating his origin as a deity of vegetation. The martyr Siāvaš is later avenged by his son, who subsequently returns to Iran.

Sūdābeh's love story with Siāvaš is reminiscent of the Inanna/Ištar story of a goddess's tragic love for Dumuzi, which leads to his death and subsequent rebirth. Siāvaš is identified with Dumuzi, and in Central Asia where his cult thrived, there are, as Skjærvø notes, "traditions and archaeological and literary evidence for his origin as a vegetation deity."[24]

Sūdābeh's lustful behavior toward Siāvaš also bears many similarities with another Mesopotamian story of Ištar, this time with the man-hero, Gilgameš. Back to her story in *Šāh-nāmeh* when Sūdābeh first sees Siāvaš, she desires him and "her heart beat faster." After a series of events, she manages to see him in private. She tells him he could be the king after his father dies and that he could possess her. Then, in an attempt to seduce him, she removes her veil and invites him to be her lover, but she will be refused by Siāvaš later on:

(ŠN, stanza 275)
ze man har če xāhī hame kām-e to

bar āyad, na pīčam[25] *sar az dām-e to*
saraš tang begrēft va yek būse čāk
be dād-o nābud agah az šarm-o bāk[26]

Take any thing you want from me
I will do it. I will not disobey you
(Then she) got his head firmly (with enthusiasm) and kissed him
And did not remember any of shame and fear.
And tries to tempt him:

(ŠN, stanza 315)
fozūn zānke dādat jahāndār šāh
biyārāyamat yāre va tāj-ō gāh

More than what the great king granted you
I shall adorn you with the crown and thrown of kingdom.[27]
An incident from the Epic of Gilgameš is strikingly similar:
And Ištar the princess raised her eyes to the beauty of Gilgameš.
"Come to me, Gilgameš, and be my lover!"
She tries to tempt him:

"When you enter our house
The wonderfully-wrought threshold shall kiss your feet!
Kings, nobles, princes shall bow beneath you."[28]
But Gilgameš (like Siāvaš) refuses Ištar's advances, reminding her of the fate of
   her previous lovers, including the vegetation god Dumuzi:
For the Dumuzi the lover of your youth
   you decreed that he should keep weeping year after year.

Thus, in both myths, the male heroes Gilgameš and Siāvaš refuse the advances of aggressive women. Ištar, like Sūdābeh, is a lustful woman more interested in sex than love. It seems that Sūdābeh represents just one aspect of the original goddess from which she is derived: an assertive personality with a strong sexual desire, vengeful, and not faithful to her husband. Her passion for Siāvaš, being illicit, is devoid of fertility. Instead, it brings only bad luck and death.

Siāvaš (Av. Siiāuuaršan-, MP Siyāwaxš) is mentioned in the Avesta in Yt 13.132 and Yt 19.71 as a *kauui-* whose name contains *aršan-*, "male." In the *Šāh-nāmeh* version of the legend of Siāvaš, the Mesopotamian goddess Ištar appears to have been replaced by a negative female figure, a woman of sorceress roots Sūdābeh, whose improper behavior and morals echo Ištar's.

The *Šāh-nāmeh*'s Siāvaš is the son of the Iranian king, Kay Kāvus, whose Avestan name is *Kauui-Usan-*, perhaps originally denoting a priest associated with a spring or well. Kay Kāvus's ancestor is Kawād, whose birth myth also connects him to water; according to the *Bundahišn*, Kawād was found in a chest (*kēwūd*) floating Moses-like in a river:

(GBd XXXV.28)

Kawād aburnāy andar kēwūd-ē(w) būd u-šān pad rōd be hišt pad kabāragān be afsard. Uzaw be dīd ud stad ud be parward ud frazand ī windidag nām nihād.

The infant Kawād was left behind chest in a river, (he) was extinguished (from cold) in the vessel. Zāb saw (him), and got (him), and raised (him) and called (him) the "found" child.[29]

This passage recalls the birth myth of Sargon II (who, incidentally, claimed that Ištar was his lover), according to which the future king was given to the river by his druid mother.[30]

As noted above, the Sūdābeh/Siāvaš story is strongly reminiscent of the Ištar/ Dumuzi myth. It is significant that in all the various versions of this myth from the Mediterranean to Central Asia, the vegetation god is not a warrior but rather a martyr, a symbol of innocence. An explanation for this could be that when the warlike Indo-Iranian raiders first began their incursions into southern Central Asia during the second millennium BCE rituals and beliefs associated with a water-river goddess and her son/lover vegetation deity were already widely spread among the people, most likely reaching the region through trade with Mesopotamia. Over time the Iranian settlers absorbed and combined these local figures with their own deities, notably Anāhitā.

One of the main components of the annual ritual cycle connected with this myth was mourning and lamentations over the death of this divine lover/son, who was considered a martyr. Women were prominent in these mourning ceremonies, screaming and beating themselves in grief in imitation of the goddess herself who has been deprived of her son.[31]

In particular, women's tears, being symbolic of water, were important. In ritual terms, the role of women in reenacting the goddess's grief also helped her divine son to return, their tears symbolizing the rain needed to bring the soil back to life. Groups of villagers with blackened faces, representing the martyred god, would appear to herald his return. In some cases, the villagers would wrap up a tree in a shroud, then raise it up and recite prayers and invocations.

These grief rituals, dramatic as they were, at the same time served as a kind of ushering in of the martyred god's subsequent rebirth.[32] At least some of the Iranian tribes who came into contact with Mesopotamian peoples by the end of the second millennium BCE adopted these mourning ceremonies, which is strange since mourning is frowned upon in Zoroastrianism. The vegetation god embodied by Dumuzi in the Mesopotamian myth survived in Iran and Central Asia under the name of Siāvaš, especially in Bukhara where his cult was prominent. In Xwarazm and Sogdiana, where people worshipped Inanna under the name of Nanai, the important role of the martyred vegetation deity Siāvaš is not surprising. What seems likely in the case of Siāvaš and the mourning rituals associated with him is that this encounter and influence from Mesopotamia had already entered Iranian culture (presumably via the trade routes) by the time of the composition of the Avesta.

In eastern Iran the martyred vegetation god gradually evolved into Siāvaš, who is known to have been the focus of an important cult in pre-Islamic Bukhara. People there sacrificed a rooster to him before dawn on the annual occasion of Nowrūz, the Iranian New Year.[33] The rooster is a sacred animal in Zoroastrian tradition, and it would seem that like the martyrdom of Siāvaš/Dumuzi, its sacrifice was considered necessary for the rebirth of nature and for fertility in the new year.

Siāvaš was an important figure among the Sakas and Sogdians, and came to be celebrated in some Iranian texts, most famously through his story in the Iranian national epic, the *Šāh-nāmeh*. In Bukhara especially, annual mourning rituals in honor of Siāvaš (or Dumuzi, as in the well-known mourning scene depicted on a wall painting from Pendjikent)[34] had a major importance right into Islamic times. Even in present-day Iran there are some mourning ceremonies for Siāvaš (Sāvūšūn), which can be traced to him.[35]

Parallels among the different versions abound. In the mourning ceremony for the Greek god Adonis, devotees carried a tree, symbolizing and connecting Adonis to the vegetation deity. Similarly, in the story of Siāvaš, following his murder his blood pours into the soil, from which a plant later grows. Moreover, according to the *Šāh-nāmeh*, "water" actively mourns Siāvaš's death:

> (ŠN stanza 2255)
> *be kīn-e Siāvaš sīah pūšad āb*
>
> *konad zār nefrīn bar Afrāsīāb.*[36]
> Due to hatred regarding Siāvaš the water wears black
> (And) in agony curses Afrāsīāb.

And when he is martyred, a plant grows up from his blood, which in Ferdowsī is still growing:

> (ŠN stanza 2255)
> *be saat gīyāī bar āmad čo (ze) xūn*
> *az ānjā ke kardand ān xūn negūn*

gīyā rā daham man konūnat nešān
ke xāni hamī xūn asyāvašān.[37]

A plant grew from his blood simultaneous
From the place that the blood poured down
I can show you the plant now
Whose name is the "blood of Siāvaš."

The stories of Adonis and Atis in Greece and Isis and Osiris in Egypt, along with their annual ceremonies, are but two examples having the same basic pattern. As noted in Chapter Three, there is also an earlier Sumerian myth about the descent of a goddess, Sud, into the underworld before being married to the god Enlil—recall that Enlil afterward changes the goddess's name to Ninlil. She was sometimes identified with Ištar, and her original name, Sud, could be connected to Sūdābeh. It has even been suggested that there is some connection between an old Chinese legend (presumably transmitted by the nomadic Sakas) and the story of Sūdābeh.[38]

In another parallel, during the Greek rituals in honor of Adonis, people grew sprouts, a form of sympathetic magic intended to revive the vegetation god. After completing the ritual they threw the sprouts into the water, which would take the vegetation deity back to his lover. An echo of this ritual can be seen today during the Iranian Nowrūz ceremonies, which include growing sprouts that are eventually cast into flowing water on *Sīzdah be-dar*, thirteen days after the New Year itself which falls at the vernal equinox.

The ritual mourning commemorating the death of a young, beautiful, virtuous man continues in Shi'ite Iran and Iraq during the 'Ashura ceremonies remembering the death of the prophet's grandson, martyred at Karbala in 680 CE. In some parts of Iran, mourners carry the figure of a tree, just as ancient Greeks did for Adonis. Across nearly all of Iran, during this annual mourning period, mourners have a ritual called *naxl-gardanī* ("palm-handling"), in which they carry a metal or wooden symbol of the palm almost as large as an actual tree itself. This "palm" is sometimes covered in black fabric.

Although in each of these myths, the god's death is due to his goddess-lover, ironically enough they are reunited following his rebirth. Modern thinking perhaps finds it difficult to accommodate the ambivalence in this divine love relationship, but we may assume that those who believed in these myths seem to have accepted the inevitable connection between death and regeneration observed in nature. By the Islamic period thus, the negative portrayal of Sūdābeh never got Siāvaš back; instead, Siāvaš's son returned to Iran, and she paid the ultimate price for her uncontrolled lust when Rostam killed her in revenge.

Certain texts from the Islamic period, including the *Fārs-nāmeh* of Ibn Balkhi and the *Tārīx-e Tabarī*, describe Sūdābeh as a witch who uses magic.[39] She is similar in this way to the Indo-Aryan goddess Diti, who also used magic. Diti's uncontrolled lust for Kašyapa is strikingly similar to that of Sūdābeh's for Siāvaš.

The Pahlavi *Book of* Ardā Wirāz (Righteous Wiraz) describes in vivid detail the horrible punishment accorded to *ǰādūgān* "witches" in the afterlife, demonstrating that in Sasanian times certain women were accused of using magic (*ǰādūgīh*) and that this was considered a serious sin (AWN 5.8/35.4/76.5/81.5). While we cannot be sure exactly what was meant in those times by "using magic," it may well have referred to a knowledge of the properties of medicinal plants—a knowledge that was largely the province of women. The situation in Sasanian Iran may have been similar to that which Carolyn Merchant has described for medieval Europe, whereby women's knowledge of herbal medicine—and its associations with goddess-based rituals and religious beliefs—became a target of severe persecution by male elites seeking to arrogate both medical and religious authority to themselves.[40]

According to the Zoroastrian texts, sorcery was considered as a demonic power created by Ahriman, and its use as one of the greatest of all sins.[41] Similarly, in popular Iranian myths and folklore, sorcery was associated largely with women, just as in many other regions of the world. Even the birth story of Zaraϑuštra in the Pahlavi *Dēnkard* describes the prophet's mother as a witch, implying that the designation was not always necessarily negative but may simply have referred to a particular kind of knowledge (Dk 7.2.6). Again, the association could be due to women's knowledge of medicinal plants, which connected them with the healing function, one of the most common functions among the goddesses we have been discussing.

It is surely no accident that the *Dēnkard* frequently pairs its use of the word *ǰādūg*, "magician" with *dēw-yazag*, "demon-worshiper," an invective used by the Zoroastrian priests against people who had retained their ancient deities and associated rituals despite official attempts to impose Zoroastrian orthodoxy (Dk 5.2.4).[42] The following passage provides an example:

(Dk 5.9.9)

Dēw-yazagīh ud ahlaw-ganīh ud ahlamōgīh ud kūn-marz ud ǰādūgīh …
Demon-Worshipping, killing the righteous, heresy (in religion), sodomy (homosexuality), performing magic …

If we accept that there are some connections between Sūdābeh and any reflection of ancient goddesses (Ištar/Inanna, and possibly Anahitā), the question arises, did people fear that if their sacrifices to the goddess did not satisfy her, she might be offended and deny them the water their plants needed to survive? Was it this they feared, the destructive aspect of the goddess that came to be expressed in the negative portrayal of many water goddesses (and possibly transferred to Sūdābeh)? Or perhaps an even deeper ambivalence toward water itself, which nourished life but could also wash it away in a flood? Or, simply, is it that the freely expressed sexual desire of the ancient goddess was no longer accepted within the religious morality?

Rūdābeh

Rūdābeh's association with water is attested by her name itself: "she of the river water;"[43] one thinks immediately of the Pahlavi word for river, *rōd*, + *āb*. Her parents' names may connect them to water as well. It may be possible to find her mother's name, Sindokht, connected to Sin = Sind, a sacred river + *dokht* = girl. Her father, Mehr (Miθra) + *āb* (water), a "non-Iranian" king, is descended from Aži-Dahhāk, a demonic dragon who *guards* the water. Rūdābeh thus belongs to the demonic world, and is referred to as "demon-born" (*dēw-zād*), "witch" (*jadū-zan*); and yet, she is simultaneously described as the most beautiful woman in all the *Šāh-nāmeh*.[44]

In the *Šāh-nāmeh*, Rūdābeh is the lover of Zāl and the mother of the hero Rostam. She is a brave, beautiful woman who lives a long life, as is typical for demigods. She is not shy to talk about her love to her parents; she fights to obtain her beloved, Zāl, and in the end she is successful. Hers is a beautiful love story, which is Islamized by Ferdowsī. It contains highly romantic scenes, such as when she lets down her hair Rapunzel-like so that Zāl may ascend it as a rope. Her pregnancy with Rostam is extraordinary as well: as a fetus Rostam grows too big to be born in the normal way, so a mythological bird, the Sīmorgh, enables a Caesarean section.

Having a superhumanly long life, a descendant of the demonic world and a foreign royal dynasty, Rūdābeh's functions are related to love and beauty, strong will, and fertility. All of these aspects enable us to perceive her as a survival of certain goddess myths and rituals that existed in ancient Iran.

Another woman in the *Šāh-nāmeh* (found as well in many other sources[45]), Katāyun, is apparently a reflex of Anāhitā. She is actually named in one passage as Nāhid (as her original foreign name), and Katāyun being the name bestowed on her by her lover/husband Goštasp (a dragon-slayer hero).

(ŠN stanza 30)

pas ān doxtar-e nāmvar gheysarā
ke Nāhīd bod nām ān doxtarā
Katayūn-aš xāndī gerān-māye šāh
do farzand-aš āmad čo tābande māh.[46]

Then, the great emperor of Rum's daughter
Whose name was Nāhīd
Was re-named as Katayūn by the great king (of Iran)
And (he) received two children (who) looked like the radiant moon.

Again, she is daughter of non-Iranian king, emperor of Rum, and is thus a foreigner. Her story resembles that of an older tale from Media, the romance of Scythian Zariadres and the princess Odatise, from which it may ultimately be derived. This tale, as told by Chares of Mytilene, features Hystaspes (Vīštāspa) and Zariadres, presented as brothers who are the children of Aphrodite and Adonis.[47]

The story shows some similarities with the later Persian stories about Zarir and Goštāsp (Zairiuuairi and Vištāspa). The Avestan *Auruuaṭ-aspa* (Zairiuuairi and Vištāspa's father) is an epithet for the sun (*tīz—asp*, "he who has a rapid horse") and that the brothers might, therefore, originally have been solar figures.[48] Boyce has suggested that this myth may have been originally connected with a love goddess such as Anāhitā.[49] The princess Odatise's home is said to be on the other side of the Tanais River, which could possibly be the river Don; the tale might thus belong to the land of Scythians.[50]

All of these connections are of course speculative, but taken as a whole they suggest a compelling pattern. In Iran's tenth-century society that had become patriarchal and monotheist, popular culture retained and preserved echoes of earlier goddess-centered worship connected with water. In this case and in the story of Katāyun, the name Nāhid seems more likely to be symbolic of some feminine quality than to refer to the goddess as such. In light of our discussion in Chapter Five regarding Anāhitā and dragons, it is interesting to note the relationship in the *Šāh-nāmeh* between Katāyun (with her possible Anāhitā connection) and the hero Goštāsp who is a dragon slayer (in the *Šāh-nāmeh*), described as having a "dragon-shaped body."[51]

The foreignness, lifestyle, and assertive character of these various *Šāh-nāmeh* women all raise some interesting questions about their origins, especially in regard to the patriarchal, Islamic society of the tenth century in which Ferdowsī lived. Although these women's names are invariably Iranian, they are emphatically described as foreigners, usually as the daughters of kings outside of Iran (although in fact their fathers have Iranian names). Rūdābeh is from Kabul to the east of Iran. She is the daughter of Mehrāb, who is said to be a descendant of the dragon-king Żaḥḥāk, who is somewhat inconsistently associated with Arabs to the West. Sūdābeh is from Hāmāvarān, associated with the western non-Iranian lands as well. Meanwhile, Tahmineh, Rostam's wife, is the daughter of the king of Samangān in Central Asia.

Why is the foreignness of these women emphasized? Is it because it was traditional for Iranians to take their women from abroad? This is an anthropological question not directly related to our discussion, but we may ponder whether in the context of the *Šāh-nāmeh* this foreignness and their free and assertive lifestyles could be connected to ancient goddess-centered beliefs and rituals, which had been increasingly suppressed by the Iranian religious elites, along with the kind of independent and assertive female personalities they represent. The society of Ferdowsī's time presumably found these strong female characters inappropriate, making it preferable to label them as non-Iranians. Ferdowsī's audience would surely have had little appreciation for the notion that these characters actually represented survivals of ancient goddesses and their characteristics.

Female Beauty in the *Šāh-nāmeh*: Divine or Human?

Descriptions of women in the *Šāh-nāmeh* usually emphasize their tallness: they are said to be "as tall as a cypress tree," with long dark hair and gazelle eyes. Where do these measurements come from?

Kia believes that this measure of beauty comes from an old tradition in eastern Iran, before the coming of the Turks. In support of her argument, Kia cites the Panjikent paintings mentioned above, which date to before the seventh century. She points out that in both paintings the female figures are exceptionally tall, have dark long hair and "gazelle" eyes, not Mongolian eyes as is the convention in later Persian paintings. The goddess depicted in the Temple 2 painting wears a crown decorated with flowers known as *nenuphar*, literally "water flower." She also wears a belt. Kia, therefore, believes that this goddess is Anāhitā, reflecting standards of beauty of the time which served as a literary model for women in the *Šāh-nāmeh*, as opposed to the Chinese-Buddhist ideal of feminine beauty seen in later Persian paintings.[52]

This theory seems plausible, especially when we consider the influence of a society's cultural symbols and reference points on local artistic representation. Artists, like anyone else, are affected by and imbued with the myths and symbols of the culture in which they grow up. Often, whether knowingly or unknowingly, they use mythological elements in their artistic production. The various art forms of Iran, past and present, offer ample evidence of this influence. The Persian miniature painting tradition is rich with reconstructed scenes from ancient Iranian myths. Often a divine figure from prehistoric times is reimagined as a hero or a mythical king, with the myth associated with that particular deity being transposed to a greater or lesser extent onto the hero.[53] Yet, the characteristics typically seen in portrayals of legendary figures in Persian paintings depict ideals of beauty based on several traditions including their myths.

The depiction of Anāhitā detailed by the writer or writers of the *Ābān Yašt* represents an ideal of female beauty, which persisted over the centuries within the collective memory of Iranian society. Khaleghi-Moghadam considers that based on the *Ābān Yašt* and later in Persian literature such as *Vīs and Rāmīn*, wearing clothing made from animal skin must have been very popular in ancient Iran.[54]

Thus, certain female characters in the *Šāh-nāmeh* who behave in ways not typical for actual Iranian women of the time are in some ways perhaps reflections of goddesses, and their visual representations could, therefore, contain elements of a distant memory of divine beauty. Such characters are invariably described as tall, despite the fact that the popular taste in pre-Islamic Iran appears to have been for women of "middle height" with "small feet" and the "almond eyes," an ideal expressed in the Middle Persian text *Husraw ī Kawādān ud Rēdag-ē* (Xosrau and the Page):

(HR 96)

gōwēd rēdag kū anōšag bawēd, zan-ē ān weh ī pad-manišn, mard dōst, u-š abzōnīh nē, bālāy mayānjīg, u-š war pahn, sar, kūn, garden hambast u-š pāy kōtah u-š mayān bārīk ud azēr pāy wišādag, angustān dagrand, u-š handām narm ud saxt-āgand, ud bēh pistān ud

u-š nāxun wafrēn, u-š gōnag anārgōn u-š čašm wādām ēwēn ud lab wassadēn ud brūg tāgdēs, <dandān> spēd, tarr, ud hōšāb ud gēsū syā ud rōšn, drāz ud pad wistarag ī mardān saxwan nē a-šarmīhā gōwēd.[55]

Rēdag says (to Husraw) "live long"; a woman best be thoughtful, like her man (husband), and not be overweight, be of middle height, broad-chested, with a well-shaped head, buttocks, (and) neck, with short legs, a thin-waist, arched feet, long fingers, soft and firm body, snowy (white) well-shaped breasts and nails, pomegranate-color (red) cheeks, almond-shaped eyes, coralline lips, arched eyebrows, white (teeth), clean and fresh, with long, bright, black hair, who does not speak shamelessly while in bed with men.

The *Pairikās/Parīs*

Since in the *Šāh-nāmeh* we often encounter the word *"parī"* in connection with a female figure's name or characteristics, it is appropriate to consider this term more carefully.

The *Pairikās* (Phl. *Parīg*), as they are called in the Avesta, are mysterious supernatural creatures said to be created by Ahriman (Aŋra-Mainyu), Ahura Mazdā's evil adversary.[56] Accordingly, the *Pairikās* are mentioned in the Avesta as demonic creatures,[57] but the term is also used as an adjective, as in *aš.pairikā-*, "accompanied by great, mighty sorceress,"[58] and *pairikauuant-*, "accompanied by witches."[59] In certain Pahlavi texts, *parīg* are mentioned among the negative creatures, usually in the company of *dēw*s (demons) and *jādūg* (witches).[60]

In the Avesta and the Pahlavi texts, the *pairikās* cause demonic harm to human beings and the other members of Ahura Mazdā's Good Creation. The *pairikās* are connected to the Sun, the Moon, and the stars, and also probably correspond to meteorites.[61] It has been suggested that one of them, the *mūš.pairikā-*, is responsible for the eclipse of the sun.[62] The Pahlavi *mūš-parīg* is connected to the sun and to the moon, according to the *Bundahišn* (GBd V 5. 4–5) as noted in Chapter Nine. Skjaervø suggests, *Mūš-parīg* may originally have been considered the demon who causes the eclipses of the moon, as is indicated by its name Mūš meaning "mouse" but originally also probably "thief," cf. OInd. *muṣ* "to steal."[63]

The insistent emphasis against the *pairikās* as demonic creatures in the Zoroastrian texts raises the suspicion that they may have once held the opposite status, beings seen as positive forces. Sarkarati states that the word *pairikā-* means "fertile" (*pairkā* from PIE *per-* to give birth), and they were originally fertility goddesses related to sexual desire and fertility.[64] Mazdāpūr as well contends that *pairikā-* once referred to an ancient mother-goddess. Her transformation can be explained by an emerging Zoroastrian morality that could not accept her, and thus demoted the *pairikās* to the status of demonic creatures. It seems that the Mazdaean priests did not accept those who insisted on keeping the old goddess-worshipping rituals. At the same time, however, the *pairikā*s' positive aspects, connected to fertility, were transferred to Anāhitā.[65] This division of aspects could account for the *pairikā*s' ambivalent nature, in the texts as well as in Iranian folklore: they were beautiful women, but who could sometimes be harmful. According to certain stories in the Iranian folkloric tradition, traveling alone beside the springs or lakes where they live, one risks becoming entrapped in their enchantments (i.e., become *parī-zadeh*).[66]

Sharifian and Atuni have suggested that the Zoroastrians' enmity against the *pairikā*s may have been due to their connection with a ritual orgy, which ran counter to Zoroastrian morality.[67] In Iranian folklore the *pairikā*s are described as sensual creatures, emphasizing their desire to copulate with their lovers who are usually heroes. "Witches" (*jādū-zanān*) are often portrayed in the same way.[68] These considerations can help explain why Sūdābeh was referred to as a *jādū-zan* and a *parī*.

The connection between the *pairikā*s and the *jādū-zanān* is very close, and thus they have sometimes been considered to be from the same origin.[69] The *jādū-zanān*, however, are usually not portrayed as having the beautiful face the *parī*s have. In her archetypical shape, the *jādū-zan* is an old ugly hag with a disgusting smell; the best-known evocation of this is the *daēnā-* encountered by evildoers when crossing the Činuuat Bridge.

According to the *Tīr Yašt*, the rain god Tištriia battles against bad years, drought, and malaise, all of which are connected to the *pairikā*s whose efforts he defeats (Yt 8.10.39–40). In fact, alongside the struggle between Tištriia and the drought demon Apaoša, *Tīr Yašt* is notable for the enmity between Tištriia and the *pairikā*s. Ahura Mazdā is said to have created Tištriia specifically for this purpose, to overcome the drought and *dūžiiāiriia* ("bad year" or "bad harvest") brought about by the *pairikā-* (Yt 8.8.51–8.53).[70] At the same time, ribald and profane people (*dūž-vačah*) say that the *pairikā-* bring good years (*hūiiāriiiā-* "good year, good harvest") for them. In the following paragraph, it is clear that the same *pairikā-* who is said to bring the bad year is also referred to as bringing the good year:

(Yt 8.51)
⁺*auuaŋʹhāi pairikaiiāi*
paitištātaiiaēca paitiscaptaiiaēca
paititarətaiiaēca paitiiaogət̰.t̰baēšaxiiāica
yā dužiiāiriia yąm
maṣiiāka auui dužuuacaŋhō
huiiāiriiąm nąma aojaite

(…) in order to withstand,
crush, overcome
and return hatred to,
that Pairikā Dužyāiryā (the bad-year witch),
whom contrarily evil-speaking men
call by name Huyāiryā (good-year).[71]

Here, the ambivalent nature of the *pairikās* is clear. This tension may arise from the divergent views of the Avestan priests, who considered the *pairikās* to be demonic, and the general population, who venerated them for their fertility functions. The *Tīr Yašt* also applies the adjective *hūiiāriiiā* to the *pairikās*, further connecting them to fertility (Yt 8.50–51). Panaino further observes that the *Tīr Yašt* contains a battle between the fixed (i.e., stable) stars, led by Tištriia/Sirius, and the shooting (i.e., unstable) stars, which are led by the *pairikā dūžiiāiriia*- who bring drought and are opposed to the cosmic order and fertility.[72]

The passage above could also show that the *pairikās* were connected to water and rain (good year/fertility=water); perhaps this is why later it was said that they live in watery places. This gives rise to certain questions: Who exactly are these supernatural creatures believed by the general population to be responsible for bringing a good harvest year? Might they be survivals of ancient fertility goddesses, who continued to exist within popular culture despite efforts by the priestly class to exterminate them?

Reading between the lines in the Pahlavi texts can provide some clues. The *pairikās* are usually mentioned along with *yātus*, who are also female demons.[73] There is a story in the *Bundahišn* where *dēvs* copulated with Yima (Jam) and his sister and thereafter gave birth to the various wild harmful creatures.[74]

In the *Dēnkard*, a female *dēv* appears to Zaraθuštra as a beautiful woman and pretends to be Spandārmad (Dk 7.57–58), reminding of the *pairikās* since they can change their shapes. The *pairikās* are shape-shifters, as we can see in later texts and stories where *parīs* have the ability to appear as humans, animals, and even pomegranates! In the *Dēnkard* passage, despite her deceptive frontal beauty, the *pairikā*'s back is crawling with snakes and other demonic creatures.

The *pairikās* of the Avesta have been identified with *apsaras* in Vedic mythology. *Apsaras* are said to have been born from water prior to the *Asuras* and the *Devas*, and are connected to fertility, love, and sexual desire.[75] All these features may be compared with those of nymphs in Greek mythology, suggesting that certain aspects at least of nymphs/*pairikās* may go back to the proto-Indo-European period.

During the Achaemenid period and later, some tribes living in Iran were referred to by Herodotus as the Parikani. They are twice mentioned as paying tribute to the Achaemenids; Herodotus places them in Media and in southwestern Iran as well. He states that they played a role in Xerxes' invasion of Greece.[76] We do not know for sure that whether there is a connection between these people and devotees of the *pairikās*. Bivar believes that the stories relating to *pairikās* all trace back to the Iranian tribe(s) called "Parikani," who, according to archeological evidence from Persepolis, lived in central Iran, near Pariz (the name of which may be derived from them), Kerman and Jiroft.[77] In Bivar's view, the Zoroastrian Magi despised these tribes as infidels.

Malekzadeh, meanwhile, states that the Parikani people lived not only in central Iran around Kerman but also in Media during the Median period. He locates these tribes throughout Iran, from Greater Xorāsān and Xwārazm in central Asia to central Iran in Kermān and Media in the north and northwest, even to the south in Balučestān. Malekzadeh suggests that like the place-name Pāriz, Forδanē in Xwārazm was also an echo of the Parikani's name.[78] He considers that the Parikani tribes were likely Iranian but did not follow Zoroastrian rituals.

By the early Islamic period, it would appear that the demonic nature attributed to the *pairikās* by the Zoroastrian priests begins to fade, with beautiful, magical *parī* figures stubbornly persisting in popular beliefs in folk stories, legends, and fairy tales, where they are often said to bring bad luck to their lovers or to people whom they love. In the *Šāh-nāmeh*, *parī*s are often equated with beautiful foreign women trying to seduce people.[79] There are several well-known stories about such figures who make love with Iranian heroes and sometimes bear them children. Occasionally, they stand as an obstacle in the hero's path, or secretly steal his horse as a means of getting him to make love.

In many of these folktales that have entered the *Šāh-nāmeh*, *parī*s are portrayed as actual human women—in the story of Tahmīneh and Rostam for example—but their supernatural precedents are not hard to detect.[80] Often, the term *parī* is applied to them as a way of emphasizing their extraordinary beauty. Rūdabeh, for example, is described as *parī-ruy* ("*parī*-faced"); similarly, Tahmīneh and Katayūn are called *parī-čehreh*, with essentially the same meaning. For Ferdowsī, a *parī* is "always a charming and pleasant figure."[81] Throughout Iranian folklore, one striking feature of the *parī*s is that they are so numerous, like the nymphs in Greek mythology. This may be due to beliefs about the water-based goddesses being so widespread, with every tiny locality having their own particular expressions of her.

The *pairikās'* connection to water is significant. Even up to modern times, Iranian popular beliefs located *parīs* within waterfalls, springs, and rivers, where they were believed to swim, as well as in wells, *qanats*, and even beneath the stairs going down to the water tanks (*āb-anbār*) in private homes.[82] In the northern Iranian provinces of Gilan and Mazadaran even today, several locales bear the name *Āb-parī*, which according to local belief are swimming places for *parīs*; the waterfalls are said to be their long hair.[83]

All this evidence would seem to indicate that *parīs/pairikās* were originally either directly connected to a water goddess, or, possibly the memory of the water-goddess cult (Anāhitā) was so strong that it remained in the collective Iranian historical memory, mixing elements with others derived from ancient *pairikā-* worship.

Folkloric tales about beautiful *parīs* are one form of evidence for these survivals; place names are another. Throughout Iran one can find sacred places whose names contain *doxtar* ("girl, daughter"), *Bībī*, or *Bānū* ("lady"), and these are usually sites associated with water. Ironically, given the Zoroastrian antagonism toward *parīs*, there would seem to be an etymological connection between the terms *parī* and Pīr, applied to Zoroastrian sacred sites such as Pīr-e sabz and Pīr-e harišt, both near Yazd.[84] Significantly, both these well-known sites are connected with legends of a royal princess who disappeared into an arid mountainside from which emerges a stream, as if miraculously. It would appear that even these important Zoroastrian shrines, which are still the object of pilgrimages today, preserve some traces of the *pairikā-* cult condemned in the Zoroastrian texts. To cite just one such possible survival, Zoroastrians in Iran (and the "Irani" Zoroastrians living in India as well) seeking the fulfillment of a wish often perform a special ritual called *jašn* or *sofre-ye doxtar-e šāh-e pariyān*—the "feast of the daughter of the *parī* king"—in which they spread a tablecloth over an area of green grass, the ritual that is not generally done by men. In cases such as this, popular beliefs and practices would seem to have outlasted the diatribes of the Zoroastrian priests.

The many similarities between Iranian belief and practices connected with *parīs* and those connected with a wide range of Indo-European water goddesses support the likelihood that many of them have pre-Zoroastrian roots.[85] The ambivalent characteristics attributed to *parīs/pairikās* in Iranian tradition suggest the presence of two layers, perhaps an older water/fertility/healing cult overlaid by a later priestly attempt, seen in the Avestan and Pahlavi texts, to demote it.

Were the *pairikās*, as Bahar questions, originally goddesses related to water, vegetation, trees, and fertility in pre-Zoroastrian times?[86] Were they perhaps a reflex of the principal goddess among the native inhabitants of Iran before the arrival of the Iranian tribes, later partially absorbed into an emerging Mazda cult, which attempted to adapt and subordinate her into its own worldview?

It is admittedly difficult to draw a clear and absolute connection between the *pairikā*s and Anāhitā. The evidence is somewhat circumstantial, but it is strong: the *pairikā*s were originally connected to the cult of an ancient, multifunctional goddess(s) of desire and fertility who was worshipped widely and under different names during the prehistoric period in the lands Iranians came to occupy. The goddess (or goddesses) in question devolved certain functions to the *pairikā*s, with some eventually accruing to the Avestan Anāhitā.

Anāhitā and the *pairikā*s thus show some similarities with the other goddesses in the region and with each other as well. The ancient goddess rituals, which probably included sacred sexual rites, were transferred to the *pairikā*s. Mythological stories connected with the *pairikā*s, emphasizing their beauty, their desire, and their free sexual behavior, were rejected according to the morality of Zoroastrianism. The *pairikā*s thus possibly transferred some of their functions (and their popularity as well) to Anāhitā, who took over their role in the popular religious life of some Iranian peoples. Over time and due to the antagonism of the Zoroastrian priesthood, the *pairikā*s were demoted in myth and legend, even as their functions and attributes survived, whether in the cult of Anāhitā or through local rituals and beliefs. The very intensity of the Zoroastrian texts' antipathy toward the *pairikā*s bears witness to the strength and endurance among the general population. Schwartz states that "The transformation seen for the *parī* in Islamic Iran to a mere beautiful, and generally benign, fairy, may be understood from the marginalization of Zoroastrian lore and tradition, whereby the older topos of the *parī(g)* as a demoness capable of assuming seductive forms yielded the fairy figure."[87] However, the popularity of the *parī(g)*s even among Zoroastrians and their connection to water seems to support the likelihood that they might have originated as fertility goddesses, as has been previously suggested.

One may note in closing that in Iran today, Parī is a popular women's name, evoking supernatural beauty. Several other common names are derived from it, including Parī-čehr, meaning "she who has the face of a *parī*."[88]

The *Dārāb-nāma*

From the Ghaznavid period there is a lengthy tale[89] about Dārāb, a mythical Iranian king, which includes a version of the Iranian Alexander romance. Dārāb was the son of Bahman, and his story has been narrated in some books such as the *Tārīx-e Tabarī, Mojmal-al tavārīx val-qasas*, and the *Šāh-nāmeh*.

The Dārāb story has ancient roots in pre-Islamic Iran. Like Moses and Qobād, Dārāb was abandoned in a river at birth. More significant to our study, it features three women who are related to Anāhitā. Dārāb's wife, Nāhīd, is daughter of Philip of Macedon and mother of Alexander. The name of the second woman is Ābān-doxt ("daughter of the waters"), and the third is her daughter, Būrān-doxt. In the *Dārāb-nāma*, Būrān-doxt is associated with water and shows a number of Anāhitā's iconographic characteristics.[90]

Hanaway believes the character of Būrān-doxt in *Dārāb-nāma* "is a popular representation" of Anāhitā, noting that it is unusual in Iranian epics for a heroic character to be as closely identified with a natural element as Būrān-doxt is with water. Her mother, Ābān-doxt, resides at Estakhr. It is Būrān-doxt who proclaims Alexander King of Persia (similar to Anāhitā's investiture of Narseh), and his seeing her bathing naked in the river can be interpreted as "a symbolic visit of Alexander to the great Anāhitā shrine at Estakhr, and his being granted a boon by the goddess."[91]

Būrān-doxt is associated with doves, hawks, and fish (possibly like Anāhitā). And like Bibi Šahrbānū, she flees foreign invaders by taking refuge in a mountain cave which miraculously opens to her. Moreover, the first component of her name, Būrān, may be related to one of Anāhitā's horses. All of these three related women and their characters together suggest a memory or survival of an Anāhitā cult in eastern Iran.[92]

Echoes of the Water Goddess and Water Rituals in Islamic Iran

As a general rule, water rituals are related to the magical practices found in myths for the control of water. Such rituals were often meant to encourage the rain to begin and turn into rivers, which should be overflowing with water. Ancient people believed that if they wanted nature to do an action, it should be encouraged through the performance of a sacred ritual. Thus, the infusion and sprinkling of water would have encouraged nature to repeat the action in its own way: that is, by raining.

In a dry country where water had always been a problem, it is not difficult to find rituals connected with it. Iranians have long been famous for their "paradise" gardens, artificially constructed oases of green in an almost dry country, kept alive by the channeling of mountain snowmelt through underground channels (*qanāts*). Iranian arts and handicrafts, moreover, feature vegetation designs which fill every empty space. All over the arid plateau of central Iran, even poor families have always had a rug in their house, thereby bringing a small reflection of paradise into their home. The need to symbolize the garden is profound, a way of coping with life in a land where water is scarce.

A number of water rituals that continued to be practiced in Iran in Islamic times are attested in historical sources. Some are still seen in Iran today, while others appear to have disappeared. As mentioned in Chapter Eight, an interesting discovery was made in 2001–2005, in two copper mines (Čale Ğār 1 and 2) in the region of Vešnave in the Iranian Western Central Plateau. Archaeologists detected a sacred cave with a small lake inside, showing indications that water rituals had been practiced there over a long period of time from around 800 BCE until the eighth century CE. These archaeologists found thousands of ceramics, jewelry, and other objects, which had all been deposited purposefully into the water. These objects also included a single bronze two-winged arrowhead.[93] The fact that this cave with its subterranean lake clearly served as an underground shrine where water-based rituals were carried out offers proof that these ceremonies did, in fact, happen in Iran. The objects found in the water were almost certainly offerings made to a water deity who, in this Iranian context, was presumably Anāhitā, and the situation resembles that of sites associated with water goddesses found all across Europe as discussed in Chapter Two.

The description of the *Čahār-šanbeh sūrī* ritual found in the seventeenth-century travelogue of Adam Olearius differs considerably from what one sees in Iran today. According to what he saw in the villages of Šamāxī and Darband, Iranians believed it to be a day of a bad luck. In order to avoid this bad luck, the villagers carried water from springs and sprayed it on their houses and on themselves; they believed that this water would wash away the bad luck of the day and change it to good luck. They tried to do this before sunrise or before noon.[94]

Olearius also mentions some ancient ruins connected to the sacred water (and thus possibly to Anāhitā), consisting of some tall but crumbling walls which remained at the top of a tall mountain, Mt. Barmakh-Angosht in Šamāxī which he personally visited. Olearius believed that in the past there must have been a large building there. Inside the walls he saw a spring with walls around it, apparently a temple.[95]

Iranian Shi'i folklore contains echoes of water rituals that may have been connected to Anāhitā in the past. For example, since water was said to have been the dowry of the prophet Muhammad's daughter Fatima (who in this case possibly replaced Anāhitā in the popular imagination), it should not be defiled. In Islamic tradition, it has been mentioned that the angels will sift the waters, and if they see any pollution they will curse the person who has caused it.[96]

In Tajikistan today at the eastern edge of the Iranian world, numerous survivals of ancient rituals are still practiced in connection with the water goddess in her Islamicized form as Fatima, the daughter of the Prophet. At a site known as Chehel Chashmeh, near the town of Shahr-e Tuz in the southwestern part of the country, where Fatima's husband Ali (the Prophet's cousin) is believed to have passed, women bring large containers to collect water they believe to ensure pregnancy and health. Still further east, in the Wakhan corridor along the Tajik-Afghan border is a site called "Bibi Fatima Hot Springs," situated in a cave on the mountainside near the village of Yamchun. Women must enter the cave completely naked and immerse themselves in the water, then touch the walls of the cave with their hands; when they emerge, they must not dry themselves with towels but rather allow the air to dry their bodies. They believe that in this way they can be assured of getting pregnant,[97] clearly an Islamicized form of an older practice associated with a water goddess.

This ritual also seems possibly related to the Zoroastrian myth according to which a young girl will bathe in the lake, which has preserved the seeds of Zaraϑuštra kept by Anāhitā, and thereafter give birth to his second son and second savior (discussed in Chapter Eight). Moreover, it reminds us of the Celtic goddess "Sulis" and her sacred spring in Bath in England with its hot mineral water, *Aquae Sulis*, which remains a popular tourist site to this day, appears to have served as the principal connection with the goddess, where her devotees requested her support (as discussed in Chapter Two).

Other locally surviving rituals would seem to have little connection with Shi'ism, but they are invariably connected to women. In the Sabzevar region of Khorasan, there is a ritual where women sprinkle water onto children from the rooftops. The fact that they sprinkle water from heights is surely significant, since it recalls Anāhitā flowing down from the celestial mountain as described in the *Ābān Yašt*.

In the traditional belief of people in small towns and villages, the waters and rivers have gender. If a river is roaring and clamorous, then people believe it is a male river; if calm, it is female. Kamreh near Khomein in Isfahan, Abadeh in Fars, and some places in the provinces of Čahār Mahal and Baxtīārī and Lorestan are examples.[98]

Some *qanāt*s (underground channels for irrigation) and wells have traditionally been considered sacred, and people believed their water to have healing properties.[99] Like rivers, some *qanāt*s in Iran have been recorded as having a gender. This is particularly noteworthy in light of the fact that in some Pahlavi texts Anāhitā possesses both genders.[100] Local people recognized the gender of *qanāt*s in different ways. In some locations, such as villages around Arak in central Iran, if the person who drilled the ground had soft-skinned hands then the *qanāt* was considered female; if his hands were rough, then the water was male. Other determinations included the amount of minerals in the water, or even the water's level. In some villages people believed that if the flow of a *qanāt* was variable, then it was male; otherwise it was female. This latter point brings to mind the fact that in the *Ābān Yašt*, Anāhitā's flow is said to be invariable, or constant. In practical terms, a variable "male" *qanāt* could cause problems; thus, the water needed to "marry to a woman" in order to become reliable.

Even today in Iran one can find "*qanāt* weddings."[101] An Iranian historian of the Qajar period, E'temad al-Saltaneh (1843–1896), mentioned this ritual as well. According to him, if a male *qanāt* does not have a wife it will go dry. People should, therefore, marry the *qanāt* to a woman (sometimes an old woman), and this woman should bathe naked in the water at least once a month.[102] Villagers celebrated this ritual exactly like a wedding, and at least one Qajar-era photograph exists of one of the "brides."[103] The main point of the ritual appears to have been for a woman to bathe in the *qanāt* (or natural stream), and for the villagers to offer food as a sacrifice to water, following an old tradition. It is possible that the idea of marrying the "male" *qanāt* was a later addition to the older ritual; it is also possible that at an earlier time the "bride" was a young girl, and only in later times replaced by a widow or old woman. On the other hand, in some villages around Yazd, a young man was married to a "female" *qanāt*.

In Sistan, another ritual existed whereby a woman was presented as a bride to Lake Hamun, in which she would bathe. This ritual, in which the bride is referred to as "Ušēdar," is clearly related to the Zoroastrian myth according to which a young girl will bathe in the lake, which has preserved the seed of Zaraθuštra, and thereafter give birth to his second son and second savior, referred to in the texts as Ušēdar.[104]

In several places in Iran on the occasion of the Islamic feast of sacrifice (*'Eid-e qurbān*), people perform the prescribed sacrifice of a lamb on the bank of a river or stream. They believe that this ceremony will give them blessing by bringing more water in the year to come. Thus, we see the Islamization of an ancient practice, whereby sacrifices were performed beside riverbanks to Anāhitā.

Another interesting ritual connected to water, *Čak-o-dūleh*, still exists among Zoroastrians in Iran.[105] Performed by a woman, this ritual is believed to bring good fortune and well-being to those who perform it. A small personal object (such as a bracelet or ring) is placed into a ceramic jar or a large pot full of water. The jar or pot then is covered by a cloth and placed under a myrtle or a pomegranate tree for the night where "it cannot see the sky/sun." The following afternoon a young virgin girl retrieves the objects from the water and returns each to its owner, while the other women recite poetry.

One may observe that placing the objects into jars symbolizes creating a cave-like or womb-like situation for the water, while the presence of women and a tree connects the ritual to the water to the notion of fertility. The personal objects are like the offerings made to the water, but in this case they are returned and blessed.

It is also interesting that the ritual is performed at night, reminding us of stanzas 94–95 in the *Ābān Yašt* where Zaraϑuštra asks Anāhitā that what would happen if her worship ceremony were to be performed by *daēuua*-worshipers after sunset. This surviving ritual would seem to be an example of Iranians preserving their ancient beliefs and practices, including a nocturnal sacrifice to the waters. In this respect, the *Čak-o-dūleh* ritual could be a sublimated continuation of the kinds of water/cave sacrifices discussed in Chapters Three and Six.

As in many cultures, in Iran bringing water from the local spring has traditionally been a woman's duty. Villagers in Xor and Biābanak in central Iran also perform a ritual of sprinkling with water, where the women go to the spring and the men spray water on each other. It is surely not accidental that so many springs around Iran have names that include the component *doxtar* ("daughter," or "girl").

Likewise up to the present day, certain folkloric tales of the islands of the Persian Gulf speak of "sea-*parīs*" (*parī-daryā'ī*), who bring good luck and calm weather.[106] To cite other possible survivals, we may recall that the tradition of "laying the *sofreh* (spread)" in Iran where traces of the ancient water-goddess rituals can often be detected. Zoroastrians in Iran (as well as the "Irani Zoroastrians" who migrated to India in nineteenth century) seeking the fulfillment of a wish often perform a special ritual called "*sofre-ye doxtar-e šāh-e pariyān*"—the "Feast of the Daughter of the King of the *Parīs*"—in which they spread a tablecloth over a specific area. This ritual cannot be performed by men.

The Parsi writer Firoza Punthakey-Mistree mentions an Indian version of this ceremony called "*sofre-ye šāh pariyā*" and another ritual with the same concept called "*sofra naxod-e mošgel gošāy* Vahram Izad" ("the spread of the problem-solving nuts") among the Zoroastrians in India.[107] Surprisingly, in the Indian name of the "*sofre-ye šāh pariyā*" the "daughter" is removed; nevertheless, traces of the water goddess are still noticeable. On the tablecloth, which is spread over the ground, there are many items including the sacred fire ("referred to as *pādšāh sāheb*s-King/Sire, and are believed by some to have the ability to communicate and grant wishes"[108]) and various foods (some of which are clearly related to fertility, fried eggs, for example).

The ceremony is performed by women at home, and foods are cooked for an unspecified deity. After completing the ritual the people pass a hand-held mirror among the participants. They each look into the mirror, and one by one they make a wish. Then they put their hand in a bowl of water and put their wet fingers to their faces. Looking in the mirror and then touching the water and putting it to the face would seem to be an imitation of some older rituals which one presumes were performed beside rivers, lakes, and springs, where one could have seen the reflection of his or her own face. Moreover, some of the food items used in this ceremony are afterward thrown into the sea. Punthakey-Mistree observes that although specifically Zoroastrian women of Iranian origin do these rituals, some Pārsi women have also adopted them during the past fifty years.[109]

In Islamic Iran, laying a *sofreh* and making a vow is very popular, mostly among women. The "*sofre-ye Bībī Se-šanbe*," the "*sofre-ye Hazrat Roghīeh*," and the "*sofre-ye Bībī Hūr*" are examples. Mirrors, fire (candles, lamps, etc.), water, and salt are common items in these rituals. In the "*sofre-ye Bībī Se-šanbe*—"the setting of Lady Tuesday"—after performing the ritual the dishes should be washed with water and this water should be thrown into running water. During the ceremony, the ritual's special story is told. No man is allowed to be present or to eat anything from the food. Even pregnant women are not allowed, in case their unborn baby is a son. One might even speculate that the storytelling component of the "*sofre-ye Bībī Se-šanbe*" could be a memory of the reciting of prayers. In any case, it is significant that ostensibly Islamic *sofreh*s in Iran also usually have something related to water.

Numerous water-sprinkling ceremonies existed throughout Iran, mostly in connection with the summer festival of Tīrgān, and in some places the practice continues even today. These ceremonies tended to be connected to Tištar/Tīr, the god of rain. In Mazandaran province in the north of Iran, a water-sprinkling ceremony related to Tīrgān continues to be practiced in some villages. This ritual is called *Tir-mā-sīzzeh-šu* in the Mazandarani language; however, while the month of Tīr falls in June according to the Iranian calendar, the Mazandarani ritual takes place in November. Abū Rayhān Birūnī, writing in the eleventh century, noted that Iranians also sprinkled water on each other during the New Year's ceremonies at Nowrūz. Perhaps the sprinkling of rosewater one sees at Nowrūz today has remained from that practice.

In general, water was considered female, and thus typically all of the ceremonies related to it, such as "asking for the rain," were performed by women, and sometimes men were not even allowed to be present. Even in rural parts of Iran today, women make female dolls for use in these rain-inducing ceremonies. The practice cuts across religious boundaries, being found among Shi'ites, Sunnis, and Armenian Christians. The doll is called the "water-bride"; it is sometimes accompanied by a male doll, used in the ceremony by young boys.[110]

In another echo of the ancient riverside sacrifice, at the end of Zoroastrian *gāhānbār* ceremonies, a portion of the sacrificial food is set aside for consumption by a dog (*qazā-ye sag*, "the dog's portion"); it is then dispersed into running water, and thus into nature. One Iranian Zoroastrian told us that when he was a child he volunteered to take some food and threw it down to the well for the water spirit.[111]

Moreover, there is a ritual connect to the Iranian New Year—Nowrūz—which occurs at the vernal equinox on or about the 21st of March, is the most important celebration of the year for all of Iranians. In every household, a table called haft-sin is laid out, with seven items beginning with the letter "*sīn*" ("s"). Each element in the rituals associated with Nowrūz has some symbolic functions and meaning. Sprouts are planted, which will be symbolically tossed into running water on the thirteenth day after Nowrūz, called "*Sīzdah be-dar*" ("The Thirteenth Outside"). All Iranians perform this ritual, which raises an interesting question: does this symbolic action have anything to do with the ancient water offering?

Recently, there have been reports in the Iranian media of some gatherings between young people in the municipal parks of a number of Iranian cities, organized mostly on Facebook, during which participants sprinkle each other with water. Perhaps these events are just meant to be fun, or perhaps they contain some ancient memory. Either way, the government authorities have found these gatherings threatening and have broken them up, making a number of arrests.

Some Iranian families maintain a ritual of running water on the occasion of Nowrūz: just before the moment of the changing of the year—calculated with astronomic precision and awaited with excitement by Iranians around the world—all the water taps in the house are turned on and left running and all the lights turned on. The New Year is ushered in with hugs, kisses, and cheers; sweets are passed around; and only then are the water taps finally turned off.

With the steady Islamization of Iranian societies from the seventh century up to the present day, the formal aspects of Iranians' religious life changed dramatically. Nevertheless, while Islamic norms including not just practices and laws but also symbols and ideas largely overwhelmed those of pre-Islamic Iran, they could not eliminate them altogether. Rather, many ancient Iranian myths and rituals were sublimated, sometimes to the extent that their original meaning and significance were forgotten. As is generally the case, the persistence of ancient cultural practices and beliefs tends to be stronger the further one is from centers of formal religious authority, that is, urban settings where "official religion" is articulated and promoted. Thus, rural areas are often fertile ground for ancient survivals. Moreover, being typically less involved in the production of formal religion, women frequently preserve old rites and notions to a greater extent than men.

With this in mind, it is not surprising to see how widespread one finds echoes of ancient Iranian rituals associated with the water goddess, Anāhitā, not just preserved in literature or in Islamicized forms where numerous adaptations to changing values and norms can be detected, but also throughout Iran today in the realm of popular traditions, especially among women. This process of sublimation and subtle survival represents the final stage of the transformation of Anāhitā as an Iranian goddess.

Conclusion

In this book we have sought to present a coherent narrative of how the Iranian water goddess known as Anāhitā evolved over the course of more than four millennia. These changes are most apparent in the textual tradition of Zoroastrianism, where Anāhitā's later portrayal in the Pahlavi texts is markedly different from how she originally appears in the Avesta. We have posed the question of whether this can be taken as a reflection of gender relations in ancient Iranian societies, or whether the presence of goddesses is merely a projection of male ideas about femininity. We wonder whether and to what extent during Sasanian times Anāhitā maintained her role as it had been articulated centuries earlier in the Avesta, and if so, whether this can be seen in any way as reflecting the actual position of women in Iranian society. Does her apparent demotion in the priestly Pahlavi texts indicate a corresponding diminution in the status of women? We cannot answer these questions with any certainty. It does seem likely that there was a discrepancy between the theological approach to religion (and specifically Anāhitā) represented in the Pahlavi texts, which were written or redacted by theologians and priests, on the one hand, and popular religion, on the other, in which the goddess may still have been a central figure of worship (particularly in fertility rites), despite the marginal role she seems to play in the official priestly sources.

We do not know for certain whether Anāhitā's importance in the religious life of Iranians over the course of three Iranian empires changed in any essential ways, or even how large a part it played in the overall religious life of Iranians. Finally, we cannot state absolutely whether or to what degree the deities, rituals, and myths of pre-Islamic Iran survived into the Islamic period, or if so, in what form. In the end, what we have proposed are suppositions and possibilities, which we have sought to support with coherent arguments, in the hope that they may serve to inspire further research in the future.

In our view, Anāhitā's historical development can be traced as follows. Originally, she is simply an Iranian goddess of water, mostly recognized by the rivers and lakes, analogous to many Indo-European river goddesses. Later, as a result of some Iranian groups migrating southwest into Elam and Mesopotamia, she acquires not just the traits of the local goddess, Ishtar, but also her centrality and her popular cult, elevating her to a new status, which is entirely at odds with the prior norms of ancient Iranian culture. Finally, with the coming of Islam she loses her formal place within the Iranian pantheon, yet traces of her survive especially in rituals and popular tales.

Rituals derived from offerings to water continue to be made by contemporary Iranians, Muslims, as well as Zoroastrians, even if they do not necessarily recognize them as such. The ancient Iranian water goddess has not been effaced by time, but still lives on in Iran, even after fourteen centuries of Islamization.

Epilogue

As the most important female deity in the Iranian pantheon, Anāhitā has been the subject of a number of studies, but none as extensive or encompassing as what has been undertaken in this study. Previous research on Anāhitā has tended to focus on specific aspects (such as linguistics or whether or not she is an "Iranian" deity), and has been largely limited to the periods of the three pre-Islamic Iranian empires. We, by contrast, have sought to incorporate the various questions addressed by previous scholars—alongside new ones of our own—within a cohesive narrative framework spanning four millennia up to the present age and drawing on a wide range of disciplines. In particular, reconstructing a proto-Indo-European water goddess through a comparison of Anāhitā with cognate figures from other cultures has not been hitherto attempted to the extent that has been done here, nor has the corpus of material on female literary and religious characters from the Islamic period previously been analyzed in terms of its possible connections to the Iranian goddess. In addition, we have advanced new arguments about the possible place of Anāhitā in Iranian and other Indo-European dragon-slaying myths.

Anāhitā emerges in history by the late Achaemenid period as one of the three principal deities of the Iranian pantheon, alongside Ahura Mazdā and Miθra; an important Avestan hymn, the *Ābān Yašt*, is composed in honor of Anāhitā, establishing her role within the Zoroastrian religion. During the course of this process she acquires additional functions, presumably from preexisting goddesses in the regions where Iranians came to live, from Central Asia (the Bactria-Margiana Archaeological Complex) to the Iranian plateau and Mesopotamia (Elamite, Sumerian, and Bablyonian). Variations on the Iranian Anāhitā are found in the religious cultures of neighboring lands, such as Armenia, Bactria, and Sogdiana. Her association with water enables us to connect her with the ancient Indo-European dragon-slaying myth as well as with the Zoroastrian savior figure, the Avestan *Saošiiant*.

The Sasanian royal family which ruled Iran from 224 to 651 CE was closely connected with the cult of Anāhitā, having been the hereditary custodians of her shrine at Eṣṭaxr during the preceding Parthian period; she remained the patron deity of the royal house throughout the Sasanian period. In the post-Sasanian

Pahlavi texts, her importance is much less than in the Avesta. Moreover, Anāhitā comes to be referred to as two distinct deities, Ardwī-sūr and Anāhīd, possessing both genders. This division and demotion are explained in light of priestly attitudes toward women and women's roles, particularly the construction of a "female" form of wisdom. We explain the ambivalence toward Anāhitā in the Pahlavi texts in terms of evidence of her connections to the planet Venus and to nocturnal *daēva* cults that were condemned by the Mazdaean priesthood.

With the coming of Islam her cult disappears, yet numerous aspects of it survive in female figures from Persian literature and through folk tales and rituals, usually Islamicized, which are often connected with water. In one important example, it is proposed that Sūdābeh and Rūdābeh, two female figures in Ferdowsī's tenth-century Persian epic, the *Šāh-nāmeh*, are mythological reflections of two aspects of female power that can be connected with the ancient cult of Anāhitā. Further examples can be found in Iranian notions of female beauty and in superstitions about fairy figures (Av. *Pairikā*s, NP *Parī*s), as well as in a number of popular rituals involving water which survive in Iran up to the present day.

In sum, this book schematizes the many progressive variations in terms of how Anāhitā was conceptualized and worshipped over time and space, in order to trace the goddess's development as a major figure in Iranian religion and the constantly evolving mix of her roles and attributes within culturally diverse communities throughout Greater Iran.

Notes

Introduction

1 Yt 5.6.
2 For a survey of temples attributed to Anāhitā in the Greek literature, see De Jong 1997, pp. 277–84; also see Chaumont 1989.
3 See Treve 1967, pp. 121–32.
4 Al-Barwari 2013.
5 Yt 5.1.
6 Mallory and Adams 2006, p. 433.
7 Y.5. and Rose 2015, p. 275.
8 Yt 5.85–7.
9 De Jong 1997, pp. 268–73.
10 Mallory and Adams 2006, p. 433.
11 Gimbutas 1982. For a critique of Gimbutas' methods, see Meskell 1995.
12 As early as a century ago, classicist Jane Harrison questioned exclusive reliance on male-authored ancient texts for the understanding of ancient religion. According to her, Hesiod's version of the Greek myths was deliberately revisionist, motivated by "the ugly malice of theological animus" (Harrison 1962, p. 285).

Chapter 1

1 The breakup of the proto-Indo-Iranian community, which is associated with Andronovo cultures of western Siberia, must have predated the earliest documented reference to their deities, which is found in a treaty from northern Mesopotamia between the Mitanni and the Hittites and dating to 1400–1330 BCE (Mallory and Adams 2006, p. 32). While most of the so-called Indo-Aryan branch moved southeastward into the India subcontinent, a small number traveled in the opposite direction and established themselves as the Mitanni ruling elite; this is proven by the fact that the names of the Indo-Iranian deities appear in the treaty in their Indo-Aryan form, demonstrating that the split from Iranian speakers had already occurred by that time (Thieme 1960).
2 Ehrenberg 1989, pp. 66–76.

3   The identification of Venus figurines with goddesses was first made by Johann
    Bachofen in the mid-nineteenth century (Bachofen 1861).

4   While a number of feminist scholars, most notably Marija Gimbutas, have
    argued that the predominance of female figurines over male ones is indicative of
    a goddess-based, matriarchal society, Douglass W. Bailey argues that, in fact, the
    majority of ancient figurines are "sexless"; according to him, the appearance of
    figurines should be seen as an emerging conceptualization of the human body as
    the "vessel of the human spirit" in Neolithic art (Bailey 2013).

5   Ucko 1968, pp. 43–4. Ehrenberg adds that they may have been intended to
    provide sexual satisfaction for the dead, or as substitutes for human sacrifices, or a
    deity who would protect people after death on their way to the underworld, or as
    images of ancestors (Ehrenberg 1989, p. 72).

6   For a discussion of the problems associated with dating and placing the proto-
    Indo-Europeans, along with methodologies for resolving them linguistically, see
    Mallory and Adams 2006, pp. 86–105.

7   Ohtsu 2010.

8   Shahmirzadi 1995, p. 136.

9   Witzel 2013.

10 Vahdati Nasab and Kazzazi 2011.

11 Archaeologist James Mellaart, who discovered the site, believed that the Neolithic
    religion of the region "was created by women," and that "The supreme Deity was
    the Great Goddess" (Mellaart 1964, pp. 30–1).

12 Ehrenberg 1989, p. 73.

13 This is the interpretation drawn by Wouter Henkelmann from his reading of the
    Persepolis Fortification Tablets (Henkelmann 2008).

14 Bahār 1997, p. 139.

15 Hinz 1973, p. 91.

16 The name "Elam" is borrowed from Hebrew (*'êlām*), which Greek *Aylam* derived
    from it. (Álvarez-Mon 2012).

17 Hinz 1973, p.18 and Bahār 1997, p. 137.

18 Hinz 1973, p. 44.

19 Hinz 1973, p. 42.

20 Hinz 1973, p. 42.

21 Hinz 1973, p. 44.

22 Hinz 1973, p. 42.

23 Potts 2013, p. 135.

24 Bahār 1997, p. 140.

25 Hinz 1973, p. 45.

26 Hallo and Simpson 1971, p. 28.

27 Kramer 1963, p. 3.

28   Bahār believed they had originally migrated from southern Iran. See Bahār 1997, p. 346.
29   These include Apsu, who was associated with all freshwater bodies, and Tiamat, the primordial goddess of the saltwater seas.
30   Crawford 1998.
31   Hinz 1973, p. 43.
32   Moore 2015, p. 31.
33   Stuckey 2001; Wakeman 1985, p. 8; Christ 1997, pp. 62–7.
34   Chaumont 1989.
35   Gnoli 2009, pp. 144–5.
36   Potts 2001, pp. 23–35.
37   Potts 2001, pp. 23–35.
38   Potts notes that "while it is true that Aelian (on the nature of animals XII.I.18) mentions a temple to Anāhitā in Elymais, there is no reason to equate this with the temple of Nane mentioned in II Maccabees." (See Potts 2001, p. 26.)
39   Bremmer 2007, p. 175.
40   Beaulieu 2018, p. 33.
41   Beaulieu 2018, p. 33.
42   Potts 2001, pp. 23–35.
43   Alvarez-Mon 2013, pp. 221–2.
44   Carter 2006, p. 325.
45   Gnoli 2009, p. 144.
46   Gnoli 2009, pp. 144–5.
47   Shenkar 2014, p. 120.
48   Grenet 2015, p. 132.
49   Grenet 2015, p.134.
50   Azarpay 1981, 134.
51   Compareti 2017, pp. 1–8
52   Azarpay 1981, 136.
53   Azarpay 1981, pp. 136–7.
54   Bremmer 2007, p. 176.
55   Potts 2001, p. 30.
56   Azarpay 1981, 134.
57   Rosenfield 1967, p. 88.
58   Azarpay 1981, p. 135.
59   Mallory and Adams 2006, pp. 431–5.
60   Aruz et al. 2007.
61   Herodotus, Book 4. 59.
62   Ustinova 1999, pp. 84–7.
63   Ustinova 1999, p. 87.
64   Jacobson 1995, p. 54; also Ustinova 1999, pp. 84–6.

Chapter 2

1   Bradley 2012, p. x.

2   Cunliffe 1997, p. 194.

3   Bradley 2012, p. 41.

4   In the Thames River, weapons from different periods have been found (Cunliffe 1997, p. 194).

5   Davidson 1988, pp. 25–7.

6   Green 1999.

7   Green 1999; Kitson 1996.

8   Ross 2005; Allason-Jones 1999.

9   Green 1999, pp. 26–40.

10   Boyce 1995.

11   Julius Caesar 1870, Book 6; also Cunliffe 1997, p. 185.

12   Cunliffe 1997, p. 185.

13   Allason-Jones 1999, pp. 107–19.

14   Cunliffe 1997, p. 199.

15   Sadovski 2017, pp. 566–99. Another word is *ap-, which also means the "current of water, river." We will discuss this word in more detail in Chapter Five.

16   Mallory and Adams 2006, p. 434.

17   Russell 1990.

18   In the domain of "waters and water-basins," one of the main words for "river, water" was *dānu- (*Av. dānu-*). See Sadovski 2017, pp. 566–99.

19   Sadovski 2017, pp. 566–99.

20   Mallory and Adams 2006, p. 126.

21   Spaeth 1996, p. 137.

22   Gibson 2013, pp. 76, 189; also Kondratiev 1998.

23   Frawley 2001; also Berresford Ellis 2002, pp. 25–31.

24   Hughes 2008, p. 166.

25   Ellis 2002, p. 25.

26   Cook 2010, p. 366.

27   Ellis 2002, p. 25.

28   Dexter 1990.

29   Guirand 1996, p. 232.

30   Bord and Bord 1985, p. 25.

31   Green 2004, p. 136.

32   Green 1992, p. 156.

33   Allason-Jones and McKay 1985, pp. 4–11.

34   Allason-Jones and McKay 1985, p. 5.

35   Jolliffe 1942, p. 58.

36 Cumont 2013.
37 Gordon 2015, p. 453.
38 Allason-Jones and McKay 1985, p. 11; also Hübner 1877.
39 Allason-Jones and McKay 1985, p. 10.
40 Jones and Mattingly, 1990, p. 277.
41 Miller 2012, p. 18.
42 Mallory and Adams 2006, p. 410.
43 Miller 2012, p. 18.
44 Yt 5.15.
45 Davidson 1999.
46 Berger 1985, p. 71.
47 Jolliffe 1942, p. 40.
48 Cunliffe 1997, p. 186.
49 This occurred with the Roman goddess Victory, who was equated to the Greek goddess Nikē; Jolliffe 1942, pp. 38–40.
50 Jolliffe 1942, p. 37.
51 O Cathasaigh 1982, pp. 78–9.
52 Gray 2009, p. 32.
53 Cusack suggests that Brigit might have been a common epithet for *all* the goddesses in pagan Ireland (Cusack 2007).
54 Jolliffe 1942, p. 46.
55 Jolliffe 1942, pp. 43 and 47–9.
56 Bitel 2001.
57 Jolliffe 1942, p. 61.
58 Jolliffe 1942, p. 61.
59 Jolliffe 1942, p. 57.
60 Strabo (64 BC to *c.* AD 24) 2014, Book XV, Chapter III, Section 14.
61 Jolliffe 1942, p. 42.
62 Jolliffe 1942, p. 58.
63 Jolliffe 1942, pp. 50–1, 54.
64 Hughes 2008, p. 229; also Berger 1985, pp. 71–2.
65 Rowley 1997, pp. 93–5.
66 Green 1999, pp. 26–40.
67 Cunliffe 1997, p. 198.
68 Green 1999, pp. 26–40.
69 Jolliffe 1942, p. 56.
70 Oakley 2006, pp. 10–11.
71 Green 1999, pp. 26–40.
72 Markey 2001.
73 Clarke and Roberts, 1996, p. 96.

74 *Metrical Dindshenchas*, v. 3, poem 2, Boand I.
75 Green 1999, pp. 26–40.
76 Kellens 1996.
77 Gavrilovic 2013.
78 The relief was kept in the National Museum of Pozarevac where it disappeared (Gavrilovic 2013, p. 251).
79 Green 1992, p. 17.
80 Green 1992, p. 18.
81 Cunliffe 1997, p. 199.
82 Cunliffe 1997, p. 199.
83 Green 1992, p. 40.
84 Including a pot filled of silver and bronze models of organs possibly to be healed by Sequana. (See Green 1992, p. 40.)
85 Davidson 1988, p. 17.
86 Green 2004, p. 47.
87 MacLeod 2011, p. 17; Green 1993; Ross 2005.
88 Allason-Jones and McKay 1985, p. 117.
89 Cunliffe 1997, p. 196.
90 Bradley 2012, p. 44.
91 Allason-Jones and McKay 1985, p. 10.
92 Media, p. 194.
93 Al-Ṭabarī (224–310 AH; AD 839–923) 1999, p. 15; also Nöldeke 1973, p. 17.
94 Nöldeke 1973, p. 4, n. 2.
95 Hubbs 1993, p. 20.
96 Tatár 2007; also A. Kernd'l et al. 1961.
97 Hubbs 1993, p. 20.
98 Ivanits 1992, p. 16.
99 Hubbs 1993, p. 20.
100 Doniger 1999, p. 1129.
101 Yurchenkova 2011.
102 Yurchenkova 2011, pp. 173–80.
103 Kuz'mina 2007, p. 105.
104 Russell 1986.
105 Russell 1987a, p. 250.
106 Strabo 2014, 12.3.
107 Chaumont 1989.
108 Russell 1986.
109 Russell 1986.
110 Chaumont 1986.
111 Chaumont 1989.

112 Boyce 1986.

113 Boyce 1986.

114 Russell 1987a, p. 241.

115 Bakuran 2014, p. 247.

116 Russell 1987a, p. 214. Also see Bakuran 2014, p. 248.

117 This information was provided by Zaza informants in October 2014 (personal communication).

118 Russell 1987a, p. 252.

119 Chaumont 1986.

120 Russell 2004, p. 383.

121 Suggested by James R. Russell, personal communication, March 15, 2015.

122 I am grateful to James R. Russell for providing this observation (personal communication, March 15, 2015).

123 Russell 2007.

124 Calzolari 2017.

125 Dumézil 1968–73; Belier, 1997, p. 10.

126 Belier 1997, pp. 217–27.

127 Hintze 2014, p. 233.

128 Wash Edward Hale has argued that in Indo-Iranian religion the term *asura* did not refer to a class of deities, but simply meant "lord" or "ruler" (Hale 1999). According to this argument, the sense of denoting a class of deities would be a later semantic development.

129 Brown 1978, p. 24.

130 Pintchman 1994, pp. 32–3.

131 Kinsley 1988, pp. 9–10.

132 Müller 1891, v. 1, p. 250.

133 RV 1.89.19; also Pinchman 1994, p. 33.

134 Hintze 2005, pp. 57–66, esp. p. 59.

135 The sole-created cow (Pahlavi *gāw ī ēk-dād*) is the fifth creation of Ohrmazd, according to the Zoroastrian texts (Boyce 1975, pp. 138–40).

136 Gignoux and Tafazzoli 1993, p. 36.

137 Müller 1891, p. 256.

138 The good/evil opposition of two sister goddesses and their offspring recall the Irish myths about the Children of Domnu and the Children of Dānu, mentioned above. An interesting parallel found in the later Persian epic tradition, the good/evil women Sūdābeh and Rūdābeh in the *Šāh-nāmeh*, will be discussed in Chapter Ten.

139 Petrosyan 2007.

140 Schwartz 2012, p. 275.

141 *Videvdat* I.3.

142   Gnoli 1993.

143   Benveniste 1933–35.

144   Bn XVII.17.14; Pakzad 2005, p. 224.

145   Mallory and Adams 2006, p. 434.

146   Müller 1891, p. 114.

147   Müller 1891, p. 115.

148   Brown 1978, p. 25.

149   Müller 1891, p. 113.

150   Watkins 2005.

151   Darmesteter also defines the word *dānu* as "water/river" (Müller 1891, p. 116).

152   Müller 1891, p. 114.

153   Lubotsky 2002, p. 11.

154   Lommel 1954.

155   Müller 1891, p. 61.

156   Boyce et al., "Anāhīd."

157   Boyce 1986.

158   In Boyce's words, "Harahvatī seems to have been the personification of a great mythical river which plunges down from Mt. Harā into the sea Vourukaša and is the source of all the waters of the world" (Boyce 1986).

159   Wilkins 1973, p. 71.

160   Bahār 1994, p. 200.

161   Ellis 2002, p. 25.

162   Kellens 2002–03, p. 323; also Skjærvø 2013a, p. 114.

163   Miller 2012, p. 18.

164   Nöldeke 1973, p. 17.

Chapter 3

1   The crystallization of the Young Avestan text occurred sometime between 600 and 500 BCE (Skjaervø 2003–04, p. 37).

2   Boyce 1982.

3   Boyce et al. 1986.

4   Skjærvø 1994. He gives the general structure on p. 211, and applies it to the *Ābān Yašt* specifically on pp. 213–15.

5   Skjærvø 1994, p. 215.

6   OInd. *ūrdhva-*, Av. *ərədwa-*. But compare Digor *urdug*, Iron *u̯r̥dig* "upright" (Thordarson 2009). It may be that at some remote time this was the name of a specific river, which gradually came to be deified.

7   Benveniste 1929, pp. 27–8, 38–9.

8   Lommel 1954, pp. 405–13.

9   Amouzgar 2001, p. 69.

10 Panaino 2000, p. 38.

11 Cheung 2007, p. 187.

12 Kellens 2002–03, p. 322.

13 Ottinger 2001, p. 360.

14 Malandra 2013, p. 108, n. 2.

15 Skjærvø 2013a, pp. 113–14.

16 Anāhitā also is said to descend down from "the height of a thousand men" (Yt.5.102), which further fits with her epithet *bərəzaitī* "high, lofty."

17 Skjærvø qualifies this, however, stating that the term derives from the Iranian root *spā-/sū-* (old Indic *śvā-/śū-*), which refers to swelling, presumably here in the sense of "overflowing with life-giving abundance." See Skjærvø 2013a, p. 114.

18 Hintze 1995, pp. 77–97.

19 Malandra (2013, p. 107) explains: "The key concept here is *āhōgēnišn*, "defilement," *āhōgēnidan* "to defile." The glosses are as follows:*anāhitā-*: 1) *anāhōgēnīd* (F5 only); 2) (*ardwīsūr*) *ī awinastāhita-*: *āhōgēnīšnīhāhiti-*: 1) Y.10.7 *āhōgēnišn(īh)*, 5.27 *āhōgēnišn* (*agarīh*); 2) Vd. 20.3 *pūityåāhityå* = *āhōgēnīdār*, 11.9 *āhōgēnišn* (*aβzar*)."

20 Boyce 1986.

21 Hertel 1927, p. 20, n. 1.

22 Gotō 2000, pp. 160–1.

23 Oettinger 2001, pp. 301–16.

24 Kellens 200–03, p. 323; see also Skjærvø 2013a, p. 114.

25 Myrhofer 1992, p. 716.

26 Malandra 2013, pp. 106–7.

27 Oettinger 2001, p. 360.

28 **an-āhitā-*, the compound *ā-hitā-* "bound."

29 Malandra 2013, p. 106.

30 De Vaan 2003, p. 66.

31 Skjærvø 2013a, p. 118.

32 Artaxerxes II A[2] Sa; Kent 1953, p. 154.

33 Ustinova 1998. Moreover, Dandamayev states that some personal names have been found in Babylonian documents which include "*ap-*" "water" as part of the name. "Appiešu" is one example (from an Iranian form **Āpaiča*, *āp* plus the hypocoristic suffix *-aiča-*). See Dandamayev 1992, p. 30.

34 Herodotus 4. 59.

35 Lincoln 2014, p. 185 (cf. Herodotus 4. 5).

36 Mark Hale, personal conversation, 2018.

37 Mayrhofer 1992, p. 81. Also see Cacciafoco 2013, pp. 73–5.

38   Mallory and Adams 2006, p. 126.

39   Mayrhofer 1992, p. 81; also Cacciafoco 2013, pp. 73–5.

40   Kitson 1997, pp. 183–240, n. 24. Yet another term, which could mean anything from a "river" to a "lake," is *wehxp* "body of water. See Mallory and Adams 2006, p. 127.

41   Sadovski 2017, p. 571.

42   Kellens 2002–03, p. 324.

43   Skjaervø 2011b, p. 85.

44   Skjærvø (2013a, p. 113) also subscribes to this interpretation, noting elsewhere (Skjærvø 2011a, p. 17) that her epithets "lofty, rich in life-giving strength, unattached" (or "unsullied") would seem to qualify an implied noun, "water" (explicit in Y 65.1).

45   *marəmnō*, athematic nom.pl from stem *marəmna-*; √*mar-* to "remember" (Bartholomae, *AirWb.* 1143), points to the priests who memorized the prayers. Macuch and Hintze: "One might consider that the final *-ō* is due to preservation in the oral tradition under the influence of the preceding *āϑrauuanō* and of the following two words which likewise end in *-ō* and stands for **marəmna*, the nom. pl.m. (with old collective ending) of *marəmna-*" (personal communication, July 6, 2017).

46   De Vaan (2003, p. 51) posits the stem **vaδairiiu-* and gives the translation "seeking marriage." This can be derived from **-iu-*, from a putative noun **vad-ar-* "marriage," containing the root √*vad-* and the Avestan *vāδaiia-* "to wed" (√*vad-* means "to conduct, lead"; the causative form connotes "marry"). Malandra also translates *kaininō vaδre.yaona* to "Maiden in marriageable position." See Malandra 1983, p. 126.

47   *carāitiš zizanāitiš*: the pregnant women whose time for giving birth is close and ask the goddess for an easy birth.

48   Yt 5.78: Some of the waters she made stand still, others she made flow forward. She conveyed (him) across a dry bed, over the (river) good *Vītaŋhaitī*.

49   Skjærvø 2007, p. 71 in "Zoroastrian Texts," unpublished typescript, https://sites.fas.harvard.edu/~iranian/Zoroastrianism/Zoroastrianism3_Texts_I.pdf.

50   Herodotus 4. 48.

51   Herodotus 4. 49.

52   There are some additional points to be made about the Sumerian roots of the river Ister-Danube, raising the possibility of a connection between this river and the Sumerian goddess Ištar. However, these are just speculations and we cannot go further without having more evidence. See Teleki 1967.

53   Nyberg 1938, p. 262.

54   Āsmān was divided into four spheres. The first (the level closest to the earth) was the star level (*star-pāyag*), then the moon (*māh-pāyag*), the sun (*xwaršēd-pāyag*),

and the *bālist ī åsmān*, the boundless light in the highest of the sky/Heaven (Pākzād 2005, IX, 2, p. 126).

55 Pākzād 2005, I A. 4, p. 26.

56 As discussed earlier, Sárasvatī, like Anāhitā and many Celtic river goddesses, was associated with both wisdom and warriors. (See Kinsley 1988, p. 57.)

57 *ažišca*, singular here, is used as plural noun, *aži-*, and Vedic *ahi-* is an Indo-Iranian word for "snake" and "dragon." *Aži* (*ažiš*) is a three-headed dragon in Yt.5.29. *Aždahā* (or *Eždehā*) is the modern Persian word for dragon. Here the word is translated as "serpents."

58 *araθnāišca/araθna-* It is not clear which insect this word meant to the author(s); to compare, the word *arāneus* in Latin means "spider." However, since the word *varənauua-* used in this stanza is translated by Malandra (1983, p. 127) as "spider" and by Skjaervø (2011a, p. 61) as "spinner," it is difficult to guess why the same meaning was repeated and which insects the author(s) meant. The word *araθna-* is used immediately after *aži-* "snake, serpent," and could be translated as "scorpion" which is actually in the arachnid group along with spiders. In New Persian (NP) these two (snakes and scorpions) are found together (as an expression) as harmful animals: "*mār va aghrab.*"

59 *vaβžaka-*: "wasp"; Cf. Pahlavi *wabz*, "wasp."

60 Hintze 2005, p. 59.

61 Or, as Oettinger (2001, p. 102) reads it, *saēte*; see also Kellens 1984, p. 91. Note that the subject of this sentence is omitted.

62 RV 7.95. 1–2: This stream Sarasvatī with fostering current comes forth, our sure defence, our fort of iron. As on a car, the flood flows on, surpassing in majesty and might all other waters. Pure in her course from mountains to the ocean, alone of streams Sarasvatī hath listened. Thinking of wealth and the great world of creatures, she poured for Nahuṣa her milk and fatness.

63 Yt 5.9.

64 Yt 5.1.

65 Yt 5.6.17–19.

66 Yt 5.13.

67 Yt 5.1–2.

68 *vīdaēuuąm- vī-* means to be opposite something.

69 Lommel (1954, p. 32) and Hoffmann (1975, p. 1/264) translate *āδū.frāδanąm-* as "stream increaser," considering that *āδū-* is related to the Avestan word *adu-* stream.

70 *gaēθō*. Oettinger (1983, pp. 36–7) translates *frāδanąm* as "the home increaser." *Gaēθō. frāδanąm* may be translated as "the world- or the being-increaser." In the Vīdēvdāt one finds this sentence: "*āat mē gaēθå frāδaiia*" (Vd 2.4); Ahura Mazdā asks Yima (Yima-xšaēta-; Vedic Yama) to increase his world for him. Throughout

the paragraph one finds the theme that "increasing" includes the development of the world. The similarity between the two forms suggests a similar meaning and concept; however, increasing the earth is Yima's duty and function, so that "world- and being-increaser" would seem to be more correct.

71   Skjaervø 2007, p.71 in "Zoroastrian Texts," unpublished typescript, see above..

72   Yt 5. 6.21–23; 7.25–27; 9.33–35; 10.37–39; 12.45–47; 13.49–51, 14.53–55; 16.61–66, 17.68–70, 18.72,74; 19.76–79; 20.81–83.

73   Skjærvø 2011a, p. 60 and Malandra 1983, p. 120.

74   Vāiiu is an ancient Indo-Iranian deity who is a hypostasis of infinite space, the atmosphere and the wind. Vāiiu is an ambivalent deity with two sides and functions. In *Yašt* 15, which is devoted to him, he appears as a mighty martial deity capable of protecting the creation of Ahura Mazdā. He can also take a deadly form, however, like the wind that brings both rain clouds (fertility) and devastating storms. Like Anāhitā, both good and evil characters fear him, and like her, he rejects his evil supplicants. And again, like Anāhitā, in the Pahlavi texts there is a clear separation and spacing between the Good Wāy (*Wāy ī weh*) and the Bad Wāy (*Wāy ī wattar*). Yima sacrifices to him on Mt. Hukairiia, where Anāhitā flows down at the height of one thousand men. The connection between these two powerful deities is considerable, but beyond the scope of the present work. The name "Vāiiu" derives from the verb *vā-* "to blow" (IE *√*h₂ueh₁*). Bartholomae, *AirWb.* 1358. Malandra 2014.

75   Yt 5. 8.29–31; Yt 15.5.19–21.

76   Yt 5. 8.29–31, 11.41–43.

77   Skjærvø 1987.

78   Yt 5.9.33–35.

79   Ahmadi 2015, pp. 238–9 and 356.

80   *mairiia-* is used in the Avesta as a negative adjective for Fraŋrasiian. It also is the demonic word for a "young man," in opposition to the Ahuric word *nar-*. These connections will be discussed in further detail in Chapter Five.

81   *hankaine*, from the stem *hankana- √kan-* "to dig," means "cave"—the underground fortress of Fraŋrasiian. His place in the *Bundahišn* is described as an underground dwelling made by magic, with four magical rivers and bright with the light of sun and moon (Bd XXXII.13).

82   Mallory and Adams 2006, p. 408; cf. Watkins 2000, p. 22.

83   Bausani 2000, p. 30.

84   Skjærvø 2003–04, p. 23.

85   Skjærvø 2011b, p. 64.

86   RV. Book 5.17.

87   Herrenschmidt and Kellens 1993.

88   Dandamayev 1992, p. 328.

89   Skjærvø 2011b, p. 65.

90   Herrenschmidt and Kellens 1993.

91   Herrenschmidt and Kellens 1993.

92   Zaehner 1955, pp. 14–15.

93   Zaehner 1955, p. 16.

94   Hintze 2014, p. 225.

95   *zaoϑrā/zaoϑra*: libations, sacrifice to water and fire.

96   *mišti zī mē hīm* ... Lommel (1954, p. 43) translates *mišti* as an adverb, "always." Note that in Pahlavi "always" is *ha-mešag*. Malandra, however (1983, p. 129), and Oettinger (1983, p. 118) both translate the word as "by/through urine," probably because in the Pahlavi translation the word *mešag* (urine) is used. Skjærvø (2005, p. 81) gives "For by (their) *care," adding the footnote: "Release of semen?"

97   *haēnā-* in Avestan normally refers to "the enemy's army." It is somewhat strange that here the term is used for Anāhitā's army. Perhaps the author(s) of the *Ābān Yašt* imagined that Anāhitā casts hail and snow upon the enemy.

98   *sūrəm/sūra-* is translated by Skjaervø (2011a, p. 62) as "rich in life-giving strength." However, the adjective would seem more appropriate in describing deities than beams.

99   *yeṅhe* could also be translated as "which," if we accept the word as *yeṅhe* gen. sg. n(eut) following *zraiiāi. vouru.kašaiia*. If we accept *yeṅhe* gen. sg. fem, then it follows Areduuī Sūrā Anāhitā and thus means "who."

100 Oettinger (1983, p. 41) and Kellens (1974a, pp. 104–6) both read this as *zuš-* (from *zū-*) and translate it as "hastily."

101 *uruuaiti-, uruuaṇt-* adj, from √*ru-* to roar (Kellens 1974a, pp. 104–105, and Idem 1984, p. 319).

102 *frašūsaṭ-* Malandra (1983, p. 120) translates this as "went away."

103 Verb √*stā-*; 3rd person, sing. middle; the participle of the present with √*stā-* shows a continuous action. *frauuaēδəmna*: adj. *fra+vaēd-* to find, "who is always to be seen."

104 The word *vaṇhāna-* is written in most texts as *vaṇhānəm* probably to coordinate with *frazušəm aδkəm vaṇhānəm*. The correct form would be *vaṇhāna* (nom. sg. fem), from √*vah-* to wear (comparing with the *frauuaēδəmna* at the beginning of the stanza) "dressed with a precious mantle" (Reichelt's translation). Oettinger (1983, p. 121) reads *vaṇhāna*. The next five lines from *arəduuī sūra anāhita* to *āzātaiiå* are a repetition of 5.78.

105 Both Skjaervø (2011a, p. 62) and Malandra (1983, p. 129) consider *frazušəm*, "with long sleeves," to describe the garment.

106 Skjærvø (2011a, p. 62) translates *bāδa yaϑa.mąm barəsmō.zasta*" as "Ever and again, when she (sacrificed to?) me with barsom in her hand." Malandra, on the other hand (1983, p. 129), gives "Holding barsom in her hand in the correct way."

(He probably follows *Yaϑa* as a conjunction, meaning "as," and *mąm* could means "measure," from √*mā* to measure. The combination *yaϑa.mąm* as an adverb could means "according to custom" or "the required measure," or as Malandra translates, "in the correct way.") *mąm* seems to mean "me," as Skjaervø translates. Kellens (1974a, p. 242) thinks that the phrase *yaϑa.mąm* with *bāδa* is used for emphasis.

107   *huuāzāta* adj.; analyzed as * *hu-ā-zāta* "noble-born" (*āzāta-* "noble").

108   Oettinger (1983, p. 121) and Kellens (1984, p. 287) both read *niiāzāna* (adj.).

109   Black and Green 1992, pp. 156–7, 169–70; also Noegel and Wheeler 2003, pp. 174–6.

110   Both Skjaervø (2011a, p. 63) and Malandra (1983, p. 130) translate *satō.straŋhąm* as "with a hundred stars." The word *straŋhąm* could be connected to "star." Oettinger (1983, p. 124) translates the phrase as "das hundert Schnüre (?) (hat)," "with a hundred strings."

111   adj. from *baβrini-*, *baβra-* "beaver."

112   For *ϑrisatanąm*: *ϑri-sata-* Skjaervø gives "three hundred" (Skjaervø 2011a, p. 63), whereas Malandra (1983, p. 130) and Oettinger (1983, p. 124) give instead "thirty beavers," *ϑrisatanąm* as pl. gen of *ϑri-saṇt-*, "thirty."

113   *carəmå* from *carəman-*; (NP *čarm-* "leather, skin") here as "the fur" of the beaver.

114   Skjaervø (2011a, p. 63) gives "about to give birth for the fourth time."

115   Malandra (1983, p. 130) and Oettinger (1983, p. 124) give the same translation, but Skjaervø (2011a, p. 63) prefers "when she is *adorned most colorful," probably *gaonōtəma* from *gaonem-*; "color."

116   Kuz'mina 2007, pp. 174–5.

117   Herodotus, Book 4.109.

118   Another connection to the beaver exists among the neighboring Finno-Ugrian peoples (a non-Indo-European linguistic group) who have a myth of the "mother-beaver." Michael Witzel's (2001) point that this provides evidence against a South Asian origin applies to the Iranian plateau as well: " the beaver is not found inside S. Asia. It occurs, however, even now in Central Asia, its bones have been found in areas as far south as N. Syria and in mummified form in Egypt, and it is attested in the Avesta (*bawri< *babhri< IE *bhebhr-) when speaking of the dress ('made up of 30 beaver skins') of the Iranian counterpart of the river goddess *sárasvatī*, *areduui sura anāhitā*: Yt 5.129 "the female beaver is most beautiful, as it is most furry: the beaver is a water animal"*yat asti baβriš sraēšta*
yaϑa yat asti gaonōtəma
(*baβriš bauuaiti upāpō*)
Avestan *baβri-* is related to the descriptive term, IE **bhebhru* 'brown, beaver' which is widely attested: O.Engl. *bebr*, *beofor*, Lat. *fiber*, Lith. *be~brus*, Russ. *bobr*, *bebr-*."

119   Malandra (1983, p. 119) also notes that Anāhitā's origin, although uncertain, could be connected to the stanza translated above (Yt 5.129). He suggests that

since in former times beavers lived in Caucasus region, so "perhaps Anāhitā was a local goddess of the extreme northwest whose cult, for whatever reasons, diffused throughout western Iran, eventually to join with that of Inanna-Ištar."

120 The development of an OIr. *aryānām waiǰah,* according to MacKenzie 1998.

121 Pākzād 2005, p. 353.

122 Amouzgar and Tafazzoli 2000, p. 44.

123 Herodotus, Book 1.131.

124 Skjaervø 2011b, p. 70.

125 Witzel 1984, p. 226; cf. Skjærvø 2005, p. 22.

126 Skjærvø 2005, p. 23.

127 One is of course reminded here of the three Dumézilian functions (Mallory and Adams 2006, p. 433).

128 Yt 5.21.85–7.

Chapter 4

1   Skjærvø 2011b, p.71.

2   Skjærvø 2011a, p. 14. Other translations of her name have been suggested: "Ārmaiti" as "holy devotion," for example, with "Spəntā" being an adjective meaning "bounteous," with her actual name being "moderation" or "piety" (Humbach 1959, Bd. I, p. 139; Nyberg 1938, p. 112).

3   Molé 1963, p. 19.

4   Skjærvø 2007, p. 59.

5   Skjærvø 2011a, p. 14.

6   Tanabe 1995, pp. 309–34.

7   Azarpay 1981, p. 139.

8   The *kusti* normally has seventy-two cords, representing the seventy-two chapters of the *Yasna.* So, why is Spandarmad's golden *kustīg* connected to thirty-three cords? Perhaps there is some connection to what Kreyenbroek mentioned in a different context: "According to the *Farḏiyāt-nāma,* one must celebrate the *Vendidād* accompanied by a *Yasna, Bāj* (i. e., *drōn*-service), and *Āfringān* of thirty-three *yazads,* in order to expiate any sin one may have committed against one of these." See Kreyenbroek 1985, p. 155.

9   My translation, adapted from Gignoux and Tafazzoli 1993 and Rashīd-Mohāsel 2010.

10 Oryān 1993, p. 225.

11 A mountain range in Iran, probably the Alborz.

12 Rāshed-Mohāsel 2009, p. 65.

13 Pākzād 2005, pp. 306–7.

14 *kāmag-dōys^ar. kāmag-* means "will, desire," and *dōys^ar* (Av. *dōiθra-*) means "eye"; the Avestan adjective *vouru.dōiθra-* "whose eyes observe widely" (Bartholomae 1904, col. 1430 "des Augen weithin gehen, weitschauend") describes the deity Saokā- (Bartholomae 1904, col. 1549). A similar idea seems to be expressed here with regard to Spandarmad. Bahār (1999, p. 191) translates the term as "wide-observer."

15 Yt 16.1 speaks about them as the two names of one deity (Kellens 1994).

16 Hintze 1995, p. 84.

17 Hintze 2003.

18 De Vaan 2003, pp. 91–2.

19 Skjærvø states that the *Dēn* in Zoroastrianism encompasses the concept of religion itself including the complete corpus of religious texts, which constituted "the Tradition" (with a capital "T") and was called the *Dēn* by the Sasanian priests. (See Skjærvø 2012, p. 23.)

20 Cantera 2016, p. 71.

21 Cantera 2016, pp. 71–3.

22 His name has been transcribed as "Wirāf" in the preliminary edition of Haug and West 1872 and in older publications; however, the Avestan form from which it derives (*Yašt* 13.101) is Virāza (Gignoux 1986).

23 Molé 1967.

24 Gignoux 1984.

25 In the transcription provided by the Titus website it is **dērand *angust* which means the "long fingers."

26 Mīr-Faxrāʾī 1993, p. 87.

27 De Jong 1997, p. 104.

28 Skjærvø 2011b, p. 71.

29 Schlerath and Skjærvø 1987.

30 Schlerath and Skjærvø 1987.

31 Boyce 1975, pp. 65–6.

32 De Jong 1997, p. 104.

33 Raffaelli 2013, p. 288.

34 Boyce and Grenet 1991, pp. 486–7, n. 629.

35 Schlerath and Skjærvø 1987.

36 Schlerath and Skjærvø 1987.

37 Kellens, "Drvāspā."

38 Skjærvø 1986.

39 Malandra 2002.

40 Skjærvø 1986.

41 Boyce et al. 1986.

42 Pākzād 2005, p. 310.

43 Op. cit., p. 294.

44 Dumézil 1945 and 1977.

45 Duchesne-Guillemin 1958, pp. 40–1 and 1962, pp. 197–202; also Widengren 1965.

46 Narten 1982, pp. 104–5;

47 Gnoli 1991, pp. 123–4.

48 Panaino 2004.

49 Narten, *Die Aməša Spəntas im Avesta*, p. 72.

50 Thieme 1970, pp. 208–16; Narten 1982, pp. 104–5; Humbach 1991; Panaino 2004.

51 Russell 2004.

52 Rose 2015, p. 275.

Chapter 5

1 De Jong 1997, p. 105.

2 De Jong 1997, p. 61.

3 Witzel 2004.

4 Panaino 2000, p. 38.

5 Dalley 2008, p. 229.

6 Bahār 1997, p. 140.

7 Voegelin 2001, p. 88.

8 Mendez 2012. Mendez speaks only of Artaxerxes' political aims, not of the Mesopotamian triangulate model specifically.

9 Bahār 1997, p. 388. It seems that for the most part, however, the Sogdians identified the Oxus with a male deity, Wakhsh.

10 Watkins 2005.

11 Bahār 1997, p. 310.

12 RV II.11.5. Vṛtra also is called "Danava," the son of the goddess Danu, as previously discussed in Chapter Four.

13 RV X.8.8–9.

14 Schwartz 2012, p. 275.

15 The word is etymologically related to words in other Indo-European languages such as Latin *anguis* (Skjaervø 1987).

16 RV 1.32.11; also Schwartz 2012, p. 275.

17 Yt 14.17.48–53.

18 Gnoli 1988.

19 Kellens 1974b.

20 Hintze 1995, pp. 77–97.

21 Hintze 1999, p. 76.

22 Hintze 1999, pp. 72–89.

23   Hintze 1995, p. 94.

24   Hintze 1995, p. 94.

25   RV II 11.5.

26   Hintze 1999, p. 78.

27   Like Anāhitā, the Vedic deity Indra also bears the epithet *śūra*- (heroic). He is the "hero" who fights fearlessly with the drought-inducing dragon in order to release the water so that it may flow back to the world (RV II 11.5). Indra slays the dragon, Vṛtra, also known as "Ahi," who kept and imprisoned the heavenly water captive (RV IV 17.7) and the dragon's mother, the goddess Danu. Vṛtra has many features in common with the Iranian Aži-Dahāka. In the *Ṛg Veda*, the dragon Vṛtra belongs to the *asura*s (who are demonic deities in the RV).

28   Humbach and Ichaporia 1998, p. 50.

29   Hintze 1994, p. 32.

30   Almut Hintze, e-mail conversation, July 20, 2016.

31   Yt 19. 6,19,40.

32   Skjaervø 1987.

33   Russell 1987b.

34   There is some discussion about the Indo-Iranian word **dhainu* (Sanskrit *dhenu*), which is usually translated as "cow." Lincoln (1976) states (following Benveniste 1969, pp. 22–3) that the word could mean "the one who gives milk," in which case it may be used for any female.

35   Skjaervø 1987.

36   *Bahman-nāmeh*, B. M. Or. 2780, fols. 180ff. Khaleghi-Motlagh (1987) accordingly suggests that "Another interpretation of the dragon-slaying by Indo-Iranian gods is that the god in question was a god of thunder and lightning, that the dragon was a black cloud, and that by slaying the dragon, the god released water impounded in its stomach to fall as rain."

37   *Bahman-nāmeh*, 180f. (Khaleghi-Motlagh 1987).

38   Saadi-nejad 2009.

39   Schwartz 2012, p. 275.

40   Skjaervø 1987.

41   Yt 19.37.

42   Yt 5.34.

43   He is often referred to as Bēwarasp in the Pahlavi texts (e.g., Dk 9.21.7; tr. West, p. 214; *Mēnōg ī xrad* 7.29, 26.34, 35, 38; tr. West, pp. 35, 60f; Bd TD1, p. 66.7–8; TD2, p. 80.6–7; tr. Anklesaria, pp. 98f; tr. West, p. 40) (Skjaervø 1987).

44   According to the *Shāh-nameh*, Żaḥḥāk will be freed at the end of time. He will attempt to cause destruction, for example, by devouring one third of the human population along with some other creatures of Ohrmazd, but he will be killed by Kərəšāspa/Kiršāsp/Garšasp.

45   Skjaervø 1987.

46 Pakzad 2005, p. 154.
47 Mayrhofer 1979, no. 123, 1/39-40.
48 Wikander 1938, pp. 21–24/58-60/84f.
49 Kellens 2013, p. 125.
50 Kellens 2013, p. 125.
51 Wikander 1938, pp. 94–6.
52 For example, in Yt 5.18.73 and Yt 13.9.37.38.
53 Pākzād 2005, pp. 394–5.
54 Bahār 1997, p. 312.
55 Pākzād 2005, p. 363.
56 It is said in the *Mēnōg ī xrad* that Ahriman created Afrasīyāb, Bēvarasp (Żaḥḥāk), and Alexander immortal, but Ahura Mazdā changed their statute (8.29–30; cf. ZWY 7.32; MX 8.29); cf. Yarshater 1984.
57 Pākzād 2005, p.156.
58 Yarshater 1984.
59 Hintze 1995, p. 94.
60 Gnoli 1988.

Chapter 6

1 Some have dated this site much later, to the Parthian period, but the question remains at present unresolved (Von Gall 1988).
2 Bahār 1997, p. 148.
3 Xenophon (*c.* 430 to 354 BC) 1968, Book VII, C.5.57 and C.6.1; also Olmsted 1948, p. 447.
4 Herodotus, Book I.131.
5 For more discussion on this see De Jong 1997, pp. 107–9.
6 De Jong 1997, p. 104 and p. 269.
7 Herodotus, Book I.131.
8 Strabo (64 BC to *c.* AD 24) 2014, 11.8. 4–5.
9 Boyce 1975, p. 74.
10 Schmitt 1970.
11 Paz de Hoz 1999.
12 Xenophon (*c.* 430 to 354 BC) 1968, V–VIII, 355.
13 Boyce, 1982, p. 147.
14 Hintze 1995, p. 94.
15 Silverman 2012, p. 58.
16 Shepard 2008, p. 140.
17 Quoted in Clement of Alexandria 1958, 5.65.3. For a new edition of Berossus see G. De Bruecker 2012.

18 Ricl 2002, p. 200.
19 Plutarch (*c.* AD 46–120) 2016, 3.1–2. Also see Chaumont 1989.
20 Plutarch (*c.* AD 46–120) 2016, 27.3.
21 De Jong 1997, p. 280.
22 Herrenschmidt and Kellens 1993.
23 De Bruecker 2012, p. 566.
24 From the De Clercq collection. See Shenkar 2014, pp. 67–8.
25 Ricl 2002, pp. 200–1.
26 Kuhrt 2013, p. 153.
27 Strabo (64 BC to *c.* AD 24) 2014, 11.14.16.
28 Pliny (AD 23–79)1944, v. 33, 82–3.
29 Plutarch (*c.* AD 46–120) 2016, 27; Tacitus 2012, 3.62; also Rose 2015, p. 257.
30 Pausanias (*c.* 100–180 CE) 1965, 7.27.5.
31 Ghirshmann 1961, p. 269.
32 Polybius (*c.* 200 to 118 BC) 2010, 10.27.
33 Isidore of Charax 1976.
34 Pliny (AD 23–79) 1944, 6.35.
35 Callieri and Chaverdi 2013, p. 694.
36 Hauser 2013, p. 734.
37 Kawami 2013, pp. 757, 763.
38 Ghirshman 1962, p. 313.
39 Herodotus, Book I. 131.
40 Strabo (64 BC to *c.* AD 24) 2014, 15.3.14.
41 Shepard 2008, p. 141.
42 Strabo (64 BC to *c.* AD 24) 2014, 15.3.14.
43 Bahār 1997, p. 100.
44 Chaumont 1989.
45 Ghirshman 1962, p. 149; also Chaumont 1989.
46 Al-Ṭabarī 1999, p. 15; cf. Nöldeke 1973, p. 17.
47 Labourt 1904, p. 71, n. 2.
48 Kavian (Kayāniān); *xvarənah-* is listed in the Avesta in *Yašt* 1.21 with *Airiiana Vaējah*, Saōka, the waters, and Anāhitā.
49 Brosius (2010) has doubted the attribution of these images as the goddess Anāhitā, arguing that they may be women of the royal house or other figures. However, given the importance of Anāhitā in epigraphic evidence and her fundamental association with the Sasanian dynasty, there seems no compelling reason to question the standard attribution in the absence of strong evidence to the contrary.
50 Humbach and Skjærvø 1983, p. 14.
51 Shepard 2008, p. 143.

52 Isadore of Charax 1976, 6.

53 Von der Osten and Naumann 1961, pp. 85–92.

54 Shenkar 2014, p. 76.

55 Canepa 2009, pp. 200–1.

56 Panaino 2015, pp. 235–57.

57 Panaino 2015, p. 248.

58 Bier 1989.

59 Duchesne-Guillemin 1971, p. 378 and pl. III, fig. 3.

60 Duchesne-Guillemin 1962, p. 333.

61 Ghirshman 1962, p. 106 and fig. 120, p. 313 and fig. 255.

62 Göbl 1968, pp. 7, 9.

63 Azarnoush 1987 and 1994.

64 Bāstānī-Pārīzī 1988.

65 Boyce 1967.

66 Bagherpour and Stöllner 2011, p.1.

67 Rose 2011, pp. 141 and 153.

68 Rose 2011, p. 143.

69 Azarpay 1975.

70 Azarpay 1981, p. 134 and p. 140, n. 61.

71 Black and Green 2003, p. 109.

72 Henning 1964, p. 252, n. 68.

73 Skjaervø 2005, p. 33.

74 Grenet and Marshak 1998, p. 8.

75 Grenet and Marshak 1998, p. 9.

Chapter 7

1   Shaked 1994, p. 97.

2   Skjærvø 2013a, p. 118.

3   Pakzad 2005, p. 141.

4   Skjærvø 2013a, pp. 113 and 117.

5   Boyce 1975, p. 308, n. 83.

6   De Jong 1995.

7   Widengren 1967.

8   Choksy 2002, p. 115.

9   Choksy 2002, p. 119.

10 Choksy 2002, p. 120.

11 Rose 2015.

12 Hintze 2003.

13 Narten 1986, pp. 292–3.

14 Hintze 2003, p. 410.

15 Hintze 2013, p. 53.

16 Macuch 2009a, pp. 135–51.

17 Macuch 2009b, pp. 251–78.

18 Macuch 2010.

19 Macuch 2010.

20 Macuch 2010, p. 207.

21 Hintze 2013.

22 Skjærvø 2005, p. 12.

23 *Āzārē, āzārdan, āzār-*: (*ʾčʾl-tnʾ*); means "to annoy" or "harass" in New Persian.

24 Pākzād 2005, pp. 194–5. I have used Pākzād's edition in making my own translation into English and have followed his chapter divisions. I have also taken consideration of Bahār's translation into modern Persian (based on three manuscripts TD1- TD2- DH; Bahār 1998).

25 *frāz ĵast:* "happened forward."

26 Pākzād 2005.

27 Yt 19.5.28–9.

28 Macuch 2009c, pp. 181–96.

29 Panaino 2015, p. 242.

30 Pākzād 2005, p. 129.

31 Pākzād 2005, p. 224.

32 Pākzād 2005, p. 308

33 This theme has a strong presence in both the Avesta (Vd 19.5) and the Pahlavi literature. As Gnoli (2003a) notes, "In the eschatological myth there is a correspondence between the sea Vouru.kaša and Lake Kaiiānsē."

34 *ābān xwarrah*: "the glory of waters."

35 Pākzād 2005.

36 8.55; 9.18; 10.15; (Rashīd-Mohāsel 2009, pp. 107, 112, and 118). In West's translation (1897), these three maidens are called "Šemīg Ābu, Šapīr Ābu and Dšnubak Ābu." These names differ from the versions given in the Avesta, where they are called *srūtaṯ-fəðriiō, vaŋhu-fəðriiå,* and *ərədaṯ -fəðriiå*, Yt 13.141–42.

37 Yt 13.62, 13.28; *Dēnkard* 7.8.1 ff; cf. Boyce 1975, p. 285; also Gnoli 2003b.

38 Rose 2015, p. 277.

39 Cereti 1995, p. 142.

40 Cereti 1995, p. 143.

41 Cereti 1995, p. 143. Here *babar* (*bpl*), "tiger," could also be read as *bplkʾ babr(ag)*: "beaver." I have translated the term as "beaver."

42 Tafazzoli 1982.

43 I have used the transcription provided by the Titus website in making my own translation: http://titus.uni-frankfurt.de/texte/etcs/iran/miran/mpers/jamasp/jamas.htm. Also see Utas 1983, p. 261.

44   Yt 5.25.108.

45   Gnoli 2003a.

46   Gnoli 2003a.

47   Pākzād 2005, p. 164.

48   Pākzād 2005, p. 329.

49   There is another spirit (*mēnog*), called *Sōg*, who is related to the moon, water, and *Ardwī-sūr:mēnog-ē(w) ī abāg Mihr ham-kār Sōg xwānēnd. hamāg nēkīh ka az abargarān ō gētīg brēhēnīd nazdist ō Sōg āyēd Sōg ō Māh abespārēd ud Māh ō Ardwīsūr abespārēd ud Ardwīsūr ō spihr abespārēd ud spihr pad gēhān baxšēd. ...* the *mēnog* who is partner with *Mīhr* is called *Sōg*. All of the goods things when created for the world by the spirits first come to the *Sōg*. The *Sōg* sends them to the moon, the moon sends them to *Ardwī-sūr*, *Ardwī-sūr* sends them to the sky, and sky disseminates them throughout the world (Bd XXVI. 26.34).

50   RV II 11.5.

51   Hintze 1999, p. 78.

52   Pākzād 2005, p. 50.

53   Anāhitā has her own role in the last scene of the Renovation: with this sacred *xᵛarənah,* the last Avestan *saošiiaṇt-* will arise from the water of Lake Kayānsē where she had kept the seed of Zaraϑuštra.

54   Pākzād 2005, p. 25.

55   Venus was considered hermaphroditic according to her position in relation to sun (Koch-Westenholz 1995, pp. 125–6).

56   *lipī:* (*lpyh*) a minute (of an arc).

57   Pākzād 2005, p. 79.

58   Venus was considered hermaphroditic according to her position in relation to the sun. See Koch-Westenholz 1995, pp. 125–6.

59   Boyce 1986.

60   Panaino 2005.

61   Pākzād 2005, pp. 79–80.

62   Panaino 2015, p. 253.

63   Panaino 2013, p. 138.

64   Panaino, "Cosmologies and Astrology," p. 251.

65   The Avestan *Satavāesa-* clearly a star divinity related to waters and rain who helps Tištriia according to Yt 8.9 and 13.43.

66   Pakzad 2005, p. 85.

67   *paymoxtān ī ān rōšnīh rāy:* "due to wearing the/that light."

68   "*wattar-*" means "worse," with the plural ending *ān*, but here it probably means "the vulgar, the populace."

69   Pākzād 2005, p. 80.

70   *gōspand-tōhmag:* here is an adj. for *māh*.

71   *murnǰēnīdārān: murnǰēnīdan, murnǰēn-:* "fatal," adj. for the *abāxtarān*.

72 The middle Persian *Gōzihr*, the imaginary dragon, from an old Iranian compound adjective **gau-čiθra* in Yt 7 as an epithet of the moon. It became the name of the imaginary dragon who stretched across the sky between the sun and the moon (Mackenzie 2002 and 1964).

73 The *muš-parīg* is considered by Skjærvø as belonging to the category of dragon/snake-like monsters, probably because of its tail. It seems to be an evil opponent of the sun, the moon, and the stars, and to have been considered as the demon who causes eclipses (Skjærvø 1987).

74 Pākzād 2005, p. 73.

75 *ēbgat*: *'ybgt'*: "devil."

76 Pākzād 2005, p. 85.

77 *āb-čihrag*: *čihr* means "face, appearance" and "nature," here *čihrag* means "nature."

78 Pākzād 2005, p. 86.

79 Malandra 2013, p. 106.

80 Koch-Westenholz 1995, pp. 125–6.

81 Primarily because its vision of the tree is clearly comparable with Nebuchadnezzar's vision of the image of the world empires (Sundermann 1988).

82 The book also deals with Ušēdar and Ušēdar-māh, the first and the second of the promised saviors, who battle with the awakened demon Żaḥḥāk (Aži Dahāka) and the great harm done to the world by this monster before his death at the hands of Garšāsp (Kərəsāspa); the section concludes with a portrayal of the final deliverance by Sōšiiāns (Rashīd-Mohāsel 1991; Sundermann 1988).

83 Cereti 1995, p. 134; Rāshed-Mohāsel 1991, p. 51.

84 Bn I.58; Pākzād 2005.

85 Madan 1911, pp. 79–80; Skjærvø 2013b; Macuch 2009a.

86 Bd III.20; Pākzād 2005.

87 Macuch 2009a.

88 Macuch 2009a, pp. 144.

89 *wattar axwān*, from *wattar*, "worse." *axw* has several meanings, among which one is "the world." So "*wattar axwān*/the worse world" could also refer to the very essence and the concept of "inferno/hell."

90 Pākzād 2005.

91 the root √*san* and the root √*zan*, preverb *ā-* + √*san* + suffix *-a*, which form *āsna*.

92 Piras 1996, p. 10.

93 Piras 1996, pp. 10–12.

94 Hintze 1994, p. 39.

95 Hintze 1994, p. 39.

96 Piras 1996, p. 13.

97 Op. cit., p. 15.

98 König 2018, pp. 56–114.

99   Op. cit., p. 1.

100   Macuch 2009a, p. 144.

101   Shaked 2013, p. 222.

102   Oryan 1993, p. 304.

103   *abē-barīh*: "being useless"; *abē*, "without," *bar*, "produce."

104   Oryan 1993, p. 304.

105   Oryan 1993, p. 304.

106   Al-Ṭabarī (224–310 AH; AD 839–923) 1999, p. 15; also Nöldeke 1973, p. 17.

107   Koch-Westenholz 1995, pp. 125–6.

108   In India, Sárasvatī protects the study of the Vedas (Boyce 1986).

109   Agat'angeghos 1976, section 22.

110   Davidson 1988, p. 26.

111   Davidson 1988, p. 26.

Chapter 8

1   Majlesī (1627–99) 1998, vol. 43, Hadīth 34.

2   Widely performed in Iran in honor and remembrance of the death of the Prophet's grandson, Husayn, who was martyred at Karbala in 680 CE.

3   Dana News 2016: "Why water is Fatima's dowry" http://www.dana.ir/news/1036039.html/چار-آبا-مه-مرهیح-ضرت-زهرا-س-است-

4   For example, Yama in the Vedas, Yima in the Avesta, and Jam or Jam-šīd in the *Šāh-nāmeh*, all derive from the same original character. In Iranian and Indian mythologies, both Yama and Jam-šīd are presented as having been rejected by the gods.

5   A high-quality color reproduction of this painting, which is now in the collection of the Aga Khan Museum in Toronto, can be found in Dickson and Welch 1981.

6   Welch 1976, p. 45.

7   Khaleghi-Motlagh 2012.

8   Dalley 2008, p. 154.

9   Dalley 1979, pp. 177–8.

10   *Enlil and Sud*, 2006. Version A, Segment A, 13–21.

11   Dalley 2008, p. 158.

12   Khaleghi-Motlagh 2012, p. 12.

13   Al-Ṭabarī (224–310 AH; 839–923 AD) 1999, v. 1, pp. 598f; Khaleghi-Motlagh 1999.

14   Näsström 1999.

15   Näsström 1999.

16   Grundy 1999.

17 Several meanings and roots for her name have been suggested, including the Avestan root *Suta.wanhu*, which means "for a good purpose" (Khaleghi-Motlagh 2012, p. 34).

18 Kellens 1974b.

19 One may note as well that in Sanskrit, *su-* means "good"; there is a Vedic goddess named Su-danu (river).

20 Justi 1963, p. 312.

21 Bahār 1997, p. 387.

22 Khaleghi-Motlagh 1999.

23 Afrāsīāb has some connection with water and drought. In two Pahlavi texts, the *Mēnog ī xrad* and the *Bundahišn*, Afrāsīāb is said to have dried up all the water from thousands of springs whose currents flowed toward Lake Kayānsē (MX 26.44; Bd XI A.11a.32). Afrāsīāb's name also, which contains the element *āb*, relates him to water-drought.

24 Skjærvø 2013c.

25 *na pīčam sar*: the negation *sar-pīčī* means to "disobey."

26 Ferdowsī 1990, v. 2, p. 221.

27 Ferdowsī 1990, v. 2, p. 223.

28 Dalley 2008, p. 77.

29 Pākzād 2005, p. 397.

30 "The Legend of Sargon, King of Agade," in King 1907, pp. 88–9.

31 Grenet 1984.

32 Saadi-nejad 2009.

33 Mazdāpūr 2002.

34 Rasuly-Paleczek and Katschnig 2005, v. 2, pp. 33–7.

35 Daneshvar 1990.

36 Ferdowsī 1990, v. 2, p. 355.

37 Ferdowsī 1990, v. 2, p. 358, n. 1.

38 Kuyaji 1974, pp. 110–11.

39 Kia 1992, p. 144.

40 Merchant 1980.

41 *Vidēvdād* 1.14.

42 Amouzgar and Tafazzoli 2000, p. 26.

43 Skjærvø 1998, p. 163.

44 Khalegi-Motlagh suggests that she is a *pairikā* (2012, p. 33).

45 These include the *Bundahišn*, the *Bahman-nāmeh*, Taʿālebi's *Ḡorar axbār moluk al-Fārs wa siyarihim*, and Mirxᵛānd's *Rawżat al-ṣafā*, among others.

46 Ferdowsī 1990, v. 5, p. 78.

47 Skjærvø 2013c.

48 Skjærvø 2013c.

49 Boyce 1955.
50 Khaleghi-Motlagh 2012, p. 57.
51 Ferdowsī 1990, v. 5, p. 25, stanza 310.
52 Kia 1992, p. 212.
53 Saadi-nejad 2009, p. 232.
54 Khaleghi-Moghadam 1996.
55 My own translation, based on the transcription from http://titus.uni-frankfurt.
    de/texte/etcs/iran/miran/mpers/jamasp/jamas.htm; also Monchi-Zadeh 1982 and
    Azarnoche 2013, pp. 41–69.
56 PIE *parikeh_a-, OPers. *parikā-, MPers. *parīg*, Sogh. *pr'ykh*, Manich. MP *parīg*,
    Khot. *palīkā-*, NP *parī*, Pashto *pēraī*, Nuristanī *pari/bari/barai*, Arm. *Parik*
    (Adhami 2010).
57 Yt 1.6.10; Yt 5.13.22.26.
58 Yt 19.41.
59 *HN* 6.
60 Dk 7.0.19 is a notable example.
61 Panaino 1990.
62 Adhami 2010.
63 Skjaervø 1987.
64 Sarkarati 1971.
65 Mazdāpūr 2002, p. 294.
66 Mazdāpūr 2002, p. 342.
67 Sharifian and Atuni 2008.
68 Examples can be found in the *Šahriyar-nāmeh/Dārāb-nāmeh*, specifically the story
    of Amīr-Arsalān.
69 Sharifian and Atuni 2008.
70 Panaino 1996.
71 Panaino 1990, part I, p. 75.
72 Panaino 1996.
73 Pākzād 2005, p.73
74 Pākzād 2005, p. 196.
75 Keith 1925; Williams 2003, p. 57.
76 Herodotus Book 7.68.
77 Bivar 1985. Other scholars have also mentioned the possible connection between
    the Parikani and "Pari" worshippers (Olmstead 1948, p. 397).
78 Malekzādeh 2002.
79 Khaleghi-Motlagh 2012, pp. 10–13.
80 Sarkarati 1971.
81 Adhami 2010.
82 Mazdāpūr 2002, p. 291.

83   Malekzadeh 2002.

84   Bahār 1997, p. 261.

85   This is the view espoused by Sarkarati (1971).

86   Bahār 1997, pp. 261–93.

87   Schwartz 2008, p. 99.

88   More such names are Parī-zād, Parī-nāz, Parī-vaš, Parī-ru, Parī-rokh, Parīā, and simply Parī (all are female names).

89   Ṭārsūsī (twelfth century) 2011.

90   Hanaway 1982a.

91   Hanaway 1982b, p. 292.

92   Hanaway 1982a.

93   Bagherpour and Stöllner 2011, p. 1.

94   Brancaforte 2004, p. 78.

95   Brancaforte 2004, p. 78.

96   Khosravi 2000.

97   Richard Foltz, personal report, May 9, 2018.

98   Sedaghat-Kish 2003.

99   Sedaghat-Kish 2003.

100   See Chapter Nine.

101   Sedaghat-Kish 2003, pp. 34–42.

102   E'temad al-Saltaneh (1843–1896) 1988.

103   Sedaghat-Kish 2003, pp. 34–42.

104   Sedaghat-Kish 2003.

105   Rose 2011, p. 153.

106   Cultural Heritage News Agency 2016.

107   Punthakey-Mistree 2013.

108   Punthakey-Mistree 2013, p. 195.

109   Punthakey-Mistree 2013, pp. 195, 203.

110   Abbasi 2007.

111   Bahman Moradian, personal communication, July 18, 2014.

Bibliography

Abbasi, Yadollah Agha, 2007. "Bārān-xāhī" ("Rain-seeking"), *Journal of the Department of Human Science and Literature*, Kerman University 12, pp. 1–20.

Adhami, Siamak, 2010. "Pairikā," *Encyclopædia Iranica*.

Agatʿangeghos 1976. *History of the Armenians*, tr. Robert W. Thomson, Albany: State University of New York Press.

Ahmadi, Amir, 2015. *The Daēva Cult in the Gāthās: An Ideological Archaeology of Zoroastrianism*, New York: Routledge.

Al-Barwārī, Hasan Ahmad Qāsim, 2013. *ʿAmārat muʿābid al-nār fī muwaqaʿ čār stīn ʿala ḍūʾ al-tanqībāt al-athariyah*, Duhok: Hawar.

Al-Ṭabarī, Muḥammad ibn Jarīr, 1999. *The History of al-Tabarī: The Sāsānids, the Byzantines, the Lakhmids, and Yemen*, vol. 5, tr. C. E. Bosworth, Albany: State University of New York Press.

Allason-Jones, Lindsay, 1999. "Coventina's Well," in Sandra Billington and Miranda Green, eds., *The Concept of the Goddess*, London: Routledge, pp. 107–19.

Allason-Jones, Lindsay, and Bruce McKay, 1985. *Coventina's Well: A Shrine on Hadrian's Wall*, Oxford: Oxbow.

Álvarez-Mon, Javier, 2013. "Khuzestan in the Bronze Age," in Potts, ed., *The Oxford Handbook of Ancient Iran*, Oxford: Oxford University Press, pp. 217–32.

Álvarez-Mon, Javier, 2012. "Elam: Iran's First Empire," in Daniel T. Potts, ed., *A Companion to the Archaeology of the Ancient Near East*, vol. 1, Chichester: Wiley-Blackwell, pp. 740–57.

Āmūzgar, Žāleh, 1380 [2001]. *Tārīx-e Irān-e bāstān*, vol. 1, Tehran: Sāzmān-e motaʾleh va tadvīn-e kutub-e ʿulūm-e ensānīye dāneshgāhhā.

Āmūzgar, Žāleh, and Aḥmad Tafażżolī, 2000. *Le cinquième livre du Denkard*, Paris: Association pour l'avancement des études iraniennes.

Āmūzgar, Žāleh, and Aḥmad Tafażżolī, 1386 [2007]. *Ketāb-e panjom-e Dēnkard*, Tehran: Moiin Publisher.

Andrés-Toledo, Miguel Ángel, 2015. "Primary Sources Avestan and Pahlavi," in Michael Stausberg and Yuhan Vevaina, eds., *The Wiley-Blackwell Companion to Zoroastrianism*, Malden: Wiley-Blackwell, pp. 519–28.

Andrés-Toledo, Miguel Ángel, 2012. "A Revision of Geldner's Critical Edition," in Alberto Cantera, ed., *The Transmission of the Avesta, (Iranica 20)*, Wiesbaden: Harrassowitz, pp. 433–8.

Aro, Sanno, and Whiting, R. M., eds., 2000. *The Heirs of Assyria: Proceedings of the Opening Symposium of the Assyrian and Babylonian Heritage Project*, Helsinki: The Neo-Assyrian Text Corpus Project.

Aruz, Joan, Ann Farkas, and Elisabetta Valtz Fino, eds., 2007. *The Golden Deer of Eurasia: Perspectives on the Steppe Nomads of the Ancient World*, The Metropolitan Museum of Art Symposia, New York: Metropolitan Museum of Art Series.

Azarnoche, Samra, 2013. *Husraw ī kawādān ud rēdag-ē* (Khosrow Fils De Kawād et un Page), Paris: Association pour l'avancement des études iraniennes.

Azarnoush, M., 1994. *The Sasanian Manor House at Hajiabad, Iran*, Florence: Monografie di Mesopotamia 3.

Azarnoush, M., 1987. "Fire Temple and Anahita Temple: A Discussion on Some Iranian Places of Worship," *Mesopotamia*, 22, pp. 391–401.

Azarpay, Guitty, 1981. *Sogdian Painting: The Pictorial Epic in Oriental Art*, Berkeley: University of California Press.

Azarpay, Guitty, 1975. "Iranian Divinities in Sogdian Paintings," *Acta Iranica*, 4, pp. 12–21.

Bachmann-Medick, Doris, 2016, *Cultural Turns: New Orientation in the Study of Culture*, Berlin: De Gruyter.

Bachofen, Johann, 1861. *Das Mutterrecht*, Basel: Benno Schwabe.

Bagherpour-Kashani, N., and Th. Stöllner, eds., *Water and Caves in Ancient Iranian Religion: Aspects of Archaeology, Cultural History and Religion*, vol. 43, Archäologische Mitteilungen aus Iran und Turan, Deutsches Archäologisches Institut, Eurasien-Abteilung, Berlin: Reimer, 2011.

Bahār, Mehrdād, 1378 [1999]. *Bundahišn*, Tehrān: Tūs.

Bahār, Mehrdād, 1376 [1997]. *Az ostūreh tā tārīkh*, Tehrān: Češmeh.

Bahār, Mehrdād, 1373 [1994]. *Jostarī chand dar farhang-e Irān*, Tehran: Fekr-e rūz.

Bailey, Douglass W., 2013. "Figurines, Corporeality, and the Origins of the Gendered Body," in Diane Bolger, ed., *A Companion to Gender Prehistory*, Oxford: Wiley, Wiley-Blackwell, pp. 244–64.

Bakuran [Kurkjian, Vahan M.], 2014 [1958]. *A History of Armenia*, Los Angeles: Indo European Publishing.

Bartholomae, Chr., 1905. *Die Gatha's des Awesta. Zarathushtra's Verspredigten*, Strassburg: K. J. Trübner.

Bartholomae, *AirWb.* = Bartholomae, Chr., 1904: *Altiranisches Wörterbuch*. Straßburg (repr. Berlin/NewYork 1979).

Bāstānī-Pārīzī, Mohamad Ebrahīm, 1368 [1988]. *Xātun-e haft qaleh*, Tehrān: Rūzbehān.

Bausani, Alessandro, 2000. *Religion in Iran*, New York: Bibliotheca Persica.

Beaulieu, Paul-Alain, 2018. *A History of Babylon, 2200 BC–AD 75*, Malden: Wiley-Blackwell.

Belier, Wouter W., 1997. *Decayed Gods: Origin and Development of Georges Dumézil's "Idéologie Tripartie,"* Leiden: Brill.

Benveniste, Emile, 1969. *Le Vocabulaire des institutions indo-européens*, Paris: Éditions de Minuit.

Benveniste, Emile, 1933–35. "L'*Ērān-vēj* et l'origine légendaire des Iraniens," *Bulletin of the School of Oriental Studies*, 7, pp. 265–74.

Benveniste, Emile, 1929. *The Persian Religion According to the Chief Greek Texts*, Paris: P. Geuthner.

Berger, Pamela, 1985. *The Goddess Obscured: Transformation of the Grain Protectress from Goddess to Saint*, Boston: Beacon Press.

Berossus, 1978. *Babyloniaca*, ed. and tr. Stanley Mayer Burstein, Malibu: Undena.

Bier, C. 1989. "Anāhīd iv: Anāhitā in the Arts," *Encyclopædia Iranica*, I/9, pp. 1003–11.

Billington, Sandra and Green, Miranda, 1999. *The Concept of the Goddess*, London: Routledge.

Bitel, Lisa M., 2001. "St. Brigit of Ireland: From Virgin Saint to Fertility Goddess," paper presented at Fordham University, New York.

Bivar, A. D. H., 1985. "A Persian Fairyland," *Papers in Honour of Professor Mary* Boyce, *Acta Iranica*, XXIV, Leiden: Brill, pp. 25–42.

Black, Jeremy, and Anthony Green, 2003. *Gods, Demons, and Symbols of Ancient Mesopotamia: An Illustrated Dictionary*, London: British Museum Press.

Bord, Janet and Bord, Colin, 1985. *Sacred Waters: Holy Wells and Water Lore in Britain and Ireland*, New York: HarperCollins.

Boyce, Mary, 1995. "Dog: in Zoroastrianism," *Encyclopædia Iranica*, vol. VII, Fasc. 5, pp. 461–70.

Boyce, Mary, 1986. "Ardwīsūr Anāhīd," *Encyclopædia Iranica*. I/9, pp. 1003–11.

Boyce, Mary, 1982. *A History of Zoroastrianism*, vol. 2, Leiden: Brill.

Boyce, Mary, 1975. *A History of Zoroastrianism*, vol. 1, Leiden: Brill.

Boyce, Mary, 1967. "Bībī Šahrbānū and the Lady of Pārs," *Bulletin of the School of Oriental and African Studies*, 30/1, pp. 30–44.

Boyce, Mary, 1955. "Zariades and Zarer," *Bulletin of the School of Oriental and African Studies*, 17/3, pp. 463–77.

Boyce, Mary and Frantz Grenet, 1991. *A History of Zoroastrianism*, vol. 3, *Zoroastrianism under Macedonian and Roman Rule*, Leiden: Brill.

Bradley, Ian, 2012. *Water, A Spiritual History*, London: Bloomsbury Publishing.

Brancaforte, E. C., 2004. *Visions of Persia: Mapping the Travels of Adam Olearius*, Cambridge, MA: Harvard University Press.

Bremmer, Jan M., 2007. *The Strange World of Human Sacrifice*, Leuven: Peeters.

Brosius, Maria, 2010. "Women i. In Pre-Islamic Persia," *Encyclopædia Iranica*.

Brown, William Norman, 1978. *India and Indology: Selected Articles*, New Delhi: Motilal Banarsidas.

Burkert, Walter, 1985. *Greek Religion*, Cambridge, MA: Harvard University Press.

Cacciafoco, Francesco Perono, 2013. "'Water Origins': The *Alb-Root in the Pre-Latine Toponymy of Ancient Liguria, *Acta* Linguistica, 7, pp. 73–5.

Callieri, Pierfrancesco and Alireza Askari Chaverdi, 2013. "Media, Khuzestan and Fars between the End of the Achaemenids and the Rise of the Sasanians," in D. T. Potts, ed., *The Oxford Handbook of Ancient Iran*, Oxford: Oxford University Press, pp. 690–717.

Calzolari, Valentina, 2017. *Apocrypha Armeniaca*, Turnhout: Brepols.

Campos Mendez, Israel, 2012. "Anahita and Mithra in the Achaemenid Royal Inscriptions," in Payam Nabarz, ed., *Anahita: Ancient Persian Goddess and Zoroastrian Yazata*, London: Avalonia, pp. 41–7.

Canepa, Mattew P., 2009. *The Two Eyes of the Earth: Art and Ritual of Kingship between Roma and Sasanian Iran*, Cambridge: Cambridge University Press.

Cantera, Alberto, 2016. "The Sacrifice (Yasna) to Mazdā. Its antiquity and variety," in Alan Williams, and Sara Stewart, eds., *The Zoroastrian Flame. Exploring Religion, History and Tradition*, London: I.B. Tauris, pp. 61–76.

Cantera, Alberto, ed., 2012. *The Transmission of the Avesta*, Wiesbaden: Harrassowitz.

Carter, Martha L., 2006. "Kanishka's Bactrian Pantheon in the Rabatak Inscription: The Numismatic Evidence," in A. Panaino and A. Piras, eds., *Proceedings of the Fifth Conference of the Societas Iranologica Europea*, Milan: Mimesis, pp. 351–8.

Cereti, Carlo G., ed., 2010. *Iranian Identity in the Course of History*, Roma: Istituto Italiano per L'Africa e L'Oriente.

Cereti, Carlo G., 1995. *The Zand ī Wahman Yasn: A Zoroastrian Apocalypse*, Roma: Istituto italiano per il medio ed estremo oriente.

Chaumont, M. L., 1989. "Anāhid iii. The Cult and Its Diffusion," *Encyclopædia Iranica*, I/9, pp. 1003–11.

Chaumont, M. L., 1986. "Armenia and Iran ii. The Pre-Islamic Period," *Encyclopædia Iranica*, II, Fasc. 4, pp. 418–38.

Chaumont, M. L., 1984. "*La route royale des Parthes de Zeugma à Séleucie du Tigre,*" *Syria*, 61/1-2, pp. 63–107.

Chaumont, M. L., 1965. "Le culte de la déesse Anāhitā (Anahit) dans la religion des monarques d'Iran et d'Armenie au Ier siècle de notre ère," *Journal Asiatique*, 253, pp. 167–81.

Chaumont, M. L., 1958. "Le culte de Anāhitā à Stakhr et les premiers Sassanides," *Revue of the History of Religions*, 153, pp. 154–75.

Cheung, J., 2007. *Etymological Dictionary of the Iranian Verb*, Leiden - Boston: Brill.

Childe, V. Gordon, 1951. Social Evolution, London: Watts.

Choksy, Jamsheed, 2002. *Evil, Good, and Gender: Facets of the Feminine in Zoroastrian Religious History*, New York: Peter Lang.

Choksy, Jamsheed, and Dubeansky, Jennifer, eds., 2013. *Gifts to a Magus: Indo-Iranian Studies Honoring Firoze Kotwal*, New York: Peter Lang.

Christ, Carol P., 1997. *Rebirth of the Goddess: Finding Meaning in Feminist Spirituality*, London: Routledge.

Christensen, Arthur, 1928. *Études sur le Zoroastrisme de la Perse antique*, København: A. F. Høst.

Clarke, David and Andy Roberts, 1996. *Twilight of the Celtic Gods: An Exploration of Britain's Hidden Pagan Traditions*, London: Blandford.

Clement of Alexandria (Titus Flavius Clemens. 150–215 CE). Translation: 1958. *Protepticus*, tr. G. W. Butterworth, Cambridge, MA: Harvard University Press.

Compareti, Matteo, 2017. "Nana and Tish in Sogdiana: The Adoption from Mesopotamia of a Divine Couple," in Touraj Daryaee, ed., *Dabir*, 1/4, Samuel Jordan Center for Persian Studies and Culture University of California: Irvine, pp. 1–8.

Compareti, Matteo, 2014. "The Representation of Zoroastrian Divinities in last Sasanian Art and Their Description According to Avestan Literature," in *Aram Zoroastrianism in The Levant and The Amorites*, vol. 26, 1&2, Oxford: Aram Publishing, pp. 139–74.

Cook, Arthur Bernard, 2010 [1914]. *Zeus: A Study in Ancient Religion*, Cambridge: Cambridge University Press.

Crawford, Harriet, 1998. *Dilmun and its Gulf Neighbours*, Cambridge: Cambridge University Press.

Cultural Heritage News Agency, 2016. "Parī- daryāʾī dar xalīj-e Fārs" (Parī- daryāʾī in the Persian Gulf), http://www.chn.ir/NSite/FullStory/News/?Id=97619&Serv=3&SGr=0.

Cumont, Franz, 2013 [1913]. *Les mystères de Mithra*, Turnhout: Brepols.

Cunliffe, Barry, 1997. *The Ancient Celts*, Oxford: Oxford University Press.

Cusack, Carole M., 2007. "Brigit: Goddess, Saint, 'Holy Woman,' and Bone of Contention," in Victoria Barker and Frances Di Lauro, eds., *On a Panegyrical Note: Studies in Honour of Garry W. Trompf*, Sydney: University of Sydney, pp. 75–97.

Dalley, Stephanie, 2008. *Myths from Mesopotamia*, Oxford: Oxford University Press.

Dalley, Stephanie, 1979. "d NIN. LÍL = mul(l)is(s)u, the Treaty of Bargaʾyah, and Herodotus' Mylitta," *Revue d'assyriologie et d'archéologie orientale*, 73, 177–8.

Dandamayev, Muhammad A., 1992. *Iranians in Achaemenid Babylonia*, Costa Mesa, CA: Mazda Publishers.

Daneshvar, Simin, 1990. *Savushun*, Washington, DC: Mage.

Darmesteter, James, 1892–3. Le Zend-Avesta, I–III, Paris, Leroux.

Darmesteter, James, 1883. *The Sacred Books of the East*, vol 23. The Zend-Avesta, Part II, The Sirozahs, Yasts, And Nyayis. Oxford: The Clarendon Press.

Davidson, H. R. Ellis, 1999. "Milk and the Northern Goddess" in Sandra Billington and Miranda Green, eds., *The Concept of the Goddess*, London: Routledge, pp. 91–106.

Davidson, H. R. Ellis, 1988. *Myths and Symbols in Pagan Europe, Early Scandinavian and Celtic Religions*, Syracuse: Syracuse University Press.

De Bruecker, G., 2012. "De Babyloniaca van Berossos van Babylon: Inleiding, editie en commentaar," unpublished Ph.D. dissertation, Groningen.

De Graef, Katrien, ed., 2013. *Susa and Elam: Archaeological, Philological, Historical and Geographical Perspectives*, Leiden: Brill.

De Hoz, Maria Paz, 1999. *Die lydischen Kulte im Lichte der griecheschen indschriften*, Bonn: Habelt.

De Jong, Albert, 1997. *Traditions of the Magi: Zoroastrianism in Greek and Latin Literature*, Leiden: Brill.

De Jong, Albert, 1995. "Jeh the Primal Whore? Observations on Zoroastrian Misogyny," in Rai Kloppenborg and Wouter J. Hanegraaff, eds., *Female Stereotypes in Religious Traditions*, Leiden: Brill, pp. 15–41.

De Menasce, J. P., 1958, *Une encyclopédie mazdéenne, le Dēnkart*, Paris: Presses universitaires de France.

De Vaan, Michiel, 2003. *The Avestan Vowels*, Leiden: Rodopi.

Devlin-Glass, Frances and McCredden, Lyn, eds., 2001. *Feminist Poetics of the Sacred: Creative Suspicions*, Oxford: Oxford University Press.

Dexter, Miriam Robbins, 1990. "Reflections on the Goddess *Donu," *The Mankind Quarterly*, 31/1–2, pp. 45–57.

Dickson, Martin and Cary Welch, Stuart Jr., 1981. *The Houghton Shah-nameh*, Cambridge: Sackler Gallery.

Doniger, Wendy, ed., 1999. *Merriam-Webster's Encyclopedia of World Religions*, Springfield, MA: Merriam-Webster.

Duchesne-Guillemin, Jacques, 1971. "Art et religion sous les Sassanides," in *Atti del Convegno Internazionale sul Tema: La Persia nel Medioevo*, Rome: Accademia nazionale dei Lincei, pp. 377–88.

Duchesne-Guillemin, Jacques, 1962. *La religion de l'Iran ancien*, Paris: Presses Universitaires de France.

Duchesne-Guillemin, Jacques, 1958. *The Western Response to Zoroaster, Ratanbai Katrak Lectures, 1956*, Oxford: Oxford/Clarendon Press.

Dumézil, Georges, 1977. *Les dieux souverains des Indo-Européens*, Paris: Gallimard.

Dumézil, Georges, 1968–73. *Mythe et Épopée*, 3 vols., Paris: Gallimard.

Dumézil, Georges, 1945. *Naissance d'Archange (Jupiter Mars Quirinus, III): Essai sur la formation de la théologie zoroastrienne*, Paris: Gallimard.

Dūstxāh, Jalīl, 1370 [1991]. *Avestā*, Tehrān: Morvarīd.

Ehrenberg, Margaret, 1989. *Women in Prehistory*, London: British Museum.

Eliade, Mircea, 1978. *A History of Religious Ideas*, vol. 1, tr. Willard R. Trask, Chicago: University of Chicago Press.

Ellis, Peter Berresford, 2002. *The Mammoth Book of Celtic Myths and Legends*, London: Robinson.

Emmerick, Ronald E. and Maria Macuch, eds., 2009. *A History of Persian Literature XVII, The Literature of pre-Islamic Iran*, London: I.B. Tauris.

Enlil and Sud, 2006. Version A, Segment A, 13-21, The Electronic Text Corpus of Sumerian Literature (ETCSL), 01.vi.2003: GC/JE, editor/technical developer: XML/TEI conversion, The ETCSL project, Faculty of Oriental Studies, University of Oxford.

E'temād al-Saltaneh, 1367 [1988]. *Meraát-al-Baladān*, ed. H. Mohaddes and A. Navā'ī, Tehrān: Tehran University.

Farridnejad, Shervin, 2015. "The Iconography of Zoroastrian Angelology in Sasanian Art and Architecture," in Neils Kutschow and Katharina Weiler, eds., *Spirits in Transcultural Skies: Auspicious and Protective Spirits in Artefacts and Architecture between East and West*, Heidelberg: Springer.

Ferdowsi, Abolqasem, 2006. *Shahnameh: The Persian Book of Kings*, tr. Dick Davis, New York: Viking.

Ferdowsi, Abolqasem, 1990. *The Shāhnāmeh (The Book of Kings)*, ed. Djalāl Khāleghī-Motlagh, 8 vols., Winona Lake: Eisenbrauns.

Fitzgerald, Timothy, 2000. *The Ideology of Religious Studies*, New York: Oxford University Press, pp. 3–32.

Foltz, Richard, 2013. *Religions of Iran: From Prehistory to the Present*, London: Oneworld.

Frawley, David, 2001. *The Rig Veda and the History of India*, New Delhi: Aditya Prakashan.

Gardner, Iain, 1995. *The Kephalaia of the Teacher: The Edited Coptic Manichaean Texts in Translation with Commentary*, Leiden: Brill.

Gavrilovic, Nadezda, 2013. "Relief of Epona from Viminacium-Certain Considerations about the Cult of Epona in Central Balkans," in Wolfgang Spickermann, ed., *Verbindung mit Leif Scheuermann*, Akten des 11. internationalen Workshops "Fontes Epigraphici Religionum Celticarum Antiquarum" vom 19.-21, an der Universität Erfurt, Mai 2011, Leidorf: Rahden, pp. 250–61.

Geiger, W., 1882. *Ostiranische Kultur im Alterum*, Erlangen: Deichert.

Geldner, K. F., 1896. *Avesta, the Sacred Books of the Parsis*, 3 vols., Stuttgart: Kohlhammer.

Geldner, K.F., 1881. Überesetzungen aus dem Avesta, II, Vendidad, 2, 15, 5, III., IV., Jasht, 5, 6, 8, 10, 13, Vendidad 13. 14, 8, 16, In: KZ, 25, pp. 179–212, 378–419, 465–590.

Ghirshman, Roman, 1962. *Persian Art: Parthian and Sassanian Dynasties*, London: Golden Press.

Ghirshman, Roman, 1961. *Iran*, Baltimore: Penguin.

Gibson, Marion, 2013. *Imagining the Pagan Past: Gods and Goddesses in Literature and History since the Dark Ages*, London: Routledge.

Gignoux, Philippe, 2005. "*Zādspram*," *Encyclopædia Iranica*.

Gignoux, Philippe,1994. "*Dēnkard*," *Encyclopædia Iranica*, VII, Fasc. 3, pp. 284–9.

Gignoux, Philippe,1986. "Ardā Wīrāz," *Encyclopædia Iranica*, II, Fasc. 4, pp. 356–7.

Gignoux, Philippe, 1986. "Sur l'inexistence d'un Bahman Yasht avestique," *Journal of Asian and African Studies*, 32, pp. 53–64.

Gignoux, Philippe, 1984. *Le Livre d'Ardā Virāz*, Paris: Editions Recherche sur les civilisations.

Gignoux, Philippe and Ahmad Tafazzoli, 1993. *Anthologie de Zadspram: Édition critique du texte Pehlevi*, Paris: Association pour l'avancement des études iraniennes.

Gimbutas, Marija, 1982. *The Goddesses and Gods of Old Europe, 6500–3500 BCE: Myth and Cult Images*, Berkeley: University of California Press.

Gnoli, Gherardo, 2009. "Some notes upon the Religious Significance of the Rabatak Inscription," in Werner Sundermann, Almut Hintze and François de Blois, eds., *Iranica 17, Exegisti monumenta, Fistchrift in Honor of Nicolas Sims-Williams*, Weisbaden: Harrassowitz, pp. 141–60.

Gnoli, Gherardo, 2003a. "Helmand River ii: In Zoroastrian Tradition," *Encyclopædia Iranica*, XII, Fasc. 2, pp. 171–2.

Gnoli, Gherardo, 2003b. "Hāmūn, ii: in Literature and Mythology," *Encyclopædia Iranica*, XI, Fasc. 6, pp. 647–8.

Gnoli, Gherardo, 1993. "Dāityā, Vaŋhvī," *Encyclopædia Iranica*, VI, Fasc. 6, pp. 598–9.

Gnoli, Gherardo, 1991. "L'Iran antico e lo Zoroastrismo," in Julien Ries, ed., *Trattato di Antropologia del Sacro, 2. L'uomo indoeuropeo e il sacro*, Milan: Jaca Book - Massimo.

Gnoli, Gherardo, 1988. "Bahrām," *Encyclopædia Iranica*, III/5, pp. 510–14.

Gnoli, Gherardo, 1974. "Politique religieuse et conception de la royauté sous les Achéménides," in *Acta Iranica* 2, Leiden: Brill, pp. 117–90.

Göbl, R., 1968. *Sasanidische Numismatik*, Braunschweig: Klinkhardt & Biermann.

Gordon, Richard 2015. "From Miθra to Roman Mithras," in Michael Stausberg and Yuhan Vevaina, eds., *The Wiley-Blackwell Companion to Zoroastrianism*, Malden: Wiley-Blackwell, pp. 451–5.

Gordon-Childe, V., 1951. *Social Evolution*, London: Watts.

Gotō, Toshifumi, 2000. "Vasistha und Varuna in RV VI{I} 88 Priesteramt des Vasistha und Suche nach seinem indoiranischen Hintergrund," in Herausgegeben von, Bernhard Forssman und Robert Plath, ed., *Indoarisch, Iranisch une die Indogermanistik*, Wiesbaden: Reichert Verlag, pp. 147–61.

Gray, L.H., 1929. *The Foundation of the Iranian Religion*, Bombay: K.R. Cama Oriental Institute.

Gray, R. Varner, 2009. *Sacred Wells: A Study in the History, Meaning and Mythology of Holy Wells and Waters*, New York: Allgora Publishing.

Green, Miranda, 2004. *The Gods of the Celts*, rev. ed., Stroud: Sutton Publishing.

Green, Miranda, 1999. "The Celtic Goddess as Healer," in Sandra Billington and Miranda Green, eds., *The Concept of the Goddess*, London: Routledge, pp. 36–40.

Green, Miranda, 1993. *Celtic Myths*, Austin: University of Texas Press.

Green, Miranda, 1992. *Symbol and Image in Celtic Religious Art*, London: Routledge.

Grenet, Frantz, 2015. "Zoroastrianism in Central Asia," in Michael Stausberg and Yuhan Vevaina, eds., *The Wiley Blackwell Companion to Zoroastrianism*, Malden: Wiley-Blackwell, pp. 129–46.

Grenet, Frantz, 1984. *Les pratiques funeraires dans l'Asie centrale sédentaire de la conquête grecque à l'islamisation*, Paris: CNRS.

Grenet, Frantz and Boris Ilich Marshak, 1998. "Le mythe de Nana dans l'art de la Sogdiane," *Arts Asiatiques*, 53, pp. 5–18.

Griffith, Ralph T. H., *The Rig Veda*, Evinity Publishing. Kindle Edition.

Grimal, Pierre, 1964. *Mythologies*, Paris: Larousse.

Gross, Rita M., 2002. "Feminist Issues and Methods in the Anthropology of Religion," in Arvind Sharma, ed., *Methodology in Religious Studies: The Interface with Women's Studies*, New York: State University of New York Press, pp. 40–66.

Grundy, Stephan, 1999. "Freyja and Frigg, "Freyja and Frigg," in Sandra Billington and Miranda Green, eds., *The Concept of the Goddess*, London: Routledge, pp. 59–67.

Guirand, Felix, 1996. The *Larousse Encyclopedia of Mythology*, London: Chancellor Press.

Hale, Wash Edward, 1999. *Asura in Early Vedic Tradition*, Delhi: Motilal Banarsidas.

Hallo, W., and W. Simpson, 1971. *The Ancient Near East*, New York: Harcourt, Brace, Jovanovich.

Hanaway, William L., 1988. "Bahman-Nāma," *Encyclopædia Iranica*, III, Fasc. 5, pp. 499–500.

Hanaway, William L., Jr., 1982a. "Ābāndokht," *Encyclopædia Iranica*, I/1, p. 61.

Hanaway, William L., Jr., 1982b. "Anahita and Alexander," *Journal of the American Oriental Society*, 102/2, pp. 285–95.

Harrison, Jane Ellen, 1962. *Prolegomena to the Study of Greek Religion*, London: Merlin Press.

Hauser, Stefan R. 2013. "The Arsacids (Parthians)", in Daniel T. Potts, ed., *The Oxford Handbook of Ancient Iran*, Oxford: Oxford University Press, pp. 728–50.

Hellholm, David, ed., 1983. *Apocalypticism*, Tübingen: Mohr.

Henkelmann, W. F. M., 2008. *The Other Gods Who Are: Studies in Elamite-Iranian Acculturation Based on the Persepolis Fortification Texts*, Leiden: Nino.

Henning, W. B., 1964. "A Sogdian God," *Bulletin of the School of Oriental and African Studies*, 28/2, pp. 242–54.

Herodotus, 1998, *The Histories*, tr. Robert Waterfield, New York: Oxford University Press.

Herrenschmidt, Clarisse and Jean Kellens, 1993. "Daiva," *Encyclopaedia Iranica*.

Hertel, Johannes, 1927. *Die Sonne und Mithraim Awesta, auf grund der awestischen feuerlehre dargestellt*, Leipzig: Haessel.

Hintze, Almut, 2015. "Zarathustra's Time and Homeland: Linguistic Perspectives," in Michael Stausberg and Yuhan Vevaina, eds., *The Wiley-Blackwell Companion to Zoroastrianism*, Malden: Wiley-Blackwell, pp. 31–8.

Hintze, Almut, 2014a. "Monotheism the Zoroastrian Way," *Journal of the Royal Asiatic Society*, 24, pp. 225–49.

Hintze, Almut, 2014b. "Avestan Research 1991–2014. Part 1: Sources and Phonology," *Kratylos*, 59, pp. 1–52.

Hintze, Almut, 2014. "YAŠTS," *Encyclopædia Iranica*.

Hintze, Almut, 2013. "On the Prophetic and Priestly Authority of Zarathstra," in Jamsheed Choksy and Jennifer Dubeansky, eds., *Gifts to a Magus: Indo-Iranian Studies Honoring Firoze Kotwal*, New York: Peter Lang, pp. 43–58.

Hintze, Almut, 2012. "On Editing the Avesta," in Alberto Cantera, ed., *The Transmission of the Avesta*, Wiesbaden: Harrassowitz, pp. 419–32.

Hintze, Almut, 2009. "Avestan Literature," in Ronald E. Emmerick and Maria Mauch, eds., *The Literature of Pre-Islamic Iran*, London: I.B. Tauris, pp. 1–71.

Hintze, Almut, 2007. *A Zoroastrian Liturgy: The Worship in Seven Chapters*, Iranica Herausgegeben von Maria Macuch, Band 12, Wiesbaden: Harrassowitz Verlag.

Hintze, Almut, 2005 [2009]. "The Cow That Came from the Moon: The Avestan Expression *mah- gaociθra-*," *Bulletin of the Asia Institute*, 19, pp. 57–66.

Hintze, Almut, 2003. Review of Choksy, *Evil, Good, and Gender, Facts of the Feminine in Zoroastrian Religious History*, *Journal of the Royal Asiatic* Society, 83/3, pp. 403–10.

Hintze, Almut, 1999. "The Saviour and the Dragon in Iranian and Jewish/Christian Eschatology," in Shaul Shaked and Amnon Netzer, eds., *Irano-Judaica* IV, Jerusalem: Ben-Zvi Institute for the Study of Jewish Communities in the East.

Hintze, Almut, 1995. "The Rise of the Saviour in the Avesta," in Christiane Reckand Peter Zieme, eds., *Iran und Turfan. Beiträge Berliner Wissenschaftler, Werner Sundermann zum 60. Geburtstag gewidmet*. Wiesbaden: Harrassowitz, pp. 77–97.

Hintze, Almut, 1994. *Der Zamyād-Yašt*, Wiesbaden: Harrassowitz.

Hinz, Walter, 1973. *The Lost World of Elam: Re-creation of a Vanished Civilization*, New York: New York University Press.

Hjerrild, Bodil, 2009. "Near Estern Equivalents to Artemis" in Tobias Fischer-Hansen and Birte Poulsen, eds., *From Artemis to Diana, The Goddess of Man and Beast*, Copenhagen: Museum Tusculanum Press, pp, 41–50.

Hoffmann, Karl, 1975. *Aufsätze zur Indoiranistik*, 2 Wiesbaden: Band, herausgegeben von J. Narten.

Hübner, E., 1877. "Der Fund von Procolitia," *Hermes: Zeitschrift für Klassiche Philologie*, 12, pp. 257–72.

Hubbs, Joanna, 1993. *Mother Russia: The Feminine Myth in Russian Culture*, Bloomington: Indiana University Press.

Hughes, Kathleen, 2008. *Early Christian Ireland – Introduction to the Sources*, Cambrige: Cambridge University Press.

Hultgård, Anders, 1983. "Forms and Origins of Iranian Apocalypticism," in David Hellholm, ed., *Apocalypticism*, Tübingen: Mohr, pp. 388–411.

Humbach, Helmut, 1991. *The Gāthās of Zarathushtra and the Other Old Avestan Texts*, 2 vols., Heidelberg: Universitätsverlag Winter.

Humbach, Helmut, 1959. *Die Gathas des Zarathustra*, Heidelberg: C. Winter.

Humbach, Helmut and Pallan R. Ichaporia, 1998. *Zamyād Yasht: Yasht 19 of the Younger Avesta: Text, Translation, Commentary*, Wiesbaden: Harrassowitz.

Humbach, Helmut and Prods O. Skjærvø, 1983. *The Sassanian Inscription of Paikuli, Part 3.1*, Restored text and translation by Prods Skjærvø, Wiesbaden: Reichert Verlag.

Isadore of Charax, 1976. *Parthian Stations*, tr. Wilfred H. Schoff, Chicago: Ares.

Ivanits, Linda J., 1992. *Russian Folk Belief*, Armonk, NY: M.E. Sharpe.

Jacobson, Esther, 1995. *The Art of Scythians: The Interpenetration of Cultures at the Edge of the Hellenic World*, Leiden: Brill.

Jamison, Stephanie W., and Brereton, Joel P., 2014, *The Rigveda: The Earliest Religious Poetry of India*, NY: Oxford University Press.

Jolliffe, Nora, 1942. "Dea Brigantia," *The Archaeological Journal*, 98, pp. 34–61.

Jones, Barri and David Mattingly, 1990. *An Atlas of Roman Britain*, Oxford: Blackwell.

Josephson, Judith, 2012. "An Analysis of the Literary Structure of the *Zand ī Wahman Yasn*," *Iranian Studies*, 45/2, pp. 243–60.

Julius Caesar, 1870. *Commentaries on the Gallic War*, tr. W. A. McDevitte and W. S. Bohn, New York: Harper.

Justi, F., 1963 [1895]. *Iranisches Namenbuch*, Hildesheim: G. Olms.

Kawami, Trudy S., 2013. "Parthian and Elymaean Rock Reliefs," in Daniel T. Potts, ed., *The Oxford Handbook of Ancient Iran*, Oxford: Oxford University Press, pp. 751–65.

Keith, A. B., 1925. *The Religion and Philosophy of the Veda and Upanishad*, Cambridge, MA: Harvard University Press.

Kellens, Jean, 2013. "Jahika et le Vocabulaire Daivique," in Jamsheed K. Choksy and Jennifer Dubeansky, eds., *Gifts to a Magus: Indo-Iranian Studies Honoring Firoze Kotwal*, New York: Peter Lang, pp. 123–7.

Kellens, Jean, 2011. "Problèmes du monothéisme vieil-avestique," lecture presented at Concordia University, Montréal, 12 May.

Kellens, Jean, 2006. *La Quatrième Naissance de Zarathushtra*, Paris: Seuil.

Kellens, Jean, 2002–03. "Le problème avec Anāhitā," *Orientalia Suecana*, 51-2, pp. 317-26.

Kellens, Jean, 2002. "Hādōxt Nask," *Encyclopaedia Iranica*, XI, Fasc. 5, pp. 457–8.

Kellens, Jean, 1996. "Drvāspā," *Encyclopædia Iranica*, VII, Fasc. 6, p. 565.

Kellens, Jean, 1994. "Dēn Yašt," *Encyclopædia Iranica*, VII, Fasc. 3, pp. 281–2.

Kellens, Jean, 1987. "Avesta: Survey of the history and the contents of the book," III, Fasc. 1, pp. 35–44.

Kellens, Jean, 1984. *Le verbe avestique*, Wiesbaden: Reichert.

Kellens, Jean, 1978. "Caractères différentiels du Mihr Yašt," in *Études Mithriaques. Actes du 2e Congrès International Téhéran, du 1er auf 8 septembre 1975*, Acta Iranica 17, Tehran and Liège: Bril, pp. 261–70.

Kellens, Jean, 1974a. *Les Noms-Racines de L'Avesta*, Wiesbaden: Reichert.

Kellens, Jean, 1974b. "Saošiiant-," *Studia Iranica*, 3, pp. 187–209.

Kent, Roland. G., 1953. *Old Persian Grammar*, New Haven: American Oriental Society, 1953.

Kernd'l, A., R. Richhardt, and W. Eisold, 1961. *Wörterbuch der russischen Gewässernamen*, Wiesbaden: Harrassowitz.

Khaleghi-Moghadam, Jalal, 1996. "The Ideal Beauty in Iranian Culture," *Īrānšenāsī*, 8/4, pp. 703–16.

Khaleghi-Motlagh, Djalal, 2012. *Women in the Shāhnāmeh*, Costa Mesa, CA: Mazda Publishers.

Khaleghi-Motlagh, Djalal, 1999. "About the Identity of Siāvaš's Mother," *Īrānšenāsī*, 66, pp. 273–8.

Khaleghi-Motlagh, Djalal, 1996. "The Ideal Beauty in Iranian Culture," *Īrānšenāsī*, 8/4, pp. 703–16.

Khaleghi-Motlagh, Djalal, 1987. "Aždahā: In Persian Literature," *Encyclopædia Iranica*.

Khosravī, M. B., 2000. "Āb dar farhang va honar va meʾmārī-ye īrānī" (Water in Iranian Culture, Art and Architecture), *Fasl-nāme-ye honar*, 42, pp. 112–20.

Kia, Khojasteh, 1371 [1992]. *Soxanān sazāvar zanān dar Šāh-nāme-ye pahlavānī* (Notes on Women in the Heroic *Šāh-nāmeh*), Tehrān: Našr-i fāxtah.

King, L. W., ed., 1907. *Chronicles Concerning Early Babylonian Kings*, London: Luzac.

Kinsley, David R., 1988. *Hindu Goddesses: Visions of the Divine Feminine in the Hindu Religious Tradition*, University of California Press.

Kitson, Peter. R., 1997. "Reconstruction, typology, and the 'original homeland" of the Indo-Europeans," in Jacek Fisiak, ed., *Trends in Linguistics Studies and Monographs 96, Linguistic Reconstruction and Typology*, Berlin & New York: Mouton de Gruyter, pp. 183–240.

Kitson, Peter. R., 1996. "British and European River Names," *Transactions of the Philological Society*, 94/2, pp. 73–118.

Koch-Westenholz, Ulla, 1995. *Mesopotamian Astrology: An Introduction to Babylonian and Assyrian Celestial Divination*, Copenhagen: Museum Tusculanum Press.

König, Götz, 2018. *Studien zur Rationalitätsgeschichte im älteren Iran. Ein Beitrag zur Achsenzeitdiskussion.* (Iranica 26), Wiesbaden, Chapter III, pp. 56–114.

Kondratiev, Alexei, 1998. "Danu and Bile: The Primordial Parents," *An Tríbhís Mhór: The IMBAS Journal of Celtic Reconstructionism* 1/4, www.imbas.org/danubile. htm.

Kotwal Firoze and Almut Hintze, 2008. *The Khorda Avesta and Yašt Codex E1*, Wiesbaden: Harrassowitz.

Kovács Teleki, Suzanne, 1967. "Sumerian Origin of the Names of the River 'Ister-Danube': A Study in Prehistory and Philology," Paper presented to the International Congress of Orientalists, University of Michigan, Ann Arbor.

Kramer, Samouel Noah, 1963, *The Sumerians: Their History, Culture, And Character*, Chicago & London, The University of Chicago Press.

Kreyenbroek, G., 1985. *Sraoša in the Zoroastrian Tradition*, Leiden: Brill.

Kuiper, F. B. J., 1960. "The Ancient Aryan Verbal Contest," *Indo-Iranian Journal*, 4/ 4 pp. 217–81.

Kuhrt, Amélie, 2013. "Can We Understand How the Persians Perceived Other Gods'/the 'God of Others'?" *Archiv für Religionsgeschichte*, 15, pp. 149–65.

Kuyaji, J. C., 1974. *Cults and Legends of Ancient Iran and China*, tr. Jalil Dustkhah, Tehran: Organization of Fine Arts.

Kuz'mina, Elena E., 2007. *The Origin of the Indo-Iranians*, Leiden: Brill.

Labourt, J., 1904. *Le Christianisme dans l'empire perse*, Paris.

Lāhījī, Shahlā, and Mehrangīz Kār, eds., 2002. *Šenāxt-e hoviat-e zan-e īrānī: dar gostare-ye pīsh-tārīx va tārīx* (The Quest of Identity: The image of Iranian women in prehistory and history), Tehrān: Roshangarān.

Lamberg-Karlovsky, C. C., ed., 1979. *Hunters, Farmers and Civilizations: Old World Archaeology*, San Francisco: W. H. Freeman.

Lincoln, Bruce, 2014. "Ancestors, Corpses, Kings and the Land: Symbolic Construction in Ancient Indis and Iran," in Touraj Daryaee, Ali Mousavi and Khodada Rezakhani, eds., *Excavating an Empire: Achaemenid Persia in Longue Durée*, Costa Mesa: Mazda Publishers, pp. 181–8.

Lincoln, Bruce, 1976. "The Indo-European Cattle-Raiding Myth," *History of Religions*, 16/1, pp. 42–65.

Lommel, Hermann, 1954. "Anahita-Sarasvati," *Asiatica: Festschrift für Friedrich Weller Zum*, 65, Leipzig: Harrassowitz, pp. 405–13.

Lommel, Hermann, 1927. *Die Yašts des Awesta*, Leipzig: J. C. Hinrichs.

Lubotsky, Alexandre, 2002. *Atharvaveda-Paippalāda, Kānda Five, Text, Translation, Commentary*, Harvard Oriental Series, Opera Minora vol. 4, Cambridge: Department of Sanskrit and Indian Studies.

Mackenzie, D. N., 2002. "Gōzihr," *Encyclopædia Iranica*, XI, Fasc. 2, p. 184.

Mackenzie, D. N., 1998. "ÊRĀN-WĒZ," *Encyclopædia Iranica*, VIII, Fasc. 5, p. 536.

Mackenzie, D. N., 1989. "Bundahišn," *Encyclopædia Iranica*, IV, Fasc. 5, pp. 547–51.

Mackenzie, D. N., 1986. *A Concise Pahlavi Dictionary*, Oxford: Oxford University Press.

Mackenzie, D. N., 1964. "Zoroastrian Astrology in the *Bundahišn*," *Bulletin of the School of Oriental and African Studies*, 27/3, pp. 511–29.

MacLeod, Sharon Paice, 2011. *Celtic Myth and Religion: A Study of Traditional Belief, with Newly Translated Prayers, Poems and Songs*, Jefferson, NC: McFarland.

Macuch, Maria, 2010. "Legal Constructions of Identity in the Sasanian Period," in Carlo G. Cereti, ed., *Iranian Identity in The Course Of History*, Roma: Istituto Italiano Per L'Africa E L'Oriente, pp. 193–212.

Macuch, Maria, 2009a. "Gelehrte Frauen: ein ungewöhnliches Motiv in der Pahlavi-Literatur," in D. Durkin-Meisterernst, Chr Reck and D. Weber, eds., *Literarische Stoffe und ihre Gestaltung in mitteliranischer Zeit. Colloquium anlässlich des 70. Geburtstags von Werner Sundermann*, Wiesbaden: Harrassowitz, pp. 135–51.

Macuch, Maria, 2009b. "Disseminating the Mazdayasnian Religion: An Edition of the Pahlavi Hērbedestān Chapter 5," in Werner Sundermann, Almut Hintze and François Blois, eds., *Iranica 17-Exegisti monumenta, Festschrift in Honour of Nicholas Sims-Williams*, Wiesbaden: Harrassowitz, pp. 251–78.

Macuch, Maria, 2009c. "Judicial and Legal Systems iii. Sasanian Legal System," *Encyclopædia Iranica*, XV, Fasc. 2, pp. 181–96.

Madan, D. M., 1911. *The Complete Text of the Pahlavi Dinkard*, 2 vols., Bombay: Society for the Promotion of Researches into the Zoroastrian Religion.

Majlesi, Mohammad Bagher, (1627–99) 1998. *Bihar ul Anwar* (Oceans of lights), ed. Mohamad Ruhani Ali-Abadi, vol. 43, *Hadith* 34. Tehran: Maham.

Malandra, William, 2014. "Vāyu," *Encyclopædia Iranica*.

Malandra, William, 2013. "Anāhitā: What's in a Name?" in Jamsheed K. Choksy and Jennifer Dubeansky, eds., *Gifts to a Magus: Indo-Iranian Studies Honoring Firoze Kotwal*, New York: Peter Lang, pp. 104–11.

Malandra, William, 2002. "Gōš Yašt," *Encyclopædia Iranica*, XI, Fasc. 2, p. 167.

Malandra, William, 1983. *An Introduction to Ancient Iranian Religion*, Minneapolis: University of Minnesota Press.

Malekzādeh, Mehrdād, 1381 [2002]. "Sarzamīn-e pariān dar xāk-e Mādestān" (The Land of the *Pari*s in Media), *Nāmeh-ye farhangestān*, 4/5, pp. 147–91.

Mallory, J. P., and Douglas Q. Adams, 2006. *The Oxford Introduction to Proto-Indo-European and the Proto-Indo-European World*, Oxford: Oxford University Press.

Markey, T. L., 2001. "Ingvaeonic *sterir 'star' and Astral Priests," *North Western European Language Evolution*, 39, pp. 85–113.

Maškūr, Mohammad Javād, 1389 [2010]. *Kār-nāmeye Ardešīr-e Bābakān*, Tehrān: Donyā-ye ketāb.

Mayrhofer, Manfred, 1992. *Etymologisches Wörterbuch des Altindoarischen*, Band. I, Heidelberg, Carl Winter Universitärverlag.

Mayrhofer, Manfred, 1979. *Iranisches Personennamenbuch*, Band. I, *Die Altiranischen Namen*, Wien: Österreichische Akademie der Wissenschaften.

Mazdapour, Katayun, 2002. "Afsāneh-ye parī dar hezār va yek shab," in Shahlā Lāhījī and Mehrangīz Kār, eds., *Šenāxt-e hoviat-e zan-e īrānī: dar gostare-ye pīsh-tārīx va tārīx (The Quest of Identity: The image of Iranian women in prehistory and history)*, Tehran: Roshangarān, pp. 290–342.

McCall, Henrietta, 1990. *Mesopotamian Myths*, Austin: University of Texas Press.

McDevitte, W. A., and W. S. Bohn, 1870. *Julius Caesar, Commentaries on the Gallic War*, Book 6. New York: Harper Brothers.

Mellaart, James, 1964. "A Neolithic City in Turkey," *Scientific American*, April, pp. 94–104.

Méndez, Isreal Campos, 2013. "Anahita and Mithra in the Achaemenid Roya Inscription," in Nabarz, Payam, ed., *Anahita: Ancient Persian Goddess and Zoroastrian Yazata*, London: Avalonia.

Merchant, Carolyn, 1980. *The Death of Nature: Women, Ecology, and the Scientific Revolution*, San Francisco: HarperCollins.

Meskell, Lynn, 1995. "Goddesses, Gimbutas and 'New Age' Archaeology," *Antiquity*, 69, pp. 74–86. *Metrical Dindshenchas*, 1991 [1903–35], ed., Edward Gwynn, Dublin: School of Celtic Studies.

Meyer, E., 1877. "Ueber einige semitische Gotter," *Zeitschriften der Deutschen Morgenländischen Gesellschaft*, 31, pp. 716–22.

Miller, D. Gary, 2012. *External Influences on English: From the Beginning to the Renaissance*, Oxford: Oxford University Press.

Mīr-Faxrā'ī, Mahšīd, 1371 [1993]. *Haδaoxta-Nask*, Tehrān: Pažohešgāh.

Molé, Marijan, 1967. *La légende de Zoroastre selon les textes pehlevis*, Paris.

Molé, Marijan, 1963. *Culte, mythe et cosmologie dans l'Iran ancien*, Paris: Presses universitaires de France.

Monchi-Zadeh, D., 1982. "Xus-rôv i Kavâtân ut Rêtak," in Jacques Duchesne-Guillemin, ed., *Monumentum Georg Morgenstierne*, vol. II. *Acta Iranica* 22, Leiden: Brill, pp. 47–91.

Moore, Dian. L., 2015. "Diminishing Religious Literacy: Methodological Assumptions and Analytical Framework for Promoting the Public Understanding of Religion," in Dinham Adam and Francis Matthew, eds., *Religious Literacy in Policy and Practice*, Bristol: Policy Press University of Bristol, pp. 27–39.

Müller, Friedrich Max, 1891–97. *The Sacred Books of the East, Vedic Hymns*, Oxford: Clarendon Press.

Nabarz, Payam, ed., 2013. *Anahita: Ancient Persian Goddess and Zoroastrian Yazata*, London: Avalonia.

Nadelhaft, Ruth, 1999. "Myth, Revision Of", in Helen Tierney, ed., *Women Studies Encyclopedia*, vol. 2, New York: Greenwood Press, pp. 967–9.

Narten, Johanna, 1986. *Der Yasna Haptaŋhāiti*, Weisbaden: Harrassowitz.

Narten, Johanna, 1982. *Die Aməša Spəṇtas im Avesta*, Wiesbaden: Harrassowitz.

Noegel, Scott, Walker, Joel, and Brannon Wheeler, eds., 2003. *Prayer, Magic, and the Stars in the Ancient and Late Antique World*, University Park: The Pennsylvania State University Press.

Nöldeke, Theodor, 1973 [1879]. *Geschichte der Perser und Arbaer Zur Zeit der Sasaniden*, Leiden: Brill.

Näsström, Britt-Mari, 1999. "Freyja: A Goddess with Many Names," in Sandra Billington and Miranda Green, eds., *The Concept of the Goddess*, London: Routledge, pp. 68–77.

Nyberg, H. S., 1938. *Die Religionen des alten Iran*, Leipzig: J. C. Hinrichs.

Oakley, G. T., 2006. *Verbeia, The Goddess of Wharfedale*, London: Dreamflesh.

O Cathasaigh, Donal, 1982. "The Cult of Brigid: A Study of Pagan-Christian Syncretism in Ireland," in James J. Preston, ed., *Mother Worship: Theme and Variations*, Chapel Hill: University of North Carolina Press, pp. 75–94.

Oettinger, Norbert, 2001. "Neue Gedanken über das nt-Suffix," in Onofrio Carruba, and Wolfgang Meid, eds., *Anatolisch und Indogermanisch*, Innsbruck: Institute für Sprachen und Literaturen der Universität Innsbruck, pp. 301–15.

Oettinger, Norbert, 1983. "Untersuchungen zur Avestischen Sprache am Beispiel des *Ardwīsūr-Yašt*," unpublished habilitation thesis, Munich: Ludwig-Maximilian Universität.

Ohtsu, Tadahiko, 2010. "Kaluraz," *Encyclopædia Iranica*, XV, Fasc. 4, pp. 409–12.

Olmstead, A. T., 1948. *History of the Persian Empire*, Chicago: University of Chicago Press.

Oryān, Saʿīd, 1371 [1993]. *Motūn-e pahlavī* (Pahlavi texts), Tehrān: National Library.

Pākzād, Fazlollāh, 2005. *Bundahišn*, Ancient Iranian Studies Series, Tehran: Center for the Great Islamic Encyclopaedia.

Panaino, Antonio, 2015. "Cosmologies and Astrology," in Michael Stausberg and Yuhan Vevaina, eds., *The Wiley Blackwell Companion to Zoroastrianism*, Malden: Wiley-Blackwell, pp. 235–57.

Panaino, Antonio, 2013. "The "Gift" of the "Givers," in Jamsheed K. Choksy and Jennifer Dubeansky, eds., *Gifts to a Magus: Indo-Iranian Studies Honoring Firoze Kotwal*, New York: Peter Lang, pp. 137–45.

Panaino, Antonio, 2005. "Tištrya," *Encyclopædia Iranica*.

Panaino, Antonio, 2004. "Hordād," *Encyclopædia Iranica*, XII/5, pp. 458–60.

Panaino, Antonio, 2000. "The Mesopotamian Heritage of Achaemenian Kingship," in Sanno Aro and R. M. Whiting, eds., *The Heirs of Assyria: Proceedings of the Opening Symposium of the Assyrian and Babylonian Heritage Project*, Helsinki: The Neo-Assyrian Text Corpus Project, pp. 35–49.

Panaino, Antonio, 1996. "Dūžyāirya," *Encyclopædia Iranica*, VII, Fasc. 6, pp. 615–16.

Panaino, Antonio, 1990–95. *Tištrya: The Avestan Hymn to Sirius*, Rome: Instituto italiano per il Medio ed Estremo Oriente.

Panaino, A., and A. Piras, eds., 2006. *Proceedings of the Fifth Conference of the Societas Iranologica Europea*, Milan: Mimesis.

Pausanias, 1965. *Description of Greece*, tr. J. G. Frazer, New York: Biblo and Tannen.

Paz de Hoz, M., 1999. *Die lydischen Kulte im Lichte der griecheschen indschriften*, Bonn: Habelt.

Petrosyan, Armen, 2007. "The Indo-European *H2ner (t)-s and the Dānu Ttribe," *Institute of Archeology and Ethnography*, 35/3, pp. 342–54.

Pintchman, Tracy, 1994. *Rise of the Goddess in the Hindu Tradition*, Albany: State University of New York Press.

Pirart, Eric, 2003. "Les parties étiologiques de l'Ardvīsūr Bānūg Yašt et les noms de la grande déesse iranienne," *Indo-Iranian Journal*, 46, pp. 199–222.

Pirart, Eric, 1997. *Syntaxe des langues indo-iraniennes anciennes*, Barcelona: Sabadell: Editorial Ausa : Institut del Pròxim Orient Antic, AUSA.

Piras, Andrea, 2000. *HĀDŌXT NASK 2*, Il Racconto Zoroastiano Della Sorte Dell'Anima, Roma.

Piras, Andrea, 1996. "*Āsna-xratu*: Innate or Rising Wisdom," *East and West*, 46/1–2, pp. 9–19.

Pliny, 1944. *Natural History*, tr. H. Rackham, Cambridge, MA: Harvard University Press.

Plutarch, 2016. *The Life of Artaxerxes*, in Koen De Temmerman and Kristoffel Demoen, eds., *Writing Biography in Greece and Rome: Narrative Technique and Fictionalization*, Cambridge: Cambridge University Press.

Polybius, 2010. *The Histories*, tr. Robin Waterfield, Oxford: Oxford University Press.

Potts, Daniel T., ed., 2013. *The Oxford Handbook of Ancient Iran*, Oxford: Oxford University Press.

Potts, Daniel T., 2013. "In the Shadow of Kurangun: Cultural Developments in the Highlands between Khuzestan and Anšan," in Katrien De Graef and Jan Tavernier, eds., *Susa and Elam: Archaeological, Philological, Historical and Geographical Perspectives: Proceedings of the International Congress Held at Ghent University, December 14–17, 2009*, Leiden: Brill, pp. 129–38.

Potts, Daniel T., ed., 2012. *A Companion to the Archaeology of the Ancient Near East*, vol. I, Chichester: Wiley-Blackwell.

Potts, Daniel T., ed., 2001. "Nana in Bactria" in Silk Road Art and Archeology 7 (S.R.A.A., VII), Jornal of the Institue of Silk Road Studies, Kamakura, pp. 23–35.

Potts, Daniel T., ed., 1997, *Mesopotamian Civilization: The Material Foundation*, London, The Athelone Press.

Preston, James J., ed., 1982. *Mother Worship: Theme and Variations*, Chapel Hill: University of North Carolina Press.

Punthakey-Mistree, Firoza, 2013. "Laying of the Sopra-e Shah Pariya," in Jamsheed K. Choksy and Jennifer Dubeansky, eds., *Gifts to a Magus*, New York: Peter Lang, pp. 195–204.

Raffaelli, Enrico. G., 2013. *The Sih-Rozag in Zoroastrianism: A Textual and Historico-Religious Analysis*, London: Routledge.

Rashīd-Mohāsel, Mohammad-Taghī, 1390 [2010]. *Vizīdagīhā ī Zādspram*, Tehrān: Cultural and Research Studies Institute.

Rashīd-Mohāsel, Mohammad-Taghī, 1389 [2009]. *Dēnkard-e Haftom* (The Seventh Dēnkard), Tehrān: Cultural and Research Studies Institute.

Rashīd-Mohāsel, Mohammad-Taghī, 1370 [1991]. *Zand ī Wahman Yasn*, Tehrān: Cultural and Research Studies Institute.

Rasuly-Paleczek, Gabriele, and Julia Katschnig, eds., 2005. *Central Asia on Display, Proceedings of the VII Conference of the European Society for Central Asian Studies, Vienna 2000*, vol. 2, Reihe: Wiener Zentralasien Studien.

Reichelt, Hans, 1968 [1911]. *Avesta Reader: Text, Notes, Glossary and Index*, Berlin: De Gruyter.

Rezania, Kianoosh, 2017. "The Dēnkard against Its Islamic Discourse" in *Der Islam* 94, Issue 2, Berlin: De Gruyter, pp. 336–362.

Ricl, Marijana, 2002. "The Cult of the Iranian Goddess Anāhitā in Anatolia before and after Alexander," *Živa Antica*, 52, pp. 197–210.

Robbins Dexter, Miriam, 1990. "Reflections on the Goddess *Donu," *The Mankind Quarterly*, 31/1–2, pp. 45–58.

Rose, Jennifer, 2015. "Gender," in M. Stausberg and Y. Vevaina, eds., *The Wiley Blackwell Companion to Zoroastrianism*, Malden: Wiley-Blackwell, pp. 141–56, 273–87.

Rose, Jennifer, 2011. "In Praise of the Good Waters: Continuity and purpose in Zoroastrian lay rituals" in N. Bagherpour-Kashani and Th. Stöllner, eds., *Water and Caves in Ancient Iranian Religion: Aspects of Archaeology, Cultural History and Religion*, vol. 43, Archäologische Mitteilungen aus Iran und Turan, Deutsches Archäologisches Institut, Eurasien-Abteilung, Berlin: Reimer.

Rosenfield, John M., 1967, *The Dynastic Arts of the Kushans*, Berkeley: University of California.

Ross, Ann, 2005. *Pagan Celtic Britain: Studies in Iconography and Tradition*, Chicago: Academy.

Rowley, Sherry, 1997. "On Saint Brigit and Pagan Goddesses in the Kingdom of God," *Canadian Women Studies*, 17/3, pp. 93–5.

Russell, James R., 2007. "The Shrine beneath the Waves," *Res: Anthropology and Aesthetics*, 51, pp. 136–156.

Russell, James R., 2004. "Pre-Christian Armenian Religion," in *Armenian and Iranian Studies*, Cambridge, MA: Harvard Armenian Texts and Studies, pp. 371–88.

Russell, James R., 1990. "Cedrenus, Georgius," *Encyclopædia Iranica*, V, Fasc. 1, pp. 108–1.

Russell, James R., 1987a. *Zoroastrianism in Armenia*, Cambridge, MA: Harvard University Press.

Russell, James R., 1987b. "Aždahā iv: Armenian Aždahak," *Encyclopædia Iranica*, III, Fasc. 2, pp. 191–205.

Russell, James R., 1986. "Armenian Religion," *Encyclopædia Iranica*, II, Fasc. 4, pp. 438–44.

Saadi-nejad, Manya, 2009. "Mythological Themes in Iranian Culture and Art: Traditional and Contemporary Perspectives," *Iranian Studies*, 42/2, pp. 231–46.

Sadovski, Velizar, 2017. "The Lexicon of Iranian" in Jared Klein, Brian Joseph, Matthias Fritz, eds., *Handbook of Comparative and Historical Indo-European Linguistics*, Berlin/Boston: De Gruyter Mouton, pp. 566–99.

Sarfarāz, A. A., 1975. "Anāhitā, mabad-e bozorg dar Bīšāpūr" (Anāhitā, the Great Temple at Bīšāpūr) in *Proceedings of the IIIrd Annual Symposium on Archaeological Research in Iran, 2nd–7th November, 1974*, Tehran, pp. 91–110.

Sarkaratī, Bahman, 1350 [1971]. "Parī," *Journal of the Departement of Literature and Humanities, University of Tabriz*, 97-100, pp. 1–32.

Schmidt, Leigh Eric, 2014. "Portents of a Discipline: The Study of Religion before Religious Studies," *Modern Intellectual History Journal*, 11/1, pp. 211–20.

Schmitt, Rüdiger, 2014. *Wörterbuch der altpersischen Königsinshariften*, Wiesbaden: Reichert.

Schmitt, Rüdiger, 2012. "Lommel, Herman," *Encyclopædia Iranica*.

Schmitt, Rüdiger, 2009. *Die altpersischen Inschriften der Achaimeniden: edition minor mit deutscher Übersetzung*, Wiesbaden: Reichert.

Schmitt, Rüdiger, 1970. "BAPZOXAPA – ein neues Anahita-Epitheton aus Kappadokien," *Zeitschrift für vergleichende Sprachforschung*, 84, pp. 207–10.

Schlerath, B. and P. O. Skjærvø, 1987. "Aši," *Encyclopædia Iranica*, vol. II, Fasc. 7, pp 750–1.

Schlerath, Bernfried, 2000. "Geldner, Karl Friedrich," *Encyclopædia Iranica*, X, Fasc. 4, pp. 394–96.

Schwartz, Martin, 2012. "Transformation of the Indo-Iranian Snake-man: Myth, Language, Ethnoarcheology, and Iranian Identity," *Iranian Studies*, 45/2, pp. 275–9.

Schwartz, Martin, 2008. "On Aiiehiiā, Afflictress of Childbirth, and Pairikā: Two Avestan Demonesses (with an Appendix on the Indo-Irania Shipwrecked Seaman)," *Bulletin of the Asia Institute*, New Series, 22, pp. 95–105.

Sedāghat-Kīsh, Jamshīd, 2003. "Qanāt-e moqaddas dar Īrān" (The Sacred Qanats in Iran), *Fasl-nāme-ye honar*, 57-58, pp. 34–42.

Shāhmīrzādī, Sādegh Malek, 1373 [1995]. *Bāstān-shenāsī-ye Īrān va Beinolnahrein va Mesr* (The Archeology of Iran, Mesopotamia and Egypt), Tehrān: Mārlīk.

Shaked, Shaul, 2013. "The Sayings of Wuzurgmihr the Sage: A Piece of Sasanian Wisdom Transmitted into Arabic," in Haggai Ben-Shammai, Shaul Shaked, and Sarah Stroumsa, eds., *Exchange and Transmission across Cultural Boundaries*, Jerusalem: Israel Academy of Sciences and Humanities, pp. 216–75.

Shaked, Shaul, 1994. *Dualism in Transformation: Varieties of Religion in Sasanian Iran*, London: School of Oriental and African Studies.

Shaki, Mansour, 1994. "Dēn," *Encyclopædia Iranica*, VII, Fasc. 3, pp. 279–81.

Sharīfiān, Mehdī, and Behzād Ātunī, 2008. "Padīdar šenasī zan-jādū," *Mythology and Sufism Studies*, 32, pp. 1–27.

Shenkar, Michael, 2014, *Intangible Spirits and Graven Images: The Iconography of Deities in the Pre-Islamic Iranian World*, Leiden: Brill.

Shepard, Jonathan, 2008. *The Cambridge History of the Byzantine Empire*, Cambridge: Cambridge University Press.

Shepherd, Dorothy G., 1980. *The Iconography of Anāhitā, Part 1*, Beirut: Faculty of Arts and Sciences, the American University of Beirut.

Silverman, Jason M., 2012. *Persepolis and Jerusalem: Iranian Influence on the Apocalyptic Hermeneutic Xenophon*, New York: T & T Clark.

Skjærvø, Prods Oktor, 2017. "The Documentation of Iranian," in Jared Klein, Brian Joseph, Matthias Fritz, eds., *Handbook of Comparative and Historical Indo-European Linguistics*, Berlin/Boston: De Gruyter Mouton.

Skjærvø, Prods Oktor, 2013a. "Anāhitā-: Unblemished or Unattached (Avestica IV)," in Jamsheed K. Choksy and Jennifer Dubeansky, eds., *Gifts to a Magus: Indo-Iranian Studies Honoring Firoze Kotwal*, New York: Peter Lang, pp. 113–22.

Skjærvø, Prods Oktor, 2013b. "Marriage ii. Next-of-Kin Marriage in Zoroastrianism," *Encyclopædia Iranica*.

Skjærvø, Prods Oktor, 2013c. "Kayāniān vi: Siiāuuaršan, Siyāwaxš, Siāvaš," *Encyclopædia Iranica*.

Skjærvø, Prods Oktor, 2012. "The Zoroastrian Oral Tradition as Reflected in the Texts," in Alberto Cantera, ed., *The Transmission of the Avesta*, Wiesbaden: Harrassowitz, 3–48.

Skjærvø, Prods Oktor, 2011a. *The Spirit of Zoroastrianism*, New Haven: Yale University Press, 2011.

Skjærvø, Prods Oktor, 2011b. "Zoroastrian Dualism," in Armin Lange et al., eds., *Light against Darkness: Dualism in Ancient Mediterranean Religion and the Contemporary World*, Göttingen: Vandenhoeck & Ruprecht, pp. 55–91.

Skjærvø, Prods Oktor, 2007. "The Avestan Yasna: Ritual and Myth," in Fereydun Vahman and Claus V. Pedersen, eds., *Religious Texts in Iranian Languages*, Copenhagen: The Royal Danish Academy of Science and Letters.

Skjærvø, Prods Oktor, 2007. "Zoroastrian Texts," unpublished typescript, https://sites.fas.harvard.edu/~iranian/Zoroastrianism/Zoroastrianism3_Texts_I.pdf.

Skjærvø, Prods Oktor, 2005–06. "The Importance of Orality for the Study of Old Iranian Literature and Myth" *Nāme-ye Irān-e Bāstān*, 5/1-2, pp. 9–31.

Skjærvø, Prods Oktor, 2005. "Introduction to Zoroastrianism," unpublished typescript, http://www.fas.harvard.edu/~iranian/Zoroastrianism/Zoroastrianism1_Intro.pdf.

Skjærvø, Prods Oktor, 2003–04. "The Antiquity of Old Avestan," *Nāme-ye Irān-e Bāstān*, 3/2, pp. 15–41.

Skjærvø, Prods Oktor. "Ahura Mazdā and Ārmaiti, Heaven and Earth in the old Avesta," *Journal of the American Oriental Society*, 122/2, pp. 399–410.

Skjærvø, Prods Oktor, 1998. "Eastern Iranian Epic Traditions II: Rostam and Bhīṣma," *Acta Orientalia Academiae Scientiarum Hungaricae*, 51, pp. 159–70.

Skjærvø, Prods Oktor, 1994. "Hymnic Composition in the Avesta," *Die Sprache*, 36, pp. 199–243.

Skjærvø, Prods Oktor, 1987. "Aždahā i: In Old and Middle Iranian," *Encyclopædia Iranica*, vol. III, Fasc. 2, pp. 191–205.

Skjærvø, Prods Oktor, 1986. *Encyclopædia*, vol. II, Fasc. 4, pp. 355–6.

Spaeth, Barbette Stanley, 1996. *The Roman Goddess Ceres*, Austin: University of Texas Press.

Stausberg, Michael and Yuhan Vevaina, eds., 2015. *The Wiley-Blackwell Companion to Zoroastrianism*, Malden: Wiley-Blackwell.

Strabo, 2014. *Geography*, tr. Duane W. Roller, Cambridge: Cambridge University Press.

Stuckey, Johanna H., 2001. "Inanna and the Huluppu Tree, an Ancient Mesopotamian Narrative of Goddess Demotion," in Frances Devlin-Glass and Lyn McCredden, eds., *Feminist Poetics of the Sacred: Creative Suspicions*, Oxford: Oxford University Press, pp. 91–105.

Sundermann, W., 1988. "Bahman Yašt," *Encyclopædia Iranica*, III, Fasc. 5, pp. 492–3.

Tacitus, 2012. *Annals*, tr. Cynthia Damon, London: Penguin.

Tafażżolī, A., 1982. "Abdīh ud sahīgīh ī Sagastān," *Encyclopædia Iranica*, I, Fasc. 2, p. 210.

Tafażżolī, A., 1354 [1975]. *Mīnū-ye karad*, Tehran: Bonyād Farhang Irān.

Tanabe, Katsumi, 1995. "Nana on Lion-East and West in Soghdian Art," *Orient*, 30/31, pp. 309–34.

Ṭārsūsī, Abu Taher Muhammad (12th century), 2011. *Dārāb-nāma Ṭārsūsī*, ed., Ḍabīh-Allāh Ṣafā, 1389[2011], Tehran: Elmi-Farhangi Publisher.

Tatár, Maria Magdolna, 2007. "The Myth of Macha in Eastern Europe," *Journal of Indo-European Studies*, 35/3, pp. 323–44.

Teleki, Suzanne Kovács, 1967. "Sumerian Origin of the Names of the River 'Ister-Danube': A Study in Prehistory and philology," paper presented to the International Congress of Orientalists, University of Michigan, Ann Arbor.

Thieme, Paul, 1970. "Die vedischen Āditya und die zarathustrischen Aməša Spənta," in Bernfried Schlerath, ed., *Zarathustra*, Darmstadt: Wege der Forschung, p. 169.

Thieme, Paul, 1960. "The 'Aryan Gods' of the Mitanni Treaties," *Journal of the American Oriental Society*, 80, pp. 301–17.

Thordarson, Fridrik, 2009. "Ossetic Language i. History and Description," *Encyclopædia Iranica*.

Trever, C., 1967. "À propos des temples de la déese Anahita en Iran sassanide," *Iranica Antiqua*, 7, pp. 121–32.

Ucko, P. J., 1968. *Anthropomorphic Figurines*, London: Smidla.

Ustinova, Yulia, 1999. *The Supreme Gods of the Bosporan Kingdom: Celestial Aphrodite and the Most High God*, Leiden: Brill.

Ustinova, Yulia, 1998. "Aphrodite Ourania of the Bosporus: The Great Goddess of a Frontier Pantheon," *Kernos*, 11, pp. 209–26.

Ustinova, Yulia, 1989. *The Supreme Gods of the Bosporan Kingdom: Celestial Aphrodite and the Most High God*, Leiden: Brill.

Utas, Bo, 1983. "The Pahlavi Treatise Avdēh u sahīkēh ī Sakistān," *Acta Antiqua Academiae Scientiarum Hungaricae*, 28, pp. 259–67.

Vahman, Fereydun and Claus V. Pedersen, eds., 2007. *Ritual and Myth: Religious Texts in Iranian Languages*, Symposium held in Copenhagen May 2002, Copenhagen: The Royal Danish Academy of Science and Letters.

Vahdati Nasab, Hamed and Mandan Kazzazi, 2011. "Metric Analysis of a Female Figurine from Tepe Sarab," *Iran*, 49, pp. 1–10.

Varner, Gary R., 2009. *Sacred Wells: A Study in the History, Meaning and Mythology of Holy Wells and Waters*, New York: Algora.

Vegas Sansalvador, Ana, 2016. "Iranian *Anāhitā-* and Greek Artemis: Three Significant Coincidences," in Dieter Gunkel, Joshua T. Katz, Brent Vine, and Michael Weiss, eds., *Sabasram Ati Srajas: Indo-Iranian and Indo-European Studies in Honor of Stephanie W. Jamison*, New York: Beech Stave Press, pp. 433–43.

Voegelin, Eric, 2001. *Order and History Volume I, Israel and Revelation*, Columbia, MO: University of Missouri Press.

Von der Osten, Hans Henning and Rudolf Naumann, 1961. *Takht-e Suleiman*, Berlin: Mann.

Von Gall, Hubertus 1988. "Das Felsgrab von Qizqapan. Ein Denkmal aus Dem Umfeld der Achämenidischen Königsstrasse," *Bagdader Mitteilungen*, 19, pp. 557–82.

Wakeman, Mary K., 1985. "Ancient Sumer and the Women's Movement: The Process of Reaching behind, Encompassing and Going Beyond," *Journal of Feminist Studies in Religion*, 1/2, pp. 7–27.

Watkins, Calvert, 2005. *How to Kill a Dragon: Aspects of Indo-European Poetics*, Oxford: Oxford University Press.

Watkins, Calvert, 2000. *The American Heritage Dictionary of Indo-European Roots*, Boston: Houghton Mifflin.

Welch, Stuart Cary Jr, 1976. *Royal Safavid Manuscripts*, New York: George Braziller.

Weller, Hermann, 1938. *Anahita, Grundlegendes zur Arischen Metrik*, Veröffentlichungen des Orientalischen Seminars der Universität Tübingen, Stuttgart-Berlin: W. Kohlhammer.

West, E. W., 1897. *Sacred Books of the East, volume 5: Dēnkard*, Oxford: Oxford University Press.

Westergaard, N. L., 1852-4. *Zendavesta, or the Religious Books of the Zoroastrians*, vol. 1, Copenhagen: Berling Brothers.

Widengren, Geo, 1967. "Primordial Man and Prostitute: A Zervanite Myth in the Sassanid Avesta," in *Studies in Mysticism and Religion Presented to Gershom G. Scholem*, Jerusalem: Magnes, pp. 227–34.

Widengren, Geo, 1965. *Die Religionen Irans*, Stuttgart: Kohlhammer.

Wikander, Stig, 1938. *Der arische Männerbund*, Lund: Ohlssons.

Wilkins, William Joseph, 1973 [1913]. *Hindu Mythology: Vedic and Purānic*, Totowa, NJ: Roman & Littlefield.

Williams, Alan V., 1990. *The Pahlavi Rivāyat Accompanying the Dādestān ī dēnīg*, 2 vols., Copenhagen: Munksgard.

Williams, George M., 2003. *Handbook of Hindu Mythology*, Oxford: Oxford University Press.

Witzel, Michael, 2013. "Iranian Migration," in D. T. Potts, ed., *The Oxford Handbook of Ancient Iran*, Oxford: Oxford University Press, pp. 423–41.

Witzel, Michael, 2004. *Linguistic Evidence for Cultural Exchange in Prehistoric Western Central Asia*, Philadelphia: Sino-Platonic Papers, 129.

Witzel, Michael, 2001. "Autochthonous Aryans? The Evidence from Old Indian and Iranian Texts," *Electronic Journal of Vedic Studies*, 7/3.

Witzel, Michael, 1984. "Sur le chemin du ciel," *Bulletin d'études indiennes*, 2, pp. 213–79.

Wolff, Fritz, 1910, *Avesta Die heiligen Bücher der parsen*, Strassburg : De Gruyter.

Xenophon, 1968. *Cyropaedia*, tr. Walter Miller, Cambridge, MA: Harvard University Press.

Yarshater, Ehsan, 1984. "Afrāsīāb," *Encyclopædia Iranica*, I, Fasc. 6, pp. 570–6.

Young, Katherine. K., 2002. "From the Phenomonology of Religion to Feminism and Women's Studies," in Arvind Sharma, ed., *Methodology in Religious Studies: The Interface with Women's Studies*, New York: State University of New York Press, pp. 17–40.

Yurchenkova, Nina, 2011. "About Female Deities in the Mythology of Finno-Ugric Peoples," *Folklore*, 47, pp. 173–80.

Zaehner, R. C., 1940. Review of Hermann Weller, *Anahita, Grundlegendes zur Arischen Metrik*, in *Journal of the Royal Asiatic Society*, 72/1, p. 89.

Zaehner, R. C., 1955. *Zurvan, A Zoroastrian Dilemma*, Oxford: Oxford University Press.

Index

Θraētaona 58, 59, 111, 113, 114, 116, 142, 143, 154
āb 115, 150, 152, 164, 220 n.23
Ābān Yašt 1, 2, 5, 26, 43–5, 48, 50–2, 56–60, 63, 64, 66–75, 81, 87, 89, 90, 94, 103, 113, 114, 116, 133, 140, 143, 157, 175, 184–6, 193, 202 n.4, 207 n.97
Abāxtarān 148
*abāxtar*s 147–9
Abdīh ud sahīgīh ī sagistān 142, 143
āb-zōhr 127, 129
Achaemenid period 1, 4, 9, 12, 14, 31, 34, 48, 104, 116, 119–23, 125, 128, 130, 133, 138, 179, 193
Aditi 27, 35–7, 41, 47
Ādityas 35, 37, 39
Afrāsiāb 59, 60, 81, 112–15, 164, 166, 220 n.23
Ahriman 36, 37, 107, 113, 137, 138, 160, 171, 176, 213 n.56
āhūiri- (ahuric) 84
Ahura Mazdā 1, 11, 14, 16, 31, 35, 43, 44, 52–8, 62–4, 67, 72–4, 78, 79, 84, 88, 91, 93, 97, 103–7, 116, 119, 121, 122, 124–6, 141, 154, 176, 177, 193, 205 n.70, 206 n.74, 213 n.56
*ahura*s 35, 61, 62
Airiiana Vaēĵah 38, 57, 70, 71
Alexander, King 181, 182, 213 n.56
al-Lāt 120
Amərətāt 77, 78, 91–3, 150
Aməšạ Spəṇtas 34, 77–9, 88, 92, 93, 101
Āmū-Daryā 115
Anāhīd 13, 127, 134, 139–41, 146–50, 157, 194
Anāhīd ī abāxtari 147–9, 157
Anahit 16, 31–4
anāhitā 47–8
Anahtakan albiwr 32
Anatolia 2, 9, 23, 31, 90, 101, 120, 123
Antiochus I 124

Antiochus III 124
Aŋra-Mainiiu/Gannāg Mēnōg 107, 110, 137
(ap-) 49
Aphrodite 32–4, 120, 123, 124, 127, 146, 173
Aphrodite-Anaitis 120
Api-Gē 17
*apsara*s 178
Aquae Sulis 26, 184
Ardā Wīrāz-Nāmag 84, 86, 135, 151, 171
Ardešīr, Sāsānian king 29, 42, 156
Ardoxšo 16, 88
Ardwī-sūr Anāhīd 13, 134, 139–47, 150, 157, 194, 217 n.49
Ard Yašt/Aši Yašt 43, 88, 89, 93
Arəduuī Sūrā Anāhitā 3, 28, 43–50, 71–5, 87, 93, 104, 112, 116
  Ābān Yašt 66–71
  and *Ardwī-sūr Anāhīd* 139–44
  chariot-riding deity 63–5
  daēuua 58–62
  fertility 65–6
  functions 50–1
  priestly function 56–8
  water/river deity 52–6
arəϑnāišca/arəϑna- 205 n.58
Argimpasa-Aphrodite Urania 17, 25
Ārmaiti 16, 79
Armenians 31–4
Arnemetia 19, 22, 26
Artaxerxes II 14, 28, 48, 101, 104, 105, 116, 121, 122, 211 n.8
Artemis 13, 120, 122, 123, 127, 130
Artemis Nanaia 14, 16
ašauuan- (righteous believers) 135
Aši 33, 43, 44, 72, 77, 78, 85, 87–91, 93, 94, 114, 138
Ašišwang 90
Āsmān 54, 204 n.54
āsna-xratu 152–4
āsn-xrad 152, 153, 155–7

www.ingramcontent.com/pod-product-compliance
Ingram Content Group UK Ltd.
Pitfield, Milton Keynes, MK11 3LW, UK
UKHW020657280225
455688UK00004B/150